Raw Food
FOR
DUMMIES®

**by Cherie Soria and
Dan E. Ladermann**

WILEY

John Wiley & Sons, Inc.

Raw Food For Dummies®

Published by
John Wiley & Sons, Inc.
111 River St.
Hoboken, NJ 07030-5774
www.wiley.com

WILEY

About the Authors

Cherie Soria (Fort Bragg, California, and Montezuma, Costa Rica) is the founder and director of Living Light Culinary Institute, a culinary school that began in 1998 and is one of the four eco-friendly businesses of Living Light International. In 1992, after studying with Dr. Ann Wigmore in Puerto Rico, Cherie learned the principles of using whole, live foods to aid in healing and rejuvenation, and she began creating a gourmet raw cuisine that rivals even the most cherished cooked foods. Her efforts sparked a revolutionary trend in culinary arts, and she's often referred to as the Mother of Gourmet Raw Vegan Cuisine. Cherie has trained thousands of raw food chefs and culinary instructors from more than 50 countries. Cherie is the author of several books, and she's among the most respected professionals in the gourmet raw culinary world.

Dan E. Ladermann (Fort Bragg, California, and Montezuma, Costa Rica) is co-owner and director of Living Light International as well as president of the Institute for Vibrant Living, a nonprofit organization dedicated to global education about organic raw vegan food and its role in vibrant living. Dan is a Certified Hippocrates Health Educator and raw vegan nutrition instructor at Living Light International.

Cherie and Dan own and operate Living Light International, which includes the Living Light Culinary Institute, the Living Light Cafe, Living Light Marketplace (shop.RawFoodChef.com), and the historic, eco-friendly Living Light Inn — all located on the beautiful Mendocino coast of northern California. They travel extensively throughout the world to promote the raw vegan lifestyle, and they've received numerous awards and accolades for Living Light International, which is recognized as one of the leading raw food businesses worldwide. Cherie and Dan's mission is to spread information about the benefits of the raw vegan lifestyle throughout the globe by training teachers, chefs, and individuals to inspire others. For more information, please visit www.RawFoodChef.com.

Dedication

We dedicate this book to everyone who's open to new approaches to eating and living in order to achieve maximum health for themselves, animals, and the planet we all share.

Authors' Acknowledgments

Sincere gratitude to Heather Dismore for her help in preparing this book for publication and to all those at John Wiley & Sons, Inc., who made this book possible: Acquisitions Editor Michael Lewis, Project Editor Jenny Larner Brown, Copy Editor Caitie Copple, and the Wiley Composition team. We owe special thanks to technical editor, Sarah Stout, for ensuring that the information in this book is accurate and complete; Emily Nolan, for testing our recipes and making suggestions to improve instructions and taste; and Angie Sheetz, for the nutritional details on each recipe.

Our deepest appreciation to cherished advisors, mentors, and colleagues: Viktoras Kulvinskas, Ann Wigmore, Dr. Brian Clement, Drs. Rick and Karin Dina, Dr. Jameth Sheridan, Brenda Davis, Vesanto Melina, Dr. Michael Klaper, and our friends at the North American Vegetarian Society who took a chance on raw foods when the word *vegan* was still a hard sell!

Eternal thanks to our wonderful staff at Living Light Culinary Institute, who care deeply about our mission to help make this a healthier, happier, greener world in which to live. Special thanks to our assistant, Terilynn Epperson, without whom we could not have met our deadlines, and to chefs Martine Lussier and Vinnette Thompson for their help with recipe development. Also thanks to Felix Schoener for his beautiful food styling on the cover of this book and to our students throughout the world who test our recipes, give us honest feedback, and continually provide us with opportunities for improvement.

Publisher's Acknowledgments

We're proud of this book; please send us your comments at http://dummies.custhelp.com. For other comments, please contact our Customer Care Department within the U.S. at 877-762-2974, outside the U.S. at 317-572-3993, or fax 317-572-4002.

Some of the people who helped bring this book to market include the following:

Acquisitions, Editorial, and Vertical Websites

Project Editor: Jenny Larner Brown

Acquisitions Editor: Michael Lewis

Copy Editor: Caitlin Copple

Contributor: Heather Dismore

Assistant Editor: David Lutton

Editorial Program Coordinator: Joe Niesen

Technical Editor: Sara Stout

Recipe Tester: Emily Nolan

Nutritional Analyst: Angie Sheetz

Editorial Manager: Christine Meloy Beck

Editorial Assistant: Alexa Koschier

Art Coordinator: Alicia B. South

Cover Photos: © Dan E. Ladermann

Cartoons: Rich Tennant (www.the5thwave.com)

Composition Services

Project Coordinator: Sheree Montgomery

Layout and Graphics: Christin Swinford

Proofreaders: Jessica Kramer, Christine Sabooni

Indexer: Claudia Bourbeau

Illustrator: Elizabeth Kurtzman

Publishing and Editorial for Consumer Dummies

Kathleen Nebenhaus, Vice President and Executive Publisher

David Palmer, Associate Publisher

Kristin Ferguson-Wagstaffe, Product Development Director

Publishing for Technology Dummies

Andy Cummings, Vice President and Publisher

Composition Services

Debbie Stailey, Director of Composition Services

Contents at a Glance

Recipes at a Glance

Table of Contents

Introduction

For more than 15 years, we've been sharing the science, alchemy, and delicious taste of raw culinary arts with people throughout the world. Our students come to us to learn how to make fabulous, health-promoting, raw food for themselves, their families, or guests in their restaurants and classrooms. Many of our students have gone on to write popular recipe books and open raw food businesses. Others are content with making delicious and nutritious meals for their friends and families. *Raw Food For Dummies* is the next step in bringing a raw plant-based lifestyle to anyone interested in it, regardless of prior experience with food preparation. Our goal is to make healthy living delicious and accessible to everyone!

About This Book

The raw food lifestyle is unique and can therefore be socially challenging at times. But the rewards are great — not only in terms of achieving amazing health and vitality but also in terms of enjoying your food and a more energetic life.

We know that people won't eat food that doesn't taste good. Who can blame them? People are sentient beings and thus motivated by senses: The smell, taste, texture, and appearance of food are important to the human experience of eating. So our mission for this book is to introduce you to raw food that's so delicious you'll want to incorporate more of it into your daily routine. The recipes in this book are varied and easy to follow, so whether you want the simplest of meals or a celebration feast, you can find it here.

A common question we get is, "What raw foods are edible and what foods shouldn't be eaten without cooking?" All fruits and leafy vegetables can be enjoyed raw, and most other vegetables can be prepared deliciously without cooking. But some starches and legumes need to be cooked to be palatable. For example, raw potatoes are too starchy to eat raw, and rice must be cooked or it can break your teeth. Most other grains and legumes can be soaked, sprouted, and eaten raw. In this book, we guide you through the preparation of many plant foods so you know your options and can make meals that suit you and your family.

Getting started with raw foods can be very easy, and our down-to-earth approach is what sets this book apart from others. We understand that most people work outside their home and need help organizing a food plan that provides the right foods when needed — at home, at work, or on the road — so we make sure that you're not left unprepared in normal life situations. We want to help you live raw, not just pass along a few tasty recipes, so we provide a bonanza of tips and suggestions for making the transition to raw foods and sticking with it — for life! We even give you lots of tips about how to set up and manage your kitchen and what foods to buy.

Conventions Used in This Book

To make this book easier to use, we've used a few conventions.

- Whenever we include a new or unfamiliar term, we put it in *italics* and include a definition nearby.

- **Bold** text gives you the most important keywords in bulleted lists or the action parts of numbered steps in non-recipe text.

- All web addresses appear in monofont. When this book was printed, some web addresses may have needed to break across two lines of text. If that happened, rest assured that we haven't put in any extra characters (such as hyphens) to indicate the break. So when using one of these URLs, just type in exactly what you see in this book, pretending that the line break doesn't exist.

Here are some additional conventions that apply to the recipes:

- All temperatures are in degrees Fahrenheit.

- Nutritional facts in each recipe are based on the ingredients as written in the book. If you make substitutions (and we highly recommend experimenting), keep in mind that the nutritional values will change according to your modifications.

- Be sure to read the recipe from start to finish before you begin preparing food. Then you can make sure to have all the ingredients, tools, and, most importantly, the time you need to make delicious meals.

- The recipes in this book are both raw and vegan. We don't use any animal products, and the food in our recipes never exceeds 118 degrees during preparation. Just keep in mind that this temp refers to the food itself, not necessarily to the air around it.

- We list *filtered water* in the ingredients list for many recipes. We recommend using pure, unchlorinated water to avoid potentially toxic chemicals and ensure you get maximum nutrition from the foods you prepare and consume. Filtered water has a more pleasant taste and does not negatively impact the flavor of recipes. If you have well water at home, you may not need to filter it. If you have city water, we recommend filtering it with a faucet attachment or pitcher system.

✔ We simply list *salt* in ingredient lists, but we recommend that you use Himalayan crystal salt because it's unbleached, contains no added chemicals, and comes from a pristine, unpolluted area of the world. Ordinary table salt and sea salt are less desirable, but if they're all you have on hand, don't let that stop you from trying out a recipe.

✔ Any spices listed in recipes should be ground unless noted. They should also be raw, if possible. You can look for raw products at the websites we list in Chapter 6, or in some cases you may be able to make your own ground spices and dried herbs using a dehydrator.

✔ Unless otherwise specified in a recipe, use medium-sized fruits and vegetables.

✔ All dried fruits should be naturally dehydrated in the sun or a low-temp dehydrator.

✔ All oils should be *cold pressed,* or extra-virgin.

✔ All lemon, lime, and orange juice should be freshly squeezed.

✔ All ingredients are organic. The recipe may simply say, *½ cup diced cucumber,* for example, but we always recommend buying organic cucumbers whenever possible.

What You're Not to Read

Although we think every word in this book is important (we did, after all, include it for a reason), you can skip over some text if you just want the basics. In particular, you can skip over the sidebars, the gray-shaded boxes. They give you background information or let you dig a little deeper into a topic. This text isn't essential for you to successfully follow a raw lifestyle, but we think it's interesting and beneficial. You can also skip anything with the Nutrition Speak icon. Text with this icon is more technical than absolutely necessary for you to understand the related content. Read it if you want to dazzle your friends with nutrition trivia at your next (raw) party.

Foolish Assumptions

When we wrote this book, we had a picture of you, our reader, in mind. Yes, we know you're a unique soul, but we had to make some general assumptions about who you are so we could make sure to meet your general information needs. We assume that at least a few of these things are true about you:

✔ You want to benefit from raw foods but don't know where to start.

✔ You want to avoid animal products and heat-processed foods, but you don't want to give up flavor or necessary nutrition.

- ✔ You're interested in adding more fresh foods to your diet and reducing the amount of processed food you consume.

- ✔ You want to improve your physical and spiritual well-being as well as the well-being of the planet.

- ✔ You have a family member or friend who has "gone raw" and you want to prepare foods you can all enjoy.

- ✔ You're willing to spend a bit of time on food preparation in return for pure, healthy, vitality-producing food.

- ✔ You're a chef or restaurant owner and see that raw food is more than a passing trend, so you want to add appealing raw options to your menu.

- ✔ You're a healthcare practitioner or nutritionist who wants to help people decide what to eat and what not to eat to enhance their nourishment.

How This Book Is Organized

Here's how the parts of *Raw Food For Dummies* break down:

Part I: Exploring the Basics of Raw Food

Part I explains the foundation of a raw food lifestyle. Here you discover how a raw diet can benefit you, including the nutritional, psychological, and environmental impact. We point out how you can eat many familiar foods in their natural raw state to improve your absorption of the nutrients these foods contain. We also explain how to get the maximum nutrition from your foods.

Part II: Embarking on Your Raw Journey

This part shows you how to make the transition to a raw or mostly raw way of eating. We help you decide how raw you want to go, with the understanding that 100 percent raw is *not* required to get immediate and lasting benefits from this lifestyle. This part includes a month-long meal plan to help you ease into planning your raw meals. And we give you the scoop on what equipment and staples you need to prepare delicious raw foods simply.

Part III: Enjoying Raw and Revitalizing Meals: The Recipes

If you thought this book was just a compilation of salad recipes, think again. In this part, we give you tons of recipes to make raw foods delicious, varied, and anything *but* boring. Find out how to make raw and nutritious smoothies, soups, salads, and snacks as well as raw versions of traditional favorites like crab cakes (crab-free, of course) and manicotti. This collection of recipes is the full meal deal, with raw appetizers, entrees, sides, and even desserts!

Part IV: Taking Your Raw Lifestyle to the Next Level

Here, you can discover how to continue to build on your increasingly raw food lifestyle. We offer tips for planning meals for family and friends — for everyday dinners and special-occasion feasts. Find tips on how to keep raw when traveling, going out to restaurants, or eating at a friend's home. We also offer some suggestions for finding other raw food enthusiasts who can keep you going strong and nourished with new raw ideas.

Part V: The Part of Tens

This part probably looks familiar to anyone who has ever picked up a *For Dummies* book. These chapters are glorified lists of important ideas. In the first one, find a list of benefits to going raw. Then we give you a list of foods best eaten raw — complete with science to back up the claims.

Icons Used in This Book

Icons help mark different kinds of information in this book, ranging from don't-forget-it-ever to interesting but not essential.

Pay particular attention when you see this icon. It alerts you to special advice that can help you make good choices and apply raw principles. If you remember nothing else, tuck away this content for recall as needed.

The Tip icon points out helpful information and tricks to save you time and frustration and smooth your raw journey.

Watch out when you see this icon. It identifies a potential problem and helps you avoid it.

This icon helps you find the nutrition-focused bits of information. If you want to know how a particular vitamin is used by your body, for example, you can find it here.

This icon flags recipes that require some preparation, usually soaking or sprouting an ingredient.

Where to Go from Here

You can start reading this book at any chapter that interests you. You don't have to start with Chapter 1 in order to understand Chapter 2, and so on. You can even skip some altogether if you're pressed for time. Here are a few recommendations for where to get started:

- If you're unfamiliar with raw foods and want a general overview of the topic, start with Chapter 1 to find out what the raw food lifestyle is, how it benefits health, and how to get started.

- If you're especially eager to eat, flip to the recipes in Part III. Chapter 8, in particular, offers simple recipes for smoothies, soups, and salads.

- If you're looking for information to help you transition from eating a traditional diet to a raw one, see the sample meal plan in Chapter 4.

- If you want to know what to stock in your raw pantry, see Chapter 5.

- If you need help finding a place to buy Himalayan crystal salt or other raw staples, Chapter 6 is a great beginning for you.

Part I
Exploring the Basics of Raw Food

The 5th Wave   By Rich Tennant

"This isn't some sort of fad diet, is it?"

In this part . . .

These chapters offer you a personal navigation system for exploring the raw food experience and getting started. Find out what's involved — and what isn't — in a raw lifestyle and why eating food in its most natural state, raw, is so beneficial to your overall health. These chapters tell you how to make sure you're getting important nutrients, including calcium, protein, antioxidants, and essential fatty acids. And we point out the power of plant-based foods for healing the body, rejuvenating energy, and slowing down the aging process.

Chapter 1

Raw Food 101

· ·

· ·

Gourmet raw foods can be just as delicious and satisfying as any food on the planet, and more and more people every day are exploring the raw food lifestyle. Many raw enthusiasts want to enjoy better personal health, whether it's looking and feeling better or healing from a major health challenge. Others want to support a friend or family member recovering from conditions like cancer, diabetes, or heart disease. And some people are simply intrigued by the concept of eating delicious food with plenty of flavor, complex texture, and natural, vibrant beauty.

Fruits and vegetables, unlike animal proteins, are delicious without much help, and they contain the nourishment your body needs to stay strong and energized.

In other words, a raw diet is power-packed with nutrients that provide plenty of protein, calcium, antioxidants, and essential fats and facilitate optimal health. The only supplements we recommend across the board for raw foodists (and many meat eaters, too) is vitamin B12 and, for those who don't get enough sunshine, vitamin D.

Of course, you don't need to eat all raw food all the time to enjoy the health benefits of the raw lifestyle. Different levels of raw are right for different people. Some choose to dedicate one meal a day to raw foods; some aim for an 80/20 split — a diet that's mostly raw; and others choose to live with only raw foods. It's a personal choice, and this book can provide the details you need to make informed decisions about what's right for you.

In this chapter, we define a raw diet and point out why it's a good idea to incorporate more raw foods into your meals. We describe the harm caused by cooking food and give you tips on how to stay nourished, balanced, and satisfied with raw, plant-based foods.

Exploring the Raw Food Lifestyle

No matter what your reason is for exploring a raw food diet, you can rev up your health, energy, and appearance by eating more raw fruits, vegetables, nuts, and seeds. The transformation that's possible when you follow a diet that's high in raw plant-based foods is truly incredible.

In this section, we point out how cooking food harms it *and* compromises your health. But there's no need to wrinkle your brow like that. We also have good news to share: Eating more raw foods can make an immediate and lasting impact on your health and vitality!

Going beyond roots and shoots: What is a raw food diet?

A raw food diet is all about abundance, not deprivation. As a raw foodist, you can eat as much delicious, health-promoting, plant-based food as you need to feel satisfied. Going raw doesn't mean you have to give up your favorite flavors and textures, because we show you how to make delicious raw meals that mimic the experience of traditional cooked foods. Our goal is to help you make healthy living delicious and satisfying.

Here are some characteristics of a raw food diet:

- ✔ Includes fresh, ripe, raw plant foods rather than processed or refined products
- ✔ May include a small amount of lightly cooked vegetables, whole grains, and legumes
- ✔ Typically contains no raw or cooked animal products
- ✔ Is high in nutrients, including vitamins, minerals, antioxidants, and phytonutrients
- ✔ Includes organic products whenever possible
- ✔ Contains a significant quantity of chlorophyll-rich green foods and other colorful plant foods
- ✔ Contains adequate complete protein from plant sources
- ✔ Contains a large proportion of foods with high water content, providing excellent hydration
- ✔ Includes raw vegetable juices
- ✔ Contains all essential fatty acids, including omega-3 fatty acids from naturally occurring plant sources

✔ Has moderate yet adequate caloric intake

✔ Contains only low to moderate amounts of sugar, which come from whole food sources

✔ Is nutritionally optimal for detoxification and healing

Flip to Chapter 3 for the nutritional details of terms such as *essential fatty acids, complete proteins, enzymes,* and *phytonutrients.*

Understanding how cooked food harms your health

Phytonutrients and antioxidants in the body are front-line defenders against cancer and other chronic illnesses. *Phytonutrients,* also referred to as phytochemicals, are health-promoting compounds that give plants their vibrant colors; phytonutrients are available only in plant foods. That's why eating fruits and vegetables representing the full spectrum of the rainbow is helpful. The thing is, phytonutrients and antioxidants are both heat and light sensitive; cooking breaks them down and reduces their power to protect.

Here are some of the other negative things that happen to food as it cooks:

✔ Vitamins, antioxidants, and phytonutrients are lost in varying degrees depending on cooking temperature and time.

✔ Proteins become *denatured,* or altered in such a way as to render them no longer useful to the body.

✔ Water in food evaporates, which leads to the loss of valuable minerals and water-soluble vitamins like vitamin C and B-complex, which help other nutrients do their jobs.

✔ Food reduces in volume but maintains its calorie count, so you end up consuming more calories by volume of food than your body needs.

✔ Food softens, making it easier to eat quickly and overeat.

✔ High heat creates toxins, especially when cooking starches and fats, and some of those toxins are *carcinogenic,* or cancer causing.

Another problem is that many foods that are alkaline when raw become acidic when cooked; this includes tomatoes. Acidity is rough on the body. For starters, it strains the kidneys, which can lead to kidney stones and kidney damage as well as bone loss and acidosis. Concentrated sweeteners (such as sugar and unripe fruit), cooked starches, and animal products also cause acidity in the body. When your body becomes too acidic, it takes calcium from your bones to neutralize the acid. That's why eating more alkaline foods helps safeguard your bones.

Additionally, raw fruits, vegetables, nuts, and seeds contain enzymes that are necessary for the digestion process. When fruits begin ripening, they actually start digesting themselves by changing their starches into simple sugars. Sugars are much easier to digest than starches, so ripe fruits are easier on the body. You can even taste your body's preference for ripe fruit when you bite into, say, a peach. A ripe one is so much sweeter. And the enzymes in the fruit that convert starch into natural sugar also aid your digestion of that food; when enzymes are destroyed by cooking, the body must work harder to digest food. Enzymes in raw foods are best preserved by keeping the food's temperature below 118 degrees.

Preserving important enzymes in whole foods is one of the primary reasons people choose to follow a raw food diet. Enzymes are necessary for every function in the body, and they're the most heat sensitive of all nutrients. Take a look at Chapter 3 for more information on how food enzymes help your body digest foods properly and why good digestion is important to good health.

When choosing food in grocery stores or restaurants, watch out for words that mean cooked. Terms like *pasteurized* and *hydrogenated* indicate that the food has been heated above the 118 degree threshold. Check out Chapter 6 for tips on reading labels to ensure that you're getting foods that are whole and in their nutritious natural state.

Boosting planetary health with vegan choices

For many raw foodists, the choice to forgo consuming animal products is an instinctive step made to minimize the negative impact of the meat industry on the planet. Growing animals for food requires huge amounts of fresh water and grazing lands, and it's totally unnecessary. With only a few exceptions — including vitamin D, which comes from the sun or a supplement, and vitamin B12, which people must get from supplementation or fortified foods, the human body can get all the nutrition it needs from plant-based sources.

Plus, because conventional farming pollutes the earth with pesticides and *genetically modified organisms* (GMOs) that get into your body when you consume the bounty, a raw plant-based diet typically supports local and organic foods, which require fewer resources from seed to spoon. So aside from the enormous human health benefits it provides, a raw vegan diet nurtures the soil, safeguards the environment, spares animals, and supports farmers.

Embracing a lifestyle, not a fad diet

Transitioning to raw food is not a process related to a temporary diet. Instead, it's a lifestyle decision with positive long-term effects that will benefit you for the rest of your life.

Unlike most diets that rely on restricting calories or carbohydrates, a raw food diet allows you to maintain your basal metabolic rate (BMR), so you can eat enough to keep your metabolism up *and* your energy high to sustain prolonged exercise and promote healthy body processes.

Your *basal metabolic rate* is the amount of calories you need to cover your basic energy needs, including breathing, keeping your heart pumping blood, maintaining brain and nervous system activity, repairing body tissues and cells, and performing other life-sustaining processes. An average adult needs to consume between 2,000 and 2,500 calories daily to ensure healthy body function and to maintain current weight.

Many traditional diets are designed to limit the amount of calories consumed in order to lose weight. In contrast, weight loss happens naturally when you transition to eating raw foods because you give yourself outstanding nutrition with foods that aren't calorie-dense. For the most part, you can eat all the raw foods you want and feel satisfied. Think about it: Have you ever heard of someone getting fat from eating too many vegetables, fruits, and sprouts?

Plus, the raw food lifestyle is so delicious. The variety of raw foods is much more exciting than the traditional low-cal options. So adding more raw fruits and vegetables to your diet means you can be better nourished, enjoy more energy, and achieve your natural body weight.

Examining Different Ways of Eating Raw

People take many different approaches to living raw, so what's optimal? Unfortunately, we can't tell you what's right for you because the answer is different for everyone, and it changes at different times of life. What feels right for you now may not make you feel best after a year or two. Your body is always evolving, and you must allow for changes in your tastes and nutritional needs. In this section, we help you figure out how raw you want to go. Finding the right balance of raw food in your life is personal.

You're a unique individual with individual needs, so tune into your body's signals to find out what foods work for you and which ones don't. Be gentle on yourself. This discovery process takes time, but you need to pay attention.

Total raw may not be realistic for you right now — or ever. Pay attention to how you feel when you choose different foods. We recommend keeping a food journal so you can record how you feel after eating certain meals. Over time, this journal can help you see patterns related to what you eat and how you feel, enabling you to find out what foods make you feel best. If you feel energetic, happy, healthy, and able to handle stress, you know you're making good food choices. Allow yourself the freedom to refine and change aspects of your diet as your needs change over time.

How much raw food do you need to consume to be considered a raw foodist and experience the benefits of the raw food lifestyle? If you enjoy and appreciate raw food, you're already a raw foodist! And if your daily diet consists of 20 percent raw food and you increase that to 50 percent, you'll notice a big difference in how you feel.

Quite often, people start a raw food journey on a very strict diet of 90 to 100 percent raw for healing, weight loss, or detox purposes. After achieving their goals, these folks tend to soften their approach and allow a few well-chosen cooked foods into their regime. Many raw foodists include some healthy cooked foods in their diet simply because of convenience when traveling, dining in restaurants, or eating in social situations. Still, most people say that the more raw food they eat, the better they feel.

Here's a general breakdown of some different ways to live raw. You may fit neatly into one category or change your regimen depending on time of year or based on what you're doing.

- ✔ **All raw all the time:** A small number of raw foodists eat only raw food and never touch anything that's cooked. Most of these folks also stay away from meat, fish, eggs, and dairy; and many don't eat oil or concentrated sweeteners, preferring instead whole-food fats and natural fruit sweeteners. A few all-raw foodists eat raw fish and raw cheese, but most are strictly raw and vegan.

- ✔ **Mostly raw vegan:** This raw foodist group is the most populous. These folks eat all raw on most days and a little cooked food on occasion or as part of a meal — a cup of cooked soup with a big salad, for example. Most of the people in this group occasionally consume carefully selected cooked foods, such as steamed vegetables, whole non-glutinous grains, and legumes, as well as fish, eggs, and dairy, but they try to ensure that raw plant-based foods make up about 80 percent of their diet.

- ✔ **Transitional raw:** These folks eat a lot of raw plant-based foods (usually at least 50 percent) and a small amount of animal protein. The remainder of their food choices tend to be healthy cooked foods.

Considering the USDA MyPlate guidance

The USDA recommendation for what and how much to eat now recognizes that a plant-based diet provides adequate nutrition and no longer insists that meat is the only form of protein. The new guidelines encourage you to make fruits and vegetables half of what you eat on a daily basis. This change is definitely a step in the right direction! But the new version of the Food Pyramid is still flawed. For starters, we think grains still carry too much weight on the chart (but we're glad that whole, gluten-free grains such quinoa, wild rice, and buckwheat are included). Instead of calling this category *Grains,* we prefer to think of it as *Starches* so that it includes potatoes, yams, beets, carrots, and winter squash. Also, the Dairy circle could be better named as *Calcium-Rich Foods* or deleted altogether, given that dark leafy greens and whole grains provide calcium plus a whole lot more. Dairy products and dairy substitutes are really not needed at all in a healthy diet.

Chapter 4 can help you decide how much raw is right for you. Just keep in mind that any increase in the percentage of raw food you consume offers health benefits. Here are a few general guidelines for a healthy daily diet:

✔ Fats should comprise 10 to 30 percent of calories.

✔ Protein should make up 10 to 15 percent of calories.

✔ Carbohydrates should make up the remaining 55 to 80 percent of calories.

Getting Proper Nutrition

Despite concern among some people, a raw food diet provides more than enough protein and calcium for healthy adults. It also offers plenty of vitamins, minerals, and antioxidants with one or two exceptions that actually apply as well to the general population: vitamin B12 and, for those who don't get enough sunshine, vitamin D.

Here are some general rules for getting the nutrients you need from raw food:

✔ Consume a wide variety of fresh, ripe, raw, organic fruits and vegetables.

✔ Eat all the colors of the rainbow to get a full spectrum of nutrients.

- ✔ Emphasize nutrient-packed green foods.

- ✔ Give enzyme- and mineral-rich sea vegetables a place in your diet.

- ✔ Enjoy a variety of raw nuts and seeds in moderation.

- ✔ Include omega-3 rich foods, including flax, chia, and walnuts.

- ✔ Soak and sprout nuts and seeds, and enjoy these foods regularly.

After you conquer the basics of meeting your body's nutritional needs, you can take your healthy eating plan to the next level by choosing to take these additional steps:

- ✔ Reduce your intake of concentrated sweets and sweeteners.

- ✔ Minimize salt intake; stick with Himalayan crystal salt if possible.

- ✔ Choose gluten-free grains, such as quinoa, millet, amaranth, and buckwheat, if you eat steamed or sprouted grains.

- ✔ Soak and sprout legumes, if you choose to include them in your diet, to make them more digestible.

- ✔ Choose organic food whenever possible to minimize chemical residues.

- ✔ Minimize or eliminate meat and dairy products from your diet.

Getting enough protein without meat

Confused about which foods provide the best protein? You're not alone. After all, the U.S. Department of Agriculture (USDA) has a category of foods called proteins that doesn't even include green leafy vegetables, which, calorie-to-calorie, have twice the amount of protein as red meat.

Don't believe it? Take a peek at the amount of protein in a 100-calorie serving of these foods:

- ✔ Broccoli: 11.2 grams

- ✔ Kale: 11 grams

- ✔ Sirloin steak: 5.4 grams

It's true that the volume of these foods are different; for 100 calories, you get 10 ounces of broccoli, 7 ounces kale, and just 2¼ ounces of steak, but calorie for calorie, your best bet is vegetables. Find out how much protein you actually need and how to get it from plant-based sources in Chapter 3 (and refer to the sidebar "Considering the USDA MyPlate guidance" for info on the new Food Pyramid).

Ask the experts: Doesn't everybody need milk?

(Cows) milk is mother nature's "perfect food" . . . for a calf! Cow's milk is designed to turn a 65-pound calf into a 400-pound cow. Dr. Michael Klaper, author of *Pregnancy, Children, and the Vegan Diet*, states, "You have no more need of cow's milk than you do rat's milk, horse's milk or elephant's milk." Even Dr. Benjamin Spock, noted pediatrician and author of *Baby and Child Care*, says, "I no longer recommend dairy products after the age of 2 years. Other calcium sources offer many advantages that dairy products do not have."

Dishing out the facts on dairy

Humans are mammals, and a few things are common to all mammals: We're warm blooded, have body hair, give birth to live young, and nurse babies. However, humans are the only mammal that continues to drink milk after being weaned. In fact, as humans leave infancy, production of the enzyme lactase, which is necessary to digest milk, declines.

But instead of listening to their bodies' insistence to get off the milk, many people take a lactase supplement so they can comfortably digest dairy products, which are totally unnecessary to a healthy diet and cause a range of health problems, including obesity and heart disease, due in part to the high amount of cholesterol and saturated fat they include. And don't think you're doing yourself a favor by choosing 2 percent milk; 35 percent of those calories are fat!

The major argument for drinking milk (and eating dairy products in general) is to ensure that you get enough calcium. But the truth is that plants provide all the calcium you need in a form that's more useful for your body — without the health risks of milk. Some of the best sources of calcium are collard greens, kale, spinach, okra, broccoli, and almonds. But you don't have to live without milk and cheese in a raw diet; flip to Chapters 9 and 11 to find out how to make these foods from delicious and heart-healthy nuts and seeds.

Staying nourished all day long

By making sure that you include plenty of fresh, colorful, nutrient-dense, high-water-content, raw plant foods in your meals throughout the day, you fuel your body to function properly all day and into old age. No matter how much raw food you consume in a day, be sure to eat meals at scheduled mealtimes and don't skip meals. Enjoying nutritious and filling foods at regular intervals makes it less likely you'll overindulge at dinner or resort to late-night snacks.

Start your day with a good breakfast; at least have a smoothie or green juice to help your body rehydrate after a night without fluids or nutrients. (Find breakfast and juice recipes in Chapters 10 and 11.)

A nourishing lunch helps curb cravings for sweets and other quick-energy foods in the afternoon. But if you do feel a need for sweets, have a piece of ripe fruit or a small handful of nuts or trail mix (recipe in Chapter 16). Keep dinner light and eat it early. Consuming foods near bedtime interferes with your ability to rest deeply because your body is working to digest your meal, which takes at least six hours and often much longer.

Integrating Raw Foods into Your Life

Embarking on a major life change can be exciting — and a little nerve-wracking, too. When a person is seriously considering "going raw," all sorts of questions run through the brain. Foremost: "What will I eat?" Salads get boring, and munching on a raw beet isn't an overly luring idea.

The good news is that there's a big wide world of delicious foods to enjoy — no cooking needed. In fact, one of the best perks of a raw diet is exploring new foods and finding creative ways of preparing old favorites. For instance, from a selection of ten fresh ingredients, you can make hundreds of different salads without repeating any. Hint: Don't use all ten in the same dish!

Make a point of trying new foods and recipes and, over time, replacing less-healthy meals with new raw favorites.

You may find that a new favorite adventure is checking out local produce markets, especially when traveling to new locations. (If this is you, be sure to check out Chapter 19 for tips on how to stay raw when you're traveling.) Dare to try something new at least once a week. Here are a few suggestions:

- ✔ Try *cherimoyas,* a sweet, white, creamy fruit that has a hint of pineapple and pear that hails from the Andes and now grows in Southern California. Just peel and eat the luscious fruit and discard the large, hard seeds, which are toxic.

- ✔ Take a chance on *durian,* a prehistoric-looking fruit that tastes like sweet onion custard. It's known in Southeast Asia as the king of fruits. Look for durian in the frozen section of Asian markets. No need to prepare it in any way; it's delicious just as it is!

- ✔ *Celery root,* also known as *celeriac,* is a crisp, slightly starchy root vegetable that tastes like celery and can grow anywhere root vegetables thrive. Shred it, puree it, or slice and eat with a dip (find dip recipes in Chapter 12).

> ✔ *Gypsy peppers* resemble spicy jalapeño chili peppers but taste like sweet bell peppers. Look for gypsy peppers at your local farmers market. Eat them with no preparation at all or stuff them with nut cheese for a savory treat. (See Chapter 9 for nut cheese recipes.)

Take a look through Chapter 7 to gain some know-how for creating satisfying raw meals. And check out the recipes in Part III to find an assortment of food ideas and step-by-step preparation instructions.

In this section, we show you that it's possible to maintain a raw food lifestyle when eating out, socializing, and even traveling. And if you still want more, go to Chapter 20 to get tips on making friends in the raw world and find out what to eat when you attend food-centered functions that are not raw-friendly.

Planning ahead

As with any major change in your diet, planning ahead for your raw lifestyle is essential to success. Keeping your refrigerator and pantry stocked with raw staples (as we suggest in Chapter 5) makes choosing wisely much easier. And because some raw recipes are a bit time-consuming, prepping key ingredients for certain meals is vital. Nuts, seeds, and grains, for instance, often need to soak overnight, and sprouting takes time. Raw breads and crackers need to dehydrate for as long as 24 hours or more. And fermenting foods like sauerkraut and cheese can require a week or more.

But don't let those timelines discourage you. We help you set up a schedule in Chapter 4 to keep these items in the hopper so you're never without them. And we flag recipes that require ahead-of-time preparation with the Plan Ahead icon. Before long, you'll have multiple batches of seeds sprouting, wheat grass growing, and cheese fermenting so you can whip up your best batch of whatever in no time!

Most of the time you won't need more than a knife and a blender to prepare your raw foods, but a food processor and dehydrator come in quite handy for some dishes. If you want long threads of what looks (and feels) like pasta, use a hand-held spiral slicer to turn veggies into noodles. And, if you want to include fruit and vegetable juices in your healthy lifestyle, a juicer is a must. Get the scoop on these and other raw kitchen tools in Chapter 5.

Dining out and staying raw

Just because you're deciding to eat more (or all) raw foods, you aren't stuck eating at home day in and day out. Many restaurants now offer vegetarian and vegan options that you can enjoy as a raw meal. If the restaurant already serves food that's fresh, organic, and minimally processed, you're likely to find healthy options.

But this isn't always the case. Uncle Bud may be in town and insist on gathering at the steak house. No problem! In Chapter 19, you can find tips on scoring a raw meal in practically any restaurant. We point out how to read a menu the raw way and suggest items to pack in, such as raw salad dressing, so you can practically guarantee yourself a filling and nutritious meal.

Keep in mind that you aren't limited to actual menu items. Check out the ingredients in a restaurant's offerings and find out what you can put together to make yourself a raw feast.

If you're lucky enough to find a bona fide raw food restaurant, like the ones in the nearby sidebar, be sure to support it with your dining dollars. Like their traditional counterparts, health-conscious raw food chefs must balance the flavor, texture, and appearance of food in order to please their guests; but raw food chefs have an additional responsibility to provide meals that contain all the nutrients required for optimal health and are easy to digest. So most raw food chefs insist on having the freshest, ripest, most nutrient-dense, seasonal, raw, organic ingredients available, and they limit fats and salt — because most raw food diners demand this level of consideration to food. Sounds like a full plate, right?

Joining the raw community

The raw lifestyle is gaining ground throughout the world and becoming more popular every day. In greater numbers all the time, people are shopping at farmers' markets and getting interested in improving their health with better food choices. This movement means that finding other people who want to consume primarily raw fruits and vegetables is much easier now than it once was.

Nevertheless, you're still a trendsetter, so you probably need to do a little research to find others who eat and live raw. Most larger cities have raw meet-up groups or raw-friendly vegetarian and vegan meet-ups, so strike up conversations at your local organic shop and farmers' markets to see what's going on in your local community. Also, go online and search for "raw food groups" and "raw food classes" to find chat groups, blogs, and classes that can help you learn more about nutrition and food preparation or just meet some like-minded people. Take a peek at Chapter 20 for more on finding a raw community or starting your own group.

Raw-friendly restaurants

Raw and raw-friendly restaurants are sprouting up all over the world. Here are some of our favorites in the U.S.:

- ✔ **118 Degrees, Costa Mesa, CA** (http://118degrees.com) serves fresh, organic, living cuisine that's presented in an artful context to be enjoyed with family and friends.

- ✔ **Au Lac, Fountain Valley, CA** (http://aulac.com) offers profoundly eye-opening raw and vegan food. Chef Ito has created remarkably delicious and fulfilling Asian-influenced cuisine, from starters to incredible desserts.

- ✔ **Café Gratitude, Los Angeles, CA** (http://cafegratitude.com) is a 100 percent organic vegan restaurant specializing in gourmet raw and cooked cuisines featuring organic produce from the restaurant's farm in Vacaville, California (Be Love Farm).

- ✔ **Karyn's Fresh Corner, Chicago, IL** (http://karynraw.com) is an organic juice bar, store, and fine-dining restaurant founded by Karyn Calabrese.

- ✔ **Living Light Cafe, Fort Bragg, CA** (www.rawfoodchef.com), located on the beautiful Mendocino coast, is an organic, gourmet, mostly raw, all vegan café with a salad bar, gourmet entrees, soups, smoothies, juices, and an amazing array of desserts. Owned and operated by yours truly (the authors of this book, Cherie Soria and Dan Ladermann), this café also offers some packaged foods online.

- ✔ **Pure Food and Wine, New York City, NY** (http://oneluckyduck.com/purefoodandwine) is a gourmet raw vegan fine-dining restaurant that also offers takeaway foods, a juice bar, and a store.

- ✔ **Quintessence, New York City, NY** (http://raw-q.com) is a gourmet, 100 percent organic, vegan, and raw restaurant with a commitment to both flavor and health.

Chapter 2

Checking Out Raw-some Foods

*T*he raw food diet is a nutrient-rich way of eating that's high in antioxidants, phytochemicals, vitamins, minerals, healthy fats, and fiber, which maximizes health and vitality. The extra good news is that following a raw food lifestyle doesn't necessarily mean that you eat *only* raw foods; for most people, that's unrealistic. But in most cases, the more raw foods you eat, the better you feel and look, especially if the few cooked foods you choose to eat are health-promoting.

In this chapter, we point out which foods are raw and which ones aren't. We also explain how eating raw foods benefits you now and over the course of your life. You can increase your energy, find a natural balance with your weight, and become healthier and more peaceful — all without feeling deprived or giving up the pleasure of eating your favorite foods.

Finding Out What's Raw and What's Not

Most health experts agree that eating fruits and vegetables is essential for good health. Even people who don't follow that advice typically don't argue its validity. However, many of the most important nutrients in produce are harmed by heat, processing, and even the passing of time in storage. That's why you get the most nutritional benefit nourishment from eating freshly harvested produce in its natural uncooked and unprocessed state.

For example, a fresh ripe tomato is clearly better for you than ketchup, which is highly processed and loaded with sugar. Yet many foods that are naturally nutritional powerhouses are no better than ketchup if they're cooked or processed. In this section we help you see what's raw and what's not, because knowing what to eat is just as important to your health and well-being as knowing what to avoid.

Choosing the good stuff

All fruits and leafy vegetables can be enjoyed raw, and most other vegetables can be eaten without cooking. But some starches and legumes need to be cooked to be palatable. For example, raw potatoes are too starchy to eat raw, and rice must be cooked or it can break your teeth, but most other grains and legumes can be soaked, sprouted, and eaten raw.

Most raw foodists choose to consume natural foods that are fresh, ripe, and grown organically in order to enjoy the highest nutrient value, the least chemical residues, and the best flavors available.

To qualify as *raw,* foods must be uncooked or processed in a way that doesn't create enough heat to destroy inherent nutrients. Many important vitamins, antioxidants, and phytonutrients are destroyed or damaged at temperatures as low as 120 to 130 degrees. The accepted temperature range for raw food is between 105 and 118 degrees.

Exploring raw food is likely to increase your awareness of some amazing fruits and vegetables that you never knew existed or that just didn't catch your attention before. The plant kingdom is a whole world of exciting foods. Here are some foods you should definitely include in your raw diet:

✔ **Leafy greens and grasses:** Eat as many greens (such as spinach, kale, and lettuce) and grasses (including wheat grass) as possible. Enjoy them in the form of green smoothies, juices, soups, and salads. If weight loss and healing are part of your health goals, make these foods and other vegetables the largest portion of your diet.

✔ **Colorful vegetables and fruits:** Whether whole, cut, or juiced, eat the full color spectrum of juicy veggies and fruits: red (peppers, tomatoes), orange (carrots, peppers), yellow (yellow squash, peaches), green (cucumbers, celery, lettuce), and blue and purple (blueberries, eggplant, purple cabbage).

Each natural color of food represents a different nutrient group of *phytochemicals,* which provide your best defenses against cancer and other chronic diseases. See Chapter 3 for more on full-spectrum eating.

✔ **Ripe fruits:** Enjoy ripe fruits and their juices as a great source of easily digestible carbohydrates and antioxidants. If weight gain is your goal or you're an athlete, eat more of these high-calorie foods, but make sure they're ripe. Unripe fruit has fewer nutrients and can cause indigestion.

✔ **Nuts and seeds:** Eat a limited amount of nuts and seeds as long as you don't have an allergy or sensitivity to these foods. Almonds, cashews, and pine nuts are great sources of essential fatty acids, protein, minerals, and other nutrients. Find recipes for nut milks and cheeses in Part III.

NUTRITION SPEAK

✔ **Legumes:** Enjoy sprouted peas, azuki beans, and lentils. Alfalfa and clover seeds are actually legumes, too. Sprout them to the leafy green stage and eat raw. We don't recommend peanuts, because they're a common allergen and very difficult to digest in their raw state.

✔ **Gluten-free grains:** Corn, which is a grain and also considered a vegetable, can be eaten raw when it's fresh or you can grind freeze-dried raw corn for use in breads (see Chapter 14). Other grains that lend themselves to raw recipes are quinoa, buckwheat, and wild rice.

Quinoa is an incredibly healthy, high-protein, nutrient-dense grain that can be sprouted and eaten raw. It's also easy to digest.

✔ **Fermented foods:** Packed with beneficial probiotics, fermented foods aid digestion. Try out our recipe for sauerkraut in Chapter 13 to get started with home fermenting.

✔ **Sea vegetables:** Foods such as sea palm, nori, and algae are high in protein and fit right into a raw diet. See Chapter 5 for a list of recommended sea veggies.

Knowing what food and drink to avoid

As you begin your raw journey, knowing what to eat is pretty important. Yet knowing what foods to avoid is helpful, too. By eliminating foods that compromise your health and replacing them with nourishing foods that strengthen your body, you feel better and enable your biological systems to function as designed.

We recommend that you avoid consuming these items:

✔ **Meat and dairy:** These animal-based products contain no fiber or phytonutrients but, unless organic, do contain lots of hormones and pesticides. If you choose to consume meat and dairy, you can limit the amount of hormones and pesticides you consume by purchasing organic, but we don't recommend these foods for optimum health.

✔ **Fried foods:** When fats and oils are heated, they become *carcinogenic* (or cancer causing) soon after they reach their individual heat threshold. Fried foods have many other negative impacts on your general health as well (see Chapter 3 for details). This no-no category includes roasted nuts and other high-fat cooked foods.

✔ **High-sugar, nutrient-free foods:** This category includes sugary beverages, candy, pastries, and other foods filled with refined sugars as well as refined wheat products, including some breads, pasta, and pizza.

✔ **Processed foods:** If a food product has a long ingredient list of components you can't pronounce, don't buy it and definitely don't eat it.

- ✔ **Alcohol:** Don't make alcohol consumption part of your daily routine. If you do drink, enjoy a glass of organic wine on occasion. Alcohol depletes the body of vitamin A, an important antioxidant, and when taken in excess, alcohol contributes to premature aging and disease.

- ✔ **Caffeine:** Caffeinated beverages, including coffee, tea, and soft drinks, are acid forming and cause overstimulation, so limit your intake to a daily cup of organic coffee (if you must have it and you're healthy). Caffeine is not recommended at all for anyone with health challenges.

- ✔ **Nonorganic foods:** Nonorganic foods are often high in pesticides, genetically modified organisms (GMO), and other components that damage health and the environment. Find more on organics in Chapter 6.

- ✔ **Chocolate:** Even raw chocolate can be overly stimulating, contain a number of harmful compounds (along with some beneficial ones), and involve high amounts of sugar. We suggest eating chocolate only on special occasions and, when you do eat it, use unsweetened raw cacao powder or carob instead to give desserts a chocolate taste. See Chapter 17 for delicious raw dessert recipes.

- ✔ **Concentrated sweets:** Desserts are not a food group . . . even though we dedicate an entire recipe chapter to them. Hey, we're human! Even whole food sweeteners, such as raw honey, can be problematic if you're experiencing health or weight challenges. Limit your intake of desserts, even raw goodies, to times of special celebration.

Are all raw foods healthy? No, raw foods are not created equal. Some are much too high in fat and sugar. So don't make *raw* the only criteria for choosing health-promoting food. Be sure to balance your food choices and not overdo the high-calorie foods — no matter what diet you follow.

Enjoying the Perks of Living Raw

Raw foods are satisfying because they're nutrient-rich. When your body's nutrition needs are met, you're less likely to crave foods. On the other hand, when you're hungry and consume foods that are filled with empty calories, your body craves more food in an attempt to get the nourishment it requires to function properly.

Ever notice how potato chips never fill you up? They have a lot of calories (thanks to generous amounts of saturated or hydrogenated fats in every bag), large amounts of salt, and very limited nutritional value. So you get all the calories that lead to weight gain and none of the nutrition that makes you healthy and satisfied. Alternately, a heaping and colorful raw salad that's loaded with minerals, phytonutrients, and antioxidants is a nutritious, filling, and satisfying snack that doesn't carry the risk of your pants no longer fitting and worse health results — like those chips do. Eating raw foods keeps you feeling light, energetic, full, and satisfied.

In this section, we describe the most important benefits of following a raw food diet, including increased energy, improved biological function, and natural weight management. But the benefits don't stop there. Living raw can also help you fend off and heal from disease (from minor infections to chronic and life-threatening conditions), enhance your mental clarity, make a positive impact on the environment, and even simplify post-meal cleanup. (See Chapter 21 for details on some of these raw-living perks.)

Feeling energetic and balanced

Think about how you felt after the last time you overate at a big holiday meal. If you're like most people, your energy plummeted and a nap ensued. More food does not equal more energy.

The relationship between *what* you eat and how you feel deserves constant awareness. Fueling your body with adequate nutrition helps you maintain a high level of energy all day long; it also supports your body's healing processes, allows you to think clearly, and helps you stay active and productive. You can eliminate, or at least minimize, the drastic up-and-down cycles of energy that many people on a conventional diet experience by eating fresh, colorful, nutrient-dense, high-water-content, raw plant foods throughout the day and by responding to the messages your body sends you.

Raw food isn't just about what you eat; it's a lifestyle decision that can help you find the ever-elusive balance — physical, mental, and emotional — that so many people seek. Some of that balance comes from being in control of your food choices and having more energy to do the things you love. The holistic perks are real; raw foodists often report that they feel better when they get up in the morning and that they're more productive and creative throughout the day than before transitioning to the raw life.

Easing digestion

Digestion and the extraction of calories and nutrients from the food you eat are necessary for survival. That's why your body prioritizes digestion over most other functions, including sleep. As soon as you eat, your biological resources focus on digestion and the process of metabolizing food.

When you start chewing food, your mouth releases digestive enzymes into your saliva. When you consume raw plant-based foods and chew adequately (or get a little help from a blender), the cell walls of the plant break down and release their food enzymes, which work with your body's digestive enzymes and reduce your *digestive load* (or the amount of resources it takes to digest food). Cooking destroys these food enzymes. Find out more about beneficial enzymes in raw food in Chapter 3.

Losing sleep over late-night snacks

Eating a big meal late at night messes up your ability to sleep well because your body needs time to digest food before pulling the shutters and letting you slumber. So try to eat several hours before bedtime and make your last meal a light raw salad, blended soup, or other easy-to- digest option. If your final meal of the day is too complex, high in fat, or abundant for the amount of activity you'll expend after eating it, then you may have trouble sleeping well. Allow yourself at least four to five hours before bedtime to digest your food.

Typically, raw food takes about 13 hours to go from ingestion to elimination. Cooked and processed foods that are high in fats and animal proteins can take up to 72 hours. One of the problems with a long period of digestion is its effect on sleep. (See the nearby sidebar "Losing sleep over late-night snacks.")

Sleep is extremely important to good health because your body does most of its healing and regeneration work while you sleep. If you're waking up at night feeling hot and unable to get back to sleep, or if you feel tired when you wake up in the morning, you may be spending a good portion of your sleep time actually digesting foods rather than getting the rest your body needs. Try eating lighter meals earlier in the evening to improve your quality of sleep.

Cleaning out the toxins

Over time, your body can build up a lot of toxins from exposure to pesticides, chemicals, pollution, drugs, processed food, and other sources. When your body is low on energy from a lack of proper nutrition and a high digestive load, it must prioritize vital functions like breathing over eliminating toxins. And if your body doesn't have adequate energy to clean out toxins, it stores them in your fat cells for later processing; the process is similar to your tendency to toss orphan items in your junk drawer or the guest-room closet.

Fortunately, you can help your body clean out the toxic clutter by simply making more healthful food choices. Eating a raw food diet supports the elimination of unnecessary, unwanted, and potentially harmful substances from your body in many ways:

- ✔ Each time you choose to eat a healthy food, you don't pick an unhealthy option. Basically, you stop acquiring junk that ends up in your closet.

- ✔ By decreasing the amount of energy required for digestion, your body can devote more energy to healing, cleansing, and rebuilding — tasks that may be long overdue. Think of this as spring cleaning.

✔ Eating raw foods provides your body with nutrients it needs to function properly. Whole natural foods are your body's cleaning supplies.

Different organs of the body — including the liver, kidneys, intestines, lungs, skin, lymphatic system, and cells — work together to neutralize, transform, and eliminate toxins. The nutrients and antioxidants that are abundant in a raw food diet support these processes.

If you're interested in cleaning out toxins quickly, take a look at Chapter 4 for details on doing a juice fast.

Improving weight management

A pleasant and sometimes unexpected perk of eating raw foods is losing weight and keeping it off. Most diets have a success rate of about 20 percent. (Success, by the way, is defined as a loss of 10 percent of body weight that's maintained for at least one year.) People who follow a raw food diet reach and maintain a healthy body weight long term for several reasons. One is the low calorie density of raw foods; another is heightened awareness of the body's signals related to food.

Getting down with calorie density

Most raw plant-based foods are nutrient rich and have a low *calorie density,* which is the number of calories in a given weight or volume of food. More calories per pound means higher calorie density, and people tend to overeat calorie-dense foods before feeling full. The result of overconsumption of calories is weight gain. Even a small amount of excess calories on a regular basis can add up over the years.

The most significant factor of calorie density in food is water content, but the presence of fiber and fat matters, too. When water is removed by cooking, dehydration, and other processing methods, food becomes more calorie dense.

When food is commercially processed, water and fiber are typically removed and replaced with low-cost fillers such as sugar, salt, and fats. This process increases the calorie density of food, making it more fattening while lowering nutritional content. Conversely, fresh raw fruits and vegetables are naturally high in water and fiber content, low in fat, nutrient dense, and low in calorie density, so you can fill up on these foods without gaining weight.

Responding to your body's signals

Raw foodists rarely worry about calories, but they do consider how much fat they eat because fat intake affects digestion; most people simply feel better and more energetic when they eat less fat. Choosing foods based on how you feel during and after eating becomes easier after you lose the desire for fried foods, processed and packaged foods, fast foods, meat, dairy, and other nutrient-deficient foods.

Tuning in to your body's signals makes it easier to tell if you're getting enough calories. You don't need a kitchen scale, measuring cup, and complicated tables to portion out every food you eat. Instead, simply eat until you feel full. When you eat healthy raw food, you can allow your body's natural satiety systems to work. *Satiety* is the state of being full, or satiated. See the "Getting satisfaction" sidebar for the inside story on satiety.

Retaining youthful vitality

The populations that live to the oldest healthy ages typically eat foods that are low in calories, fat, and animal products. These long-lasting people consume plant-based foods containing high levels of nutrients and fiber. Sounds like the raw food diet, right? Fruits and vegetables, sprouts, and juices are low in calorie density and create the least amount of free radicals in your body. These foods are also high in antioxidants that neutralize free radicals that damage other cells in your body.

Free radicals are uncharged molecules that are highly reactive and unstable. They attack healthy cells like biological gangsters. The body can handle free radicals with an adequate armory of antioxidants, but if free radicals overpower the antioxidant force and damage your body's live cells, then disease and accelerated aging can set in.

Overeating and consuming high amounts of cooked fats create free radicals; environmental pollution, radiation, cigarette smoke, and herbicides do, too. So the more antioxidants you can eat to defend your body, the better! Of course, you can buy pills and superfoods to help reduce free radicals, too, but the best approach is to avoid polluting your body in the first place.

Getting satisfaction

Satiety is controlled by two main mechanisms in your body: stretch receptors and nutrient receptors. The *stretch receptors* in the stomach and intestines tell your brain when you've have had enough to eat. When eating a diet that's high in calorie-dense processed foods, it's very easy to overeat before your stomach says, "Enough already!" If you eat nutritious raw foods, which are high in water content and low in calorie density, your stomach can detect when you've have had enough food. It sends the appropriate signals to your brain before you have a chance to consume too many calories. The *nutrient receptors* signal when you've received enough nutrients. When you eat processed foods that are low in nutrition, your body knows it's still deficient and continues to call out, "Feed me, feed me!" With raw foods, your body can easily detect that its nutritional needs have been met, and you can trust its signals

Saving money

A significant hurdle for people to overcome when they transition to living on raw organic foods is the perceived higher cost. People simply believe that they can't afford to make the change from highly processed convenience foods. Well, we believe you can't afford *not* to. For starters, consider the money you can save over the course of your life on healthcare and prescription medicine by becoming healthier and more active!

And if you think organic groceries are expensive, just think about how much organic produce you can buy for the cost of coronary bypass, which can easily exceed $100,000.

Too many people overlook the enormous financial drain on our national and personal budgets for fighting disease and providing medical care to a malnourished and lethargic population. The U.S. spends nearly $3 trillion every year on healthcare. Yet you can reduce your chances of suffering a devastating, chronic food-related health problem, including obesity, diabetes, and heart disease, just by following an organic raw food diet.

In addition to the money you can save on healthcare by nourishing your body with raw foods, you can cut your immediate food budget with these tips:

✔ Grow a kitchen garden. Find out how in Chapter 7.

✔ Buy local produce in season, shop sales at farmers' markets, and use online resources to stretch your grocery dollars. Get more money-saving tips in Chapter 6.

✔ Take advantage of membership clubs like Costco or Sam's Club. Most now carry fresh and organic foods.

✔ Know which foods are best to purchase organic and which ones you can buy conventional without added exposure to harmful pesticides. Get the rundown in Chapter 6.

✔ Reduce the cost of eating out by taking food with you when you're away from home. See Chapter 19 for suggestions.

✔ Go to raw potlucks or host your own. Find networking and planning help in Chapter 20.

On a personal level, when you're considering your food choices in light of your health and energy levels, be sure to factor in missed work, productivity loss, and the state of your relationships along with medical bills and drug costs. The real costs of life's most basic decisions aren't always obvious.

Pure water, pure body

No matter what food regimen you follow — raw, vegan, vegetarian, conventional, or whatnot — drinking plenty of clean, unchlorinated water is critical. Your body and cells require proper hydration to function efficiently. Tap water in most cities in the U.S. is free of the pathogens that plague much of the world, but it still includes other harmful substances, including toxic pesticides and chemicals such as chlorine, which kills beneficial probiotics. At a minimum, filter your drinking water with a carbon filter to remove chlorine. And don't forget, the water you put *on* your body is important, too. When you wash and bathe, you expose your largest detoxification and elimination organ, your skin, to whatever chemicals are in the water. Find advice on water filtration systems in Chapter 5.

Chapter 3

Getting Essential Nutrients

. . . .

In This Chapter

▶ Getting the real story on protein

▶ Eating foods of every color of the rainbow

▶ Being smart about the foods you choose

▶ Finding out what nutrients a raw diet provides (and lacks)

. . . .

A raw food lifestyle can be great fun — and very satisfying — if you understand the basics of good nutrition, learn simple food-preparation techniques, and identify natural whole foods that you enjoy. Raw foodists revel in freedom from counting calories, measuring portions, and craving can't-haves. Because a raw plant-based diet provides nearly all the nutrients you need, this way of life fosters balance and satisfaction.

Your body relies on the food you eat to provide an assortment of nutrients to fuel its ability to function. In order to achieve and maintain vibrant health, your cells require a steady stream of carbohydrates, essential fats, protein, minerals, and vitamins. You also need a good digestive system to break down and utilize the essential nutrients. If you can't digest your foods well, the nutrients they provide aren't *bioavailable,* or usable by the body. Raw diets are naturally designed to support health and meet nutrient requirements.

In this chapter, we show you how a diet of raw food can meet most of your nutritional needs. We introduce you to the concept of full-spectrum eating and point out how to supplement your diet as needed. We also reveal food combinations that optimize digestion, which further improves overall health.

Procuring Plenty of Protein

The prevailing question about a raw food diet (and vegetarian and vegan diets, too) is: Where do you get your protein? The fact that this question comes up so much is baffling to those who know that protein is not an elusive nutrient. The rampant concern about protein deficiency reveals a widespread misconception that people need to drink lots of milk and eat lots of meat to get enough protein. Yet some of the largest and strongest animals in the world, including silverback gorillas, horses, and elephants, thrive on a plant-based diet, and very few people wonder where they get their protein.

A good indication of how much protein we really need is seeing the amount that newborn babies — who are at the stage of life when humans develop and grow fastest — require when their only nutritional requirement is nature's perfect food: mother's milk. Six percent of the calories in breast milk are from protein.

Most health organizations throughout the world recommend that 4.5 to 10 percent of a person's daily calories come from protein. Some people require more protein than others, because of age and levels of activity, so this standard errs on the side of excess. But all the protein you need is available from plant-based nutrition.

As a percentage of total calories, here's how much protein each kind of plant-based food provides:

- ✔ **Fruits:** 6 percent
- ✔ **Nuts and seeds:** 11 percent
- ✔ **Grains:** 12 percent
- ✔ **Vegetables:** 18 percent
- ✔ **Legumes:** 30 percent

Eating a variety of plant foods and consuming enough calories to support your level of activity enables you to get plenty of protein.

Another, slightly different way that protein requirements are often presented is in terms of body weight. The recommendation is to consume 0.8 grams of protein for every kilogram of body weight per day. A kilogram is 2.2 pounds, so a 160-pound adult requires 58 grams of protein. A 2,000 calorie per day diet composed of 12 percent calories from protein provides 60 grams of protein, and this requirement is easily met on a raw food diet. Fortunately, measuring amounts of protein and studying tables is unnecessary when you eat a full-spectrum raw food diet.

Pandering to protein pushers

Much of the misinformation and confusion about human protein requirements is based on animal studies using rats in the early 1900s. Later, in the 1950s, research on the protein requirements of humans revealed that rats and humans have different protein requirements and that plant-based foods provide all the essential amino acids (the building blocks of protein) and complete protein in the amount that humans need.

Still, the powerful and highly profitable meat and dairy industries are happy to reinforce misconceptions about the requirement for meat and dairy in the human diet, and these industries are aided through generous subsidies and other supports by the United States Department of Agriculture (USDA). The federally funded National School Lunch program, for instance, spends more on dairy products than any other food item, and the USDA still includes milk as a required beverage in this program despite research showing that milk not only lacks nutritional benefits but actually has an adverse effect on health. The USDA has an inherent conflict of interest. On one hand, it's supposed to encourage Americans to eat healthfully, but it's also designed to support agricultural profits. Unfortunately, profit often prevails, compromising health awareness.

Figuring Out Full-Spectrum Eating

You may already know that full-spectrum lighting is good for you, but do you know that *full-spectrum eating* — choosing foods based on variety of color — is one of the best things you can do for your health? The compounds that give fruits and vegetables their natural and vibrant colors also infuse these plants with nutrients. So eating foods with a variety of natural colors ensures that you ingest the range of nutrients you need for optimal health.

Phytonutrients, a class of extremely beneficial compounds found only in plants (*phyto* means *plant* in Greek), give plants their variety of textures, flavors, color, and fragrance. When eaten, phytonutrients boost the immune system and provide anti-inflammatory, antiviral, antibacterial, and cellular-repair benefits. Certain families and colors of plants tend to contain specific groups of phytonutrients. Figure 3-1 provides a sampling of the various phytonutrients (and the biological benefits they provide) that are available in various foods grouped by color.

Phytonutrients are sensitive to heat, and they're quickly compromised or even destroyed when exposed to temperatures above their heat threshold. Like most of the nutrients that your body needs, phytonutrients are *synergistic,* meaning that they work better with companion nutrients than alone. Therefore, eating a variety of natural, whole, raw foods helps your body take advantage of all the available food power.

Color	Foods	Phytonutrients (with benefits)
Red	Tomatoes, red bell peppers, pink grapefruit, cherries, raspberries, red grapes, strawberries, red apples, watermelon	Resveratrol (anti-cancer, cardio-protective) Lycopene (reduces risk of stomach and prostate cancers)
Orange	Carrots, yams, sweet potatoes, orange bell peppers, squash, pumpkin, apricots, cantaloupe, mangoes, oranges	Carotenoids (provide vitamin A, protect DNA, may protect against breast, colorectal, lung, prostate, and uterine cancers)
Yellow	Corn, yellow bell peppers, lemons, grapefruit, oranges, peaches, nectarines, pears, pineapple	Flavonoids (protect against cardiovascular disease and cancer) Lutein, zeaxanthin (antioxidant, anti-cancer, anti-viral, may help fight cataracts and macular degeneration) Beta carotene (helps vision, the immune system, and skin)
Green	Broccoli, leeks, leafy greens (arugula, kale, lettuce, parsley, watercress, Swiss chard, collard greens, mustard greens, beet greens, cabbage), Brussels sprouts, bok choy	Isothiocyanates (prevent lung, esophageal, and other cancers) Indole-3-Carbinol (anti-cancer) Thiocyanates, Sulforaphane (anti-cancer) Zeaxanthins and lutein (antioxidant, anti-cancer, anti-viral, may help fight cataracts and macular degeneration)
Blue/Indigo	Blueberries, grapes, plums, bilberries, black mission figs	Anthocyanins and bioflavonoids (antioxidant, anti-inflammatory, improve night vision, prevent and treat macular degeneration and cataracts)
Purples/Violet	Purple cabbage, purple cauliflower, eggplant, beets, raspberries, grapes, strawberries, blackberries, plums	Lycopene (reduces risk of prostate and stomach cancers) Terpenes (activate body's protective enzymes, protect eyes, act as antioxidants, modify hormones, help block cholesterol absorption, protect cellular differentiation) Anthocyanins (antioxidant, anti-cancer, reduce LDL cholesterol, and have other heart-healthy properties)
White	Cauliflower, cabbage, radishes, chives, leeks, scallions, garlic, shallots, onions	Allyl Sulfides (reduce risk of stomach and colon cancers) Quercetin (antioxidant, natural anti-histamine, and anti-inflammatory) Isothiocyanates (anti-cancer)

Figure 3-1:
Eating foods of differ-ent colors provides a variety of different nutrients.

Sizing Up the Food Groups

When you first begin replacing cooked and processed foods with whole raw plant-based foods, you may need to fend off cravings for fast foods, processed snacks, and fatty meals. Emotional connections to and cravings for certain foods can be strong, but your attraction to cooked and nutritionally deficient foods lessens as you continue eating nourishing foods. As your body becomes healthier, it better communicates its real needs.

The number one trick for enjoying sustained energy and good health is to eat an abundance of foods that have low calorie density and high levels of nutrition. And the best choices are foods straight from the Earth. So when you want a snack, reach for raw fruits and vegetables; enjoy these foods as they are or juice 'em and drink! Also be sure to drink plenty of pure water between meals. Water not only keeps you hydrated but also creates a sense of fullness that controls hunger and keeps you alert.

In Chapter 7 and Part III, we provide detailed instructions for preparing healthy and satisfying goodies that can take the place of your previous go-to foods. Initially you may feel drawn to raw foods that are high in nuts and fats, but this desire tends to pass as you continue on the raw food way. In this section, we describe the benefits of different food groups, including fruits, vegetables, nuts, seeds, grains, and legumes to help you choose foods that improve your health and well-being.

Be sure to consult your doctor or holistic health practitioner for guidance and support regarding specific food choices to meet your nutritional needs and to make adjustments to prescription medication that may be needed as your health improves.

Figuring in fruits

According to most botanists, anything containing a seed is a fruit. That includes cucumbers, zucchini, peppers, and tomatoes — foods considered by most people to be vegetables. Fruits, both sweet and nonsweet varieties, are a great source of calories and nutrients. They should comprise a large portion of your diet, but fruits should not be the sole component of your diet.

The typical nutritional breakdown of a fruit looks like this:

- ✔ **Carbohydrates:** 89 percent
- ✔ **Protein:** 6 percent
- ✔ **Fats:** 5 percent

Fruits are low in fats and proteins and full of simple carbohydrates, making them easy to digest and a terrific source of energy. The protein level of fruit is lower than vegetables, but fruits can supply most, if not all, the essential amino acids you need. Citrus fruits in particular are very high in vitamin C, which is important for the production of collagen, connective tissue, muscles, bones, teeth, and a strong immune system. Many fruits are also high in the critical B vitamins, including B9 (folic acid).

If you're experiencing *Candida* (yeast overgrowth) or have a medical challenge such as cancer, experts often recommend reducing or eliminating sweet fruits from your diet because of their high sugar content. Always consult with a qualified health practitioner and nutrition expert if you're experiencing any major health issues.

Vindicating vegetables

Vegetables require more digestive energy than fruits because the protein and fat content in vegetables is higher and the carbohydrates are more complex.

The typical nutritional breakdown of vegetables looks like this:

- ✔ **Carbohydrates:** 73 percent
- ✔ **Protein:** 18 percent
- ✔ **Fats:** 9 percent

An entire book could be written about the health benefits of the vegetable kingdom alone, but here are a few good examples of the outstanding nutrition these foods offer:

- ✔ The cabbage family of plants, also known as cruciferous vegetables (or brassica) — Napa cabbage, green and purple cabbage, Brussels sprouts, bok choy, kale, broccoli, and cauliflower — are superstars of the plant kingdom when it comes to cancer-fighting properties. These foods are high in vitamin A, vitamin C, calcium, carotenoids, folic acid, and antioxidants and chemicals that boost DNA repair.
- ✔ Garlic contains *allicin,* which has antibacterial properties that help the body fight bacterial infections.
- ✔ Gingerroot, turmeric, and galangal are culinary and medicinal herbs that contain *gingerol,* which is known for reducing nausea and dizziness.
- ✔ Onions have *quercetin,* an antioxidant that neutralizes the damage potential of free radicals on cells and DNA. Quercetin is also an anti-inflammatory that may help protect you against heart disease and cancer.
- ✔ Green peas, snap peas, and green beans are good sources of protein, iron, magnesium, potassium, zinc, vitamin C, and B vitamins (except B12).
- ✔ Dark leafy greens, including kale, spinach, and romaine lettuce, are high in protein and packed with vitamins K, C, E, and many of the Bs. Packed with important minerals such as calcium, iron, potassium, and magnesium, dark leafy greens are also loaded with phytonutrients that protect the health of eyes and cells.
- ✔ Root vegetables such as carrots, beets, and yams offer an abundance of dietary fiber, beta carotene, other antioxidant phytonutrients, and an array of vitamins.
- ✔ Stalk vegetables, including asparagus, celery, and fennel bulb are often used medicinally for their cleansing properties. They're a rich source of fiber, potassium, vitamin C, and more.

Enjoying nuts and seeds

Nuts and seeds can add flavor and texture to raw meals and snacks and make them extra delicious and nutritious. When eaten in moderation (a palmful each day), nuts reduce the risk of diabetes and lower cholesterol levels and risk of heart disease. Nuts are rich in folic acid and other B vitamins as well as vitamin E, copper, potassium, magnesium, L-arginine, and zinc — all great nutrition for the heart.

Consume nuts and seeds raw or after soaking and sprouting them to remove the enzyme inhibitors that interfere with digestion. Instead of eating roasted nuts and seeds (and the carcinogens created by roasting), enjoy seasoned and dehydrated soaked and sprouted raw nuts and seeds as a crunchy snack or salad topping. See Chapter 7 for recommended soaking times for different kinds of nuts and seeds, and find delicious recipes in Chapter 13.

Brazil nuts contain exceptionally high levels of selenium, which is important for production of thyroid hormones and proper immune-system function. Selenium also helps prevent coronary artery disease, liver cirrhosis, and cancers. Eating a single 5-gram Brazil nut each day provides enough (174 percent of the recommended daily amount) of this trace element.

Including grains and legumes

Most grains, especially glutenous grains like wheat, rye, and barley, are not a major component of most raw diets because, cooked or raw, these foods are problematic. Here's why:

- ✔ Most grains contain *gluten,* a protein that an increasing number of people can't tolerate. Gluten is one of the most common allergens. Even people who don't have a diagnosed gluten intolerance or celiac disease may be gluten sensitive and experience symptoms such as indigestion, aching and stiff joints, skin problems, headaches, lethargy, and gas.

- ✔ Processed, refined, and cooked grains are low in vitamins and other nutrients. Even raw whole grains containing gluten create an acidic state in the body, which can lead to serious health consequences, including osteoporosis, kidney damage, and calcium loss.

- ✔ Grains contain *opioids,* addictive compounds that block pain receptors and trigger feelings of euphoria — one of the reasons people are continually drawn to them. But after an initial uplift, grains leave you feeling lethargic.

- ✔ Grain products tend to be bland tasting on their own, so people often pair them with sugar and unhealthy fats. This fix leads people to consume even more fat and other nutritionally devoid calories.

- ✔ Over-consumption of refined grain-based products leads to blood sugar imbalances and weight gain.

The best grains to eat are whole grains such as millet, quinoa, amaranth, and buckwheat, which are all gluten-free and can be soaked, sprouted, and eaten raw.

What's up with wheat-grass juice?

One ounce of wheat-grass juice contains the nutritional equivalent of more than two pounds of fresh fruits and vegetables. Plus, wheat-grass juice is very similar in molecular structure to red blood cells, so consuming this juice enhances the blood's capacity to carry oxygen to every cell of the body. The juice boosts energy by counteracting nutritional deficiencies and removing waste products that congest cells, blood, tissues, and organs. It also assists people seeking to lose weight by improving blood circulation and stoking the metabolic rate, suppressing appetite, and enhancing digestion.

Wheat-grass juice has been credited with the following benefits:

- Preventing gray hair and hair loss
- Relieving constipation
- Increasing resistance to radiation
- Accelerating healing of sores and wounds
- Reducing blood pressure

Legumes, which include peanuts, lentils, beans, and soybean products such as tofu, are a combination of starch and protein. They can cause gas, bloating, and other symptoms of indigestion. However, many raw foodists consume sprouted lentils, chickpeas, mung beans, and peas (cooked and raw) as a protein source. Green peas, lentils, mung, and azuki beans are also excellent sources of iron, zinc, and B vitamins (except B12).

Considering meat and dairy

All the protein and calcium you need is available in a plant-based diet — without animal products, which contain no dietary fiber and are proven to contribute to cancer, heart disease, diabetes, Alzheimer's, and other degenerative diseases. Eating meat and dairy is a personal choice, not a dietary necessity, and the choice comes with health consequences. Because so many people embrace a raw lifestyle due to poor health, lack of energy, or weight challenges, they often dive in feet first, beginning their raw journey eschewing all animal proteins.

However, some raw foodists, especially those just "testing the waters" choose to add more raw plant foods to their diet while continuing to eat some animal products. These people still feel tremendous benefits of the raw foods, especially if they cut down on the amount of meat and dairy they eat.

If you choose to eat animal products as a raw foodist, we don't recommend eating meat that's raw or cooked at high temperatures. Stewing meat is best; in fact, water cooking is the safest way to cook in general. And although unpasteurized dairy products are available in many places, dairy products present health risks — whether they're cooked or not. But after you find out how to make delicious nut milk, cheese (see Chapter 9), and even ice cream (see Chapter 17), we think you'll easily replace dairy products with these healthy alternatives.

You can find a growing assortment of raw foods — in addition to the whole fruits and vegetables that have always been available — in local grocery stores throughout the country. Even restaurants are offering more raw and vegan options. If you don't see something you want on the menu, ask for it. Most restaurants are willing to accommodate dietary requests. See Chapter 19 for more suggestions for staying raw when dining out.

Including Elusive Nutrients in Your Plan

All nutrients are important to your body's ability to function, and consuming a wide variety of vitamins and minerals is important because they tend to work best in combination. In other words, nutrients have a synergistic relationship. Vitamin C, for example, enhances the body's absorption of iron, and vitamin D enables calcium to help build strong bones. So it follows that nutrient-dense whole foods facilitate more biological action and achieve greater health results than any few standalone nutrients — ingested as supplements, for instance — can manage on their own.

In this section, we describe the power and support network of some of the most vital and elusive nutrients your body needs, including B12, D, calcium, probiotics, healthy fats, and enzymes.

Getting enough vitamin B12

Vitamin B12 is critical to good health. This nutrient is involved with maintenance of nerve cells; production of protective myelin sheaths around nerves, genetic material (DNA), red blood cells, and serotonin; and the breakdown of homocysteine, which is necessary for heart health. Vegans (people who don't eat any animal products) and a fair portion of the general population can only get this essential vitamin by taking a supplement or eating B12-fortified foods.

All reputable vegan and raw food experts recommend taking a vitamin B12 supplement or, at minimum, being tested regularly for homocysteine or methylmalonic acid (MMA) levels, which can indicate a B12 deficiency. This applies to everyone. Vegans and vegetarians aren't the only ones at risk for B12 deficiency; about 40 percent of the population overall need more B12, especially people over 50.

Supplementation is easy and inexpensive. Here are some ways to do it:

✔ Eat fortified foods such as vegetarian support formula nutritional yeast and certain green superfoods like chlorella.

✔ Take a *sublingual* (under the tongue) B12 pill or use a sublingual spray.

Overdosing on B12 isn't possible, so you can eat fortified foods and green superfoods in addition to taking a sublingual vitamin B12 pill!

Some people claim that eating a raw, near-raw, or vegetarian diet can provide an adequate intake of vitamin B12 without supplements or B12-fortified foods. It's simply not true. To ensure you have adequate levels of B12 in your system, take a supplement.

Using nutritional yeast

The easiest way to supplement vitamin B12 with fortified food is to add Red Star Vegetarian Support Formula nutritional yeast to your food. Or you can get nutritional yeast in bulk from a food co-op or natural food store. Just be sure to get one that's labeled *Vegetarian Support Formula,* which means it's fortified with B12.

Here are some daily dosage options for nutritional yeast. Choose one:

✔ Powdered form: 1 tablespoon

✔ Mini-flakes: 1½ tablespoons

✔ Large flakes: 2 tablespoons

For maximum absorption, split your dosage between two servings each day.

Several recipes in Part III call for nutritional yeast, including nut cheese (Chapter 9) and nacho cheese sauce (in the recipe for Nacho-Cheese Kale Chips in Chapter 16). You can also sprinkle it on salads, sauces, sauerkraut, and other foods to add a slightly cheesy taste. Kids really love the flavor.

Some not-raw vegan foods, including fortified soymilk and rice milk, are also enriched with vitamin B12.

Trying out supplements

If you choose to get your B12 in pill form, we suggest taking it *sublingually,* so it dissolves under your tongue, which allows better absorption than if you swallow it. Take it once a day or once a week depending on your personal preferences.

Here's the typical B12 sublingual pill dosage recommendation for raw vegans:

- ✔ **Daily:** At least 10 mcg
- ✔ **Weekly:** 2,000 mcg

The weekly dose is considerably higher than the daily dose because a relatively small percentage of vitamin B12 is absorbed when taken in high doses, and you want to ensure that your body absorbs the needed amount. Vitamin B12 isn't toxic, so your body eliminates any excess in your system.

Exposing a need for vitamin D

Vitamin D, the sunshine vitamin, helps people absorb and process calcium, and too-low levels of this vitamin are associated with increased cancer risks. Humans produce vitamin D from adequate sun exposure or gain it by eating fortified foods, including some cereals and commercially processed dairy milk, and/or supplementation.

If you're fortunate enough to live at a latitude of around 35 degrees or less and get at least 10 to 15 minutes of good sun exposure on your face, hands, arms, or legs each day, then your body may be producing an adequate amount of vitamin D. If not, you probably need to supplement.

Vitamin D is not reliably available from unfortified foods, and if you're on a whole food plant-based diet, then you probably aren't consuming any vitamin D–fortified foods. So if you're not getting proper sun exposure, you may want to consider taking a vitamin D supplement. Just keep in mind that many vitamin D supplements are derived from animal sources, so look for a vegan source if avoiding animal products is important to you and follow the manufacturers' recommended dose.

Concentrating on calcium

Calcium is an important mineral for bone health and other body functions. Fortunately, like cows and elephants, people can get plenty of calcium from a plant-based diet. Collards, kale, mustard greens, turnip greens, broccoli, Chinese cabbage, okra, bok choy, sesame seeds, sunflower seeds, and figs are all excellent sources of calcium. In fact, leafy greens provide more calcium than milk, and the human body absorbs the calcium in plant foods better than the calcium received from dairy products.

Vitamin D plays an important role in calcium absorption and utilization, so be sure to get your needed supply of vitamin D to help your body process the calcium you're consuming. Along with adequate calcium intake, weight-bearing exercise (including walking) also improves bone health.

The body's calcium balance is negatively affected by smoking and ingesting excess animal protein, sodium, caffeine, alcohol, and phosphorus. Strongly consider a calcium supplement if any of these risk factors apply to you.

Fermenting foods for active probiotics

A fully functional digestive system is critical to proper nutrient absorption. If you're not digesting the nutrients, vitamins, and minerals in your food, then you're probably not absorbing enough nutrition to maintain good health. This is where probiotics come in. *Probiotics* are the beneficial bacteria that live and produce themselves naturally in the intestinal tract in healthy people. But chlorine in tap water and antibiotics — both designed to kill pathogens and bacteria — reduce the probiotics and good bacteria in your system. Therefore, many people lack enough probiotics to achieve full digestion.

Fermented foods, including sauerkraut (recipe in Chapter 13) and nut and seed cheeses (recipes in Chapter 9), are not only delicious and a wonderful addition to your diet; they're also rich in probiotics that are necessary for good health. If you prefer to take probiotics in pill form, supplements are easy to find in most health specialty markets.

Making friends with fats

Fatty acids are critical to many body processes, including cell production, transportation, and absorption of fat-soluble vitamins (A, D, E, and K), and hormone regulation. *Essential fatty acids* are fats that the body cannot produce; these nutrients should be consumed in moderation.

Humans must get two essential fatty acids from diet:

- ✔ **Omega-6, linoleic acid (LA):** Animal-based foods and processed foods (including oil from corn, cottenseed, soybean, safflower, sesame, sunflower, and grape seed), and many nuts and seeds contain omega-6 fats. Nuts and seeds contain a reasonable amount of this nutrient and are the best source of omega-6.

- ✔ **Omega-3, alpha-linolenic acid (ALA):** Omega-3 fatty acids are in leafy greens, fruits, vegetables, flax, hemp and chia seeds, cold-water fish, and walnuts. Among the different forms of omega-3 fatty acids are ALA, EPA, and DHA. When you consume plant foods, you get ALA, and your body converts it into EPA and DHA and then uses it.

If you think of a see-saw with omega-3 fats (which reduce inflammation) on one end and omega-6 fats (which promote inflammation) on the other, you want to keep the seesaw exactly balanced or to keep the omega-3 side heavier — that is, consume an equal amount or a higher amount of 3 than 6. This ratio allows your hormones, cell membranes, and nervous system to function properly.

On a standard American diet, however, people eat 15 or more times omega-6 than 3 (the wrong side of the seesaw is in the air), which leads to chronic inflammation and other health problems. An abundance of omega-6 fats also interferes with your body's ability to convert ALA to the needed EPA and DHA forms.

DHA (a form of omega-3) is extremely important for pregnant and nursing women as well as for infants and young children. DHA is available in cold-water fish and fish oils, but these sources contain environmental contaminants such as mercury, dioxin, and PCBs that become concentrated in fats and tissues. Cold-water algae is a good source for DHA.

Exploring enzymes

In order to digest and assimilate food, the body needs digestive enzymes. These enzymes are produced primarily by the pancreas and also come from eating raw and living foods in their natural state.

Any form of cooking or processing — including pasteurization, irradiation, microwaving, steaming, boiling, frying, and baking — destroys the natural enzymes in food. To keep foods raw and their enzymes active, the temperature of food cannot exceed 113 to 118 degrees, which is well below typical cooking temperatures.

Enzymes break down food, allowing nutrients to be adequately absorbed in the digestive tract. What you eat is important, but the best diet in the world doesn't do much good if your body can't use the nutrients in the food. Plus, food that's not properly digested becomes a burden on your detoxification and elimination systems. Incompletely digested food that's absorbed by your body can trigger an *autoimmune response,* a biological reaction in which your immune system attacks and destroys healthy human tissue that has a similar amino-acid sequence to unrecognized substances.

Many raw nuts and seeds contain enzyme inhibitors that protect these foods from premature sprouting and germination. Soaking and sprouting nuts and seeds deactivate the enzyme inhibitors and begin germination, essentially creating a living food and making it more digestible. Find more information on soaking and sprouting in Chapter 7.

The body devotes a tremendous amount of its precious energy to produce enzymes for digestion. You can relieve your body of some of this work by eating raw plant foods, chewing them well, and soaking and sprouting nuts and seeds to deactivate enzyme inhibitors — actions that maximize the volume of enzymes you get from food.

Adding superfoods

When people refer to *superfoods,* they're usually talking about foods that offer very high nutritional benefit and negligible, if any, downsides. Some people think of cacao as a superfood because it contains antioxidants, but cacao also contains alkaloids and stimulants that are addictive. For that reason, we don't consider it a superfood.

Goji berries and acai berries are considered superfoods because of their high *ORAC value (oxygen radical absorbance capacity),* which is a measure of antioxidant value. But plenty of other fruits contain a high level of antioxidants, too, including blueberries, blackberries, and raspberries.

Get your berries fresh, frozen, or in powder form and add them to your water or smoothie as a flavor and nutrition booster.

Combining Foods to Aid Digestion

Food combining is a practice in which certain foods are eaten together and in a certain order to optimize digestion, which results in better nutrition and more available energy. Although not based on peer-reviewed science, here are some food-combining habits you may want to try:

- ✔ **Eat foods with the highest water content first.** Watery foods are fast-moving and start digesting quickly. If you eat them later in a meal, they may get stuck behind a food that's slower to digest, which can lead to fermentation. Eat juicy fresh fruits alone or before heavier food.

- ✔ **Limit high-sugar foods when eating high-protein foods.** The combination of sweet fruit and proteins such as nuts can cause gas, because fruits digest so much more quickly than nuts. Nut cheese, yogurt, and milks are easier to digest than whole nuts.

- ✔ **Limit the number of fats in a meal.** Stick to one fat source per meal if possible, to simplify digestion.

- ✔ **Don't combine starch with proteins.** The body must work long and hard to digest a starch-and-protein combination, so it can cause gas and bloating. Eating reasonable portions can help to mitigate this problem.

- ✔ **Limit intake of liquids right before or after eating.** Water and other beverages dilute your digestive juices, interfering with digestion, so don't drink more than a few ounces of liquid in the half hour before or after eating.

- ✔ **Eat happily.** Stress and negative emotions don't mix well with any food and can compromise your ability to digest, so don't bring them to the table.

Another way to aid digestion is to always chew your food to a mush. We like to say, "Juice your food and chew your juice." It's a good idea no matter what type of food you're eating.

Part II
Embarking on Your Raw Journey

The 5th Wave   By Rich Tennant

"I SAID, I DON'T KNOW WHY WE NEED A FOOD
DEHYDRATOR WHEN WE ALREADY
OWN A CLOTHES DRYER!"

In this part . . .

The chapters in this part provide a step-by-step guide for transitioning to a mostly or totally raw lifestyle — at your own pace. Find out how to set up your pantry and kitchen to make preparing delicious raw meals easier and more enjoyable. We point out how (and for how long) to store your foods for maximum nutrition and food safety. We even offer a sample menu for your first month of eating raw, and it includes recommendations for when to prepare foods in bulk to make mealtimes easier. These chapters are full of tips on what to buy, where to shop, and how to prepare truly satisfying raw meals.

Chapter 4

Going Raw

*V*ery few people strive to eat a diet of 100 percent raw foods. The amount of raw foods you choose to eat in relation to other food options is a personal choice that's often based on specific goals. Sometimes those goals center on health issues or weight challenges; other times they're based on a desire to end food addictions. Only you know what's best for you.

The most important thing to remember when embarking on a raw food lifestyle or integrating raw foods into your cuisine — just like when you begin any other change in life — is to avoid putting unrealistic expectations on yourself. A moderate approach helps with transitions and improves your chances of making positive change stick. When going raw, slowly add more whole, plant-based foods to your diet. Find foods you enjoy and allow a natural transition to occur. You'll be craving salads and green juice before you know it!

In this chapter, we help you consider how raw you want to go and offer suggestions for easing into a raw foods lifestyle. We even provide you with a sample 31-day menu for your first month raw. Follow this sample or use it as a guide to create your own plan. We point out the benefits of detoxifying your body with fasts and cleanses and tell you how to do it. And yes, we also provide some tips for introducing your friends and family to the wonderful and nourishing world of raw cuisine.

Easing, Not Rushing, into Raw

Most raw foodists say that they eat *high raw*, meaning that the majority of their meals are raw. And most of these folks don't feel guilty when they consciously eat something cooked, because high-raw individuals tend to consume foods (cooked and raw) that are nutritious and promote health.

It takes months, sometimes years, to reach a point where you prefer to eat mostly raw food. For some, a pure and total raw diet is the goal, but it's not for everyone. What's most important is for individuals to make deliberate and healthful — yet comfortable — choices about the food they eat.

As you become motivated to make the transition to raw foods, you may consider jumping in feet first and cutting out all cooked foods from your diet for a while just to experience what it feels like. That's perfectly fine, of course. But you can enjoy tremendous improvement in health by eating a diet that's just half raw and eliminating some of the unhealthiest foods in your current diet.

Identifying an ideal ratio of cooked to raw food to consume is tough. Some people say that 80 percent of your daily calories should come from raw foods, but that depends on what makes up the other 20 percent. If it's potato chips and sour cream dip, then the diet isn't very health promoting. But if that 20 percent consists of healthy cooked foods, such as steamed vegetables and whole, gluten-free grains or legumes, then good health isn't compromised.

If you're choosing a raw food diet due to a life-threatening health challenge such as cancer, heart disease, extreme high blood pressure, or diabetes, then a quick transition to this healing diet may be more beneficial than a slow approach. If you're pursuing a raw life for other reasons, then a gradual transition may be more suitable.

In this section, we point out the emotional components of eating and highlight the attachment many people have to eating cooked food. We also describe situations in which eating cooked foods may be preferable to certain raw options. Most importantly, this section is where you can find guidance for moving toward a mostly raw food diet in a way that make sense for you.

Understanding the attachment to cooked foods

No one knows exactly why humans began cooking food. It may have been accidental; perhaps a piece of food dropped into a communal fire and someone ate it, liked the experience, and convinced others to try. Or cooking may have been an attempt to preserve food between hunts. Whatever the case may be, we know that humans have looked to fire with a feeling of safety and protection for thousands of years. We're the only animal that doesn't instinctively fear fire. Instead, we've harnessed the fiery element and used it to warm our shelters and provide basic provisions for survival, including cooking foods that are not otherwise edible or meant for human consumption.

Now, since the advent of refrigeration, most plant-based foods don't need to be cooked. Sure, the cooking process makes some foods easier to chew, but cooking decreases the nutritional value of food, particularly antioxidants, like vitamin C and folate.

If you're transitioning to raw foods and have digestive issues or dental problems, try blending and juicing fruits and veggies to make foods easier on your system and to (ahem) smooth the transition. See how-to details for using your juicer in Chapter 7.

The fact is, many humans continue to cook foods because that's how they're used to eating them. Your past experience with food plays an important role in your sense of comfort and satisfaction regarding food. In other words, if you were brought up eating cooked foods and the eating experience involved happiness and emotional bonding, then you likely gravitate toward cooked foods, especially when in need of emotional soothing. If you have fond memories of eating salads, then that's the food that soothes your heart!

For those who love a plate of hearty lasagna and other traditional favorites, the good news is that producing raw food meals with flavors, textures, and appearances that resemble many of those cooked foods is as easy as (raw) pie. We show you how to do it in this book!

Going all raw: Is it necessary?

In a word: no. You do not need to eat all raw food all the time to experience the benefits of raw foods on your health. In fact, some cooked foods are better for you than some raw foods when eaten every day or in large amounts.

Here are some things to consider when assessing the nutritional value of a cooked food:

- ✔ **What food is being cooked?** Whole plant foods such as quinoa and other whole grains as well as root vegetables and legumes such as lentils and azuki beans — if prepared without added oil, salt, and/or sugar — are healthier when cooked than many gourmet raw foods that are high in fat and sugar.

We don't recommend that you eat raw animal products, because bacterial contamination can make you very sick. Cooked or raw, animal protein is a proven catalyst for some of the worst health challenges: heart disease, cancer, and stroke. Yet some raw foodists eat small amounts of cooked meat, cooked or raw fish, and/or raw dairy products and maintain good health, but these people tend to make careful nutritional choices about their food, and raw plant foods make up the majority of their diet.

✔ **How is the food being cooked?** Of all the cooking methods used for plant foods, we prefer steaming. This method results in the least amount of nutrient loss because the water temperature cannot exceed the temperature of steam. Compared to boiling, far fewer nutrients are leached into the water during steaming.

Broccoli, for example, contains tons of folate. Boiling broccoli florets for 5 minutes results in a loss of 45 to 64 percent of the folate, but 0 to 17 percent of folate is lost by steaming broccoli for 5 to 15 minutes.

✔ **How long is the food being cooked?** The amount of nutrient loss during cooking over a set period of time varies with each fruit and vegetable; each nutrient reacts differently to cooking, too. In general, water-soluble vitamins (such as folate, B-complex, and vitamin C) are harmed much quicker than fat-soluble nutrients (such as A, D, and E). But fat-soluble vitamins are eliminated much more slowly than water-soluble vitamins, so the body doesn't need to get these from food sources every day.

✔ **At what temperature is the food being cooked?** Grilling and baking food with high heat creates toxic chemical reactions in the food. Low temperatures are always better for retaining nutrients. In general, food that stays below 118 degrees is considered raw.

✔ **Who's eating the food?** Some people, particularly the elderly and those with impaired digestive systems, have trouble digesting raw foods from the cruciferous, or Brassica, family, which includes broccoli, cabbage, kale, and Brussels sprouts. For them, steaming these foods and getting some of the nutritional benefits may be better than avoiding them altogether. Another option is fermenting these foods, which creates even more health benefits (see Chapter 7 for info on fermenting foods and Chapter 13 for our Sauerkraut recipe).

✔ **How clean is the water supply?** When traveling to areas where the quality of water used to wash food contains harmful bacteria or is otherwise suspect, raw produce may not be clean. To avoid the risk of getting sick, you may want to steam or boil your food.

When making food choices, try to focus on nourishing your body with the most healthful options available at any given time. It's far better to eat a plate of steamed kale every day than to fill up on raw cheesecake instead. We know that kale is no match for cheesecake and every food plan needs a place for desserts, but even raw cheesecake is high in fat and a bit difficult to digest, so enjoy it sparingly. The point is that lightly cooked nutritious foods are better choices than some high-fat raw foods.

Setting Up a Raw Food Plan for Your First Month

A gradual transition to raw foods gives you time to adjust to the physical and emotional changes you'll likely experience while making this lifestyle change. During the early days of your transition, you may struggle to control cravings for foods that are cooked or unhealthy. Especially if you experience emotional stress, reverting to previous unhealthy eating habits is more likely. It's a problem particularly for people who try to transition too quickly or who haven't yet found their balance with raw foods for another reason. Having a plan in place helps to reduce impulsive decisions related to food, so we created a sample 31-day menu to get you started.

When raw food becomes ingrained into your lifestyle and your cravings are a thing of the past, making appropriate and healthy food choices is much easier, even in the midst of stress. In fact, good nutrition makes controlling emotions and maintaining balance easier when things get tough. Until you reach that point, consider keeping a food and feelings journal to record what you eat. Note how you feel before and after you make various food choices. You may discover that certain feelings impact certain food choices, and this exercise also enables you to monitor your body's response to different foods. As your body becomes healthier, you may see that it's easier to trust the signals and cravings it sends you.

Thinking ahead is the key to success with a raw food lifestyle, so this plan (Figure 4-1) includes advance preparation tips that make it possible to enjoy delicious and satisfying raw foods such as bread, crackers, cheese, and even creamy desserts. To make it all work, simply follow the steps, do the shopping, and spend some quality time in your kitchen a few days each week.

Here are few pointers for following this menu:

- All the recipes listed in the menu are included in Part III. Find a complete list of recipes with page numbers in the Recipes at a Glance section at the beginning of the book.

- The few days prior to Day 1 requires a lot of food prep because there's no reserve from the week before. Spend a couple of days preparing your condiments, sauces, and staple foods so you have the basics like crackers, cheese, bread, and milk.

Sample Menu
First 31 Days of Raw Food

SUNDAY	MONDAY	TUESDAY	WEDNESDAY	THURSDAY	FRIDAY	SATURDAY
Food prep prior to start: * Shop. * Soak and dehydrate walnuts for brownies. * Start sprouts. * Soak almonds for milk. * Soak oat groats for oatmeal. * Soak seeds for Onion–Caraway Seed Bread, Sweet Pepper Sesame Chips, and Buckwheat Granola. * Make chips, bread, granola, Sweet Red Pepper and Zucchini Hummus, Cashew Mayonnaise, and two dressings. * Start Sauerkraut.	1 **Breakfast:** Green Smoothie, Cinnamon Oatmeal, and Almond Milk **Snack:** To-Live-For Green Juice **Lunch:** Salad with toppings, Sweet Red Pepper and Zucchini Hummus, and Sweet Pepper Sesame Chips **Dinner:** Better-Than-Eggs Salad Sandwich on Onion–Caraway Seed Bread and green salad with dressing	2 **Breakfast:** Green Smoothie, Buckwheat Granola, and Almond Milk **Snack:** To-Live-For Green Juice **Lunch:** Salad with sprouts, avocado, toppings, and dressing and Sweet Pepper Sesame Chips **Dinner:** Zucchini Pasta with Cashew Dill Sauce and green dinner salad with dressing or Green salad, cooked whole grains or legumes, and steamed vegetables	3 **Breakfast:** Green Smoothie, Cinnamon Oatmeal, and Almond Milk **Snack:** To-Live-For Green Juice **Lunch:** Salad with toppings, Sweet Red Pepper and Zucchini Hummus, and Sweet Pepper Sesame Chips **Dinner:** Avocado and tomato sandwich on Onion–Caraway Seed Bread with Cashew Mayonnaise and Vitality Soup or Massaged Kale Salad, sprouted or cooked quinoa, and steamed vegetables	4 **Breakfast:** Green Smoothie, Buckwheat Granola, and Almond Milk **Snack:** To-Live-For Green Juice **Lunch:** Salad with toppings and Sweet Pepper Sesame Chips **Dinner:** Wraps with Better-Than-Eggs Salad filling, sprouts, and tomato and Massaged Kale Salad with dressing **Food prep:** * Freeze bananas for ice cream snacks. *Check/harvest Sauerkraut.	5 **Breakfast:** Green Smoothie, Cinnamon Oatmeal, and Almond Milk **Snack:** To-Live-For Green Juice **Lunch:** Salad with toppings and avocado and bread or chips **Dinner:** Salad, leftovers, or out **Food prep:** * Soak almonds for milk.	6 **Breakfast:** Green Smoothie, Buckwheat Granola, and Almond Milk **Snack:** To-Live-For Green Juice **Lunch:** Salad with sprouts, toppings and Sweet Pepper Sesame Chips **Dinner:** Out **Food prep:** * Make brownies or other snack, Almond Milk, and sauces for ice creams or other snacks. * Soak oat groats.
7 **Breakfast:** Green Smoothie, Buckwheat Granola, and Almond Milk **Snack:** To-Live-For Green Juice **Lunch:** Salad with toppings and Sweet Pepper Sesame Chips **Dinner:** Out **Food prep:** * Start sprouts. * Make Pine Nut Parmesan Cheese, Not-Salmon Pâté, two salad dressings, Marinara Sauce, and condiments of choice (freeze some).	8 **Breakfast:** Green Smoothie, Cinnamon Oatmeal, and Almond Milk **Snack:** To-Live-For Green Juice **Lunch:** Salad with toppings, Not-Salmon Pâté, and Sweet Pepper Sesame Chips **Dinner:** Zucchini Pasta with Marinara Sauce and Pine Nut Parmesan and green salad with dressing	9 **Breakfast:** Green Smoothie, Buckwheat Granola, and Almond Milk **Snack:** To-Live-For Green Juice **Lunch:** Salad with toppings, Sauerkraut, and Onion–Caraway Seed Bread **Dinner:** Not-Salmon Pâté Tomato Sliders and Massaged Kale Salad or Green salad, cooked whole grains or legumes, and steamed vegetables	10 **Breakfast:** Green Smoothie, Cinnamon Oatmeal, and Almond Milk **Snack** To-Live-For Green Juice **Lunch:** Salad with toppings, Not-Salmon Pâté, and Sweet Pepper Sesame Chips **Dinner:** Spinach Manicotti with Béchamel (or leftover Marinara) and green salad with dressing or Massaged Kale Salad or green salad, sprouted or cooked quinoa, and steamed vegetables	11 **Breakfast:** Green Smoothie, Buckwheat Granola, and Almond Milk **Snack:** To-Live-For Green Juice **Lunch:** Salad with toppings, Sauerkraut, and Onion–Caraway Seed Bread **Dinner:** Not-Salmon Pâté sandwich or wrap with green salad **Food prep:** * Soak buckwheat for granola.	12 **Breakfast:** Green Smoothie, Cinnamon Oatmeal, and Almond Milk **Snack:** To-Live-For Green Juice **Lunch:** Salad with toppings, avocado, and Sweet Pepper Sesame Chips **Dinner:** Salad, leftovers, or out **Foodprep:** * Shop. * Rinse and sprout buckwheat. * Soak almonds for milk.	13 **Breakfast:** Green Smoothie, Buckwheat Granola, and Almond Milk **Snack:** To-Live-For Green Juice **Lunch:** Salad with toppings and Sweet Pepper Sesame Chips **Dinner:** Out **Food prep:** * Make Almond Milk, Buckwheat Granola, and a snack or dessert. * Soak and peel almonds for cheese.

Figure 4-1: A sample raw food plan for your first 31 days of living raw.

SUNDAY	MONDAY	TUESDAY	WEDNESDAY	THURSDAY	FRIDAY	SATURDAY
14 **Breakfast:** Green Smoothie, Buckwheat Granola, and Almond Milk **Snack:** To-Live-For Green Juice **Lunch:** Salad with Sweet Pepper Sesame Chips **Dinner:** Out *Food prep:* * Start sprouts. * Make Lemony Zucchini Bisque, Sweet Red Pepper and Zucchini Hummus, Dolmas, two dressings, Almond Feta Cheese, and Garlic-Herb Croutons.	**15** **Breakfast:** Green Smoothie, Cinnamon Oatmeal, and Almond Milk **Snack:** To-Live-For Green Juice **Lunch:** Salad with toppings and Sweet Pepper Sesame Chips **Dinner:** Horiatiki salad, Dolmas, Sweet Red Pepper and Zucchini Hummus, and Lemony Zucchini Bisque with Shaved Fennel	**16** **Breakfast:** Green Smoothie, Buckwheat Granola, and Almond Milk **Snack:** To-Live-For Green Juice **Lunch:** Salad with toppings and Onion–Caraway Seed Bread **Dinner:** Zucchini Pasta with Basil Pesto, Great Greek Olives, and leftover bisque or Green salad, cooked whole grains or legumes, and steamed vegetables	**17** **Breakfast:** Green Smoothie, Cinnamon Oatmeal, and Almond Milk **Snack:** To-Live-For Green Juice **Lunch:** Salad with toppings, Sauerkraut, and Sweet Pepper Sesame Chips **Dinner:** Full-meal salad with dressing, leftover Dolmas, Almond Feta Cheese, and Lemony Zucchini Bisque with Shaved Fennel or Massaged Kale Salad, sprouted or cooked quinoa, and steamed vegetables Food prep: * Soak seeds for seasoned seeds.	**18** **Breakfast:** Green Smoothie, Buckwheat Granola, and Almond Milk **Snack:** To-Live-For Green Juice **Lunch:** Salad with toppings, Sauerkraut, and Onion–Caraway Seed Bread **Dinner:** Lettuce wraps with veggies and leftover tomato pesto *Food prep:* * Dehydrate seasoned seeds for salad toppings. * Soak oat groats for oatmeal.	**19** **Breakfast:** Green Smoothie, Cinnamon Oatmeal, and Almond Milk **Snack:** To-Live-For Green Juice **Lunch:** Salad with toppings, Sauerkraut, and Sweet Pepper Sesame Chips **Dinner:** Salad, leftovers, or out *Food prep:* * Shop. * Rinse oat groats. * Soak almonds for milk.	**20** **Breakfast:** Green Smoothie, Buckwheat Granola, and Almond Milk **Snack:** To-Live-For Green Juice **Lunch:** Salad with Sweet Pepper Sesame Chips **Dinner:** Out *Food prep:* * Soak and peel almonds for feta cheese. * Make Jalapeño-Onion Corn Bread and snacks or desserts.
21 **Breakfast:** Green Smoothie, Cinnamon Oatmeal, and Almond Milk **Snack:** To-Live-For Green Juice **Lunch:** Salad with Sweet Pepper Sesame Chips **Dinner:** Out *Food prep:* * Start sprouts. * Soak seeds for Onion–Caraway Seed Bread * Make Sauerkraut. * Make Caesar Dressing, Italian Herb Dressing, and Basil Pesto. * Make Beefy Barbeque filling and bread.	**22** **Breakfast:** Green Smoothie, Buckwheat Granola, and Almond Milk **Snack:** To-Live-For Green Juice **Lunch:** Salad with toppings, Sauerkraut, and Onion–Caraway Seed Bread **Dinner:** Creamy Red Bell Pepper–Chipotle Soup, Jalapeño-Onion Corn Bread, and Caesar Salad	**23** **Breakfast:** Green Smoothie, Cinnamon Oatmeal, and Almond Milk **Snack:** To-Live-For Green Juice **Lunch:** Salad with toppings, Sauerkraut, and Onion–Caraway Seed Bread **Dinner:** Zucchini Pasta with Basil Pesto and green salad with Italian Herb Dressing or Green salad, cooked whole grains or legumes, and steamed vegetables	**24** **Breakfast:** Green Smoothie, Buckwheat Granola, and Almond Milk **Snack:** To-Live-For Green Juice **Lunch:** Salad with toppings, Sauerkraut, and Sweet Pepper Sesame Chips **Dinner:** Beefy Barbeque Sandwich and Massaged Kale Salad or Massaged Kale Salad, sprouted or cooked quinoa, and steamed vegetables	**25** **Breakfast:** Green Smoothie, Cinnamon Oatmeal, and Almond Milk **Snack:** To-Live-For Green Juice **Lunch:** Salad with toppings and Onion–Caraway Seed Bread **Dinner:** Lettuce wraps with leafy greens and Beefy Barbeque filling and green salad	**26** **Breakfast:** Green Smoothie, Buckwheat Granola, and Almond Milk **Snack:** To-Live-For Green Juice **Lunch:** Salad with toppings and Sweet Pepper Sesame Chips **Dinner:** Salad, leftovers, or out *Food prep:* * Shop. * Plan next week's/ month's menu. * Peel and soak almonds for cheese.	**27** **Breakfast:** Cinnamon Oatmeal, and Almond Milk **Snack:** To-Live-For Green Juice **Lunch:** Green salad with Sweet Pepper Sesame Chips **Dinner:** Out *Food prep:* * Prep snacks or dessert.

SUNDAY	MONDAY	TUESDAY	WEDNESDAY
28	29	30	31
Breakfast: Green Smoothie, Cinnamon Oatmeal, and Almond Milk	**Breakfast:** Green Smoothie, Buckwheat Granola, and Almond Milk	**Breakfast:** Green Smoothie, Cinnamon Oatmeal, and Almond Milk	**Breakfast:** Green Smoothie, Buckwheat Granola, and Almond Milk
Snack: To-Live-For Green Juice	**Snack:** To-Live-For Green Juice	**Snack:** To-Live-For Green Juice	**Snack:** To-Live-For Green Juice
Lunch: Salad with Sweet Pepper Sesame Chips	**Lunch:** Green salad with toppings and Onion–Caraway Seed Bread	**Lunch:** Green salad with toppings and Sweet Pepper Sesame Chips	**Lunch:** Salad with toppings and Onion–Caraway Seed Bread
Dinner: Out	**Dinner:** Green Burrito, Caesar Salad, Pico de Gallo, Guacamole, and Sweet Pepper Sesame Chips	**Dinner:** Green salad with Mexican leftovers and Gazpacho or Green salad, cooked whole grains or legumes, and steamed vegetables	**Dinner:** Root-Vegetable Raw-violi using frozen Basil Pesto or Massaged Kale Salad, sprouted or cooked quinoa, and steamed vegetables
Food prep: * Start sprouts. * Make Caesar Dressing and one other dressing, Refried Bean Pâté for Green Burrito, and Pico de Gallo. * Prep items for next week's menu.			

✔ Moving forward, advance food prep generally takes a few hours each week. Handle easy food prep during the week and knock out the more intensive prep on the weekends.

✔ Thursday and Friday meals use leftovers, and midweek meals are more creative, offering a simple cooked vegan meal option, too.

✔ Each day of the week shows pretty much the same breakfast, mid-morning snack, and lunch. That may sound boring, but it's not. No two smoothies or salads need to be the same.

✔ Dinner on Saturday and Sunday nights allows for eating out. Feel free to substitute another night's dinner if you go to a potluck or don't eat at home on a different night.

✔ To minimize time in the kitchen

 • Make two or three batches of crackers at a time; they can stay fresh for the entire month.

 • Make breads in large batches and freeze them until needed.

 • Make a week's supply of Almond Milk for cereals and freeze half.

 • Sauces and condiments freeze well, so prepare double batches and freeze some so they're handy when you need them.

Making Mealtime a Family Affair

Preparing raw meals is a great family project that can include members of almost any age. After all, little ones aren't in danger of burns when there's no heat in the kitchen. And when children are encouraged to be creative in the kitchen and participate in food preparation, they tend to be more interested in eating the foods being served.

People in general — adults, children, and those in between — often more readily accept changes when they're included in the decisions. So use meal-preparation time to slow down, catch up with each other, and engage your whole family in the move toward healthier living.

Find tasks for family members that are creative and fun. Giving children a mealtime job and letting them take pride in contributing to the family's well-being as you transition to a raw lifestyle is especially important. Most kids love juicing, blending, and decorating plates and tables. Sprouting is also fun for kids because sprouts grow so fast. From one day to the next, there's a visible difference; that's exciting. And when the sprouts are ready, children tend to be more interested in eating them if they've watched them grow. Take a look at Chapter 7 for details on growing sprouts in your kitchen garden.

Here's a list of other ways to get family members involved in the kitchen:

- ✔ **Get input when planning menus.** Depending on how many people are in your household, consider giving each family member one night each week to pick a favorite meal. Find menu-planning tips in Chapter 18.

- ✔ **Shop for food together.** Ask each person to choose a new fruit or vegetable. People tend to be more receptive to trying food that they pick.

- ✔ **Ask members of the family to wash the produce after shopping.**

- ✔ **Solicit opinions when tasting recipes for seasonings.** Adjust the flavor as needed to suit your family's tastes.

- ✔ **Assign someone to peel vegetables.** If age appropriate, family members can cut, dice, or julienne vegetables for recipes.

- ✔ **Get help with measuring ingredients**. Many children enjoy adding measured ingredients to mixing bowls and blenders.

- ✔ **Appoint a garnisher.** Enjoying food involves more than tasting it. Make food look beautiful to add to the pleasure.

- ✔ **Make cleanup a family job.** One of the things raw foodists love most about preparing this cuisine is *not* cleaning up greasy pots and pans! Raw foods usually rinse clean with no fuss and a little soap.

Always prepare food with love. Don't go into the kitchen when you're in a foul mood; make together time in the kitchen a positive and enjoyable experience. If you're just not feeling the love (it happens to the best of us), take a few minutes to adjust your attitude before walking into the kitchen.

Detoxifying: Out with the Old!

In the modern world, you're continually bombarded with pollutants and substances that are harmful to your health; toxins hit you through the foods you eat, the air you breathe, and the water you drink. Food additives, household chemicals, beauty products, alcoholic beverages, medications, and even poor digestion can all add to the toxic load you carry.

Bodies store toxins in fat cells and must expend precious energy and resources to detoxify and eliminate these harmful substances. Toxins are stored in fat tissue, sometimes for years, until the fat is burned; but when the body is burning calories, fat is the last to go.

Detoxing — through fasting or cleansing — helps you get to these hard-to-reach corners of your system because your body isn't receiving many new calories. Your system finds the fat, burns it, and disposes of the toxins hiding out there. Removing the toxic buildup in your system can make a huge difference in your health and support your transition to a raw food lifestyle.

In this section, we point out the signs of toxic buildup and describe fasting and cleansing, two methods used to detoxify your body, gain control of emotional eating, and manage cravings:

- *Fasting* is the practice of abstaining from food or radically limiting your intake of fiber for a period of time.
- *Cleansing* refers to the elimination of unwanted and potentially harmful substances from the body.

Feeling the toxic burden

The immune system generally does an amazing job with the cleansing process to keep people healthy and able to fight off disease — that is, unless the system gets overburdened by toxins. Sometimes the first sign of toxic overload is lethargy or a need for more sleep. Problems with skin, digestion, and other bodily functions can also arise to alert you of a problem.

Many different kinds of cleansing programs exist. If your program does its job, you'll likely experience some common symptoms of detoxification, especially in the early stages of the cleansing. Detox symptoms include headaches, diarrhea, flatulence, increased body odor, nausea, increased perspiration, runny nose, and skin breakouts and rashes. After all, you're eliminating toxins; they leave your body via bowel movements, gases, skin, and breath. Don't be alarmed. A thorough cleaning isn't pretty at first, but the process is worth it.

You may wonder why you'd bother with a fast or cleanse if you're transitioning to a mostly raw diet anyway because raw foods are naturally cleansing. A main benefit of cleansing before making changes to your diet is the quicker abatement of cravings for unhealthy foods. Detoxifying your body enables you to feel health improvements more quickly. And, for many people, feeling truly healthy and energetic makes it much easier to stay committed to nutritious food choices. And soon, the heavy and unpleasant feeling of popular but nutrition-deficient foods like chips and fried foods is no longer tempting at all, making it easy to avoid them.

Choosing a detoxification program

Undergoing a fast or cleanse successfully depends on your particular situation. Even the best, most effective, and most reputable detox plans are not suitable for everyone.

We don't recommend any type of fast or cleansing program for children, elderly people, or anyone with compromised health. If a special circumstance warrants a detoxification program for a person in one of these groups, the program should only be conducted under the guidance of a knowledgeable and trusted healthcare professional.

Consider these questions when you're evaluating a detoxification program:

- ✔ Does the program meet my needs and fit into my daily routine?
- ✔ Is the program based on good science?
- ✔ Do I have adequate time for rest if the program requires it?
- ✔ How will this program affect me and others near me?
- ✔ Does the program require supervision by a doctor to monitor my medication intake or for any other reason?
- ✔ Do I need to purchase any special equipment, like a juicer or special foods, to follow the program?
- ✔ How will I follow up the program when it ends?

Detoxing requires determination and dedication. It leads to a certain amount of discomfort, and you need to be prepared for that.

Conducting a cleanse

A cleansing program typically excludes junk foods and other consumables that are devoid of (or low in) nutrition. A cleansing diet includes only simple raw foods with fiber, and it can be sustained over a long period of time with rewarding benefits. A cleanse is technically different from a fast, which contains no fiber, only liquids. So a fast is a type of cleansing program, but a cleansing diet is not necessarily a fast.

Feeling the results of a cleanse typically takes longer than the results of a fast because cleansing programs tend to be less intense than fasts, which usually require some expert supervision, especially if you're on medication or have health challenges.

We recommend undergoing a cleansing program prior to attempting a fast in order for you to prepare your body and mind for the sacrifice and detoxification process. In this section, we describe two popular and gentle cleansing programs: herbal therapy and a green smoothie cleanse.

Trying herbal therapy

The raw food diet itself is a type of cleanse, but if you want to take your cleaning a step further, consider herbal therapy. This regimen involves taking herbs for a period of one to three weeks while continuing to eat a light diet of low-fat raw foods, soups, juices, and smoothies.

For this popular program, you can purchase commercially prepared combinations of herbs that are designed to accelerate the detoxification process and remove accumulated waste from your system. A lot of different herbal products are on the market, and some are better suited for some people than others. Read the labels carefully to see which one seems to fit your needs best; but don't give up if the one you purchase gives you gas or diarrhea. Just try a different brand and see if it suits your system better. Follow the manufacturer's directions and don't try to speed things up by taking more than the recommended amount.

Feasting on green smoothies

Probably the most gentle detox diet is the green smoothie diet. In this cleaning program, you consume only green smoothies for a set period of time that usually ranges from 15 to 30 days. All you need is a blender and a supply of fresh organic fruits and vegetables.

You can blend any combination of fruits and vegetables and make your smoothie extra delicious with herbs and spices (find smoothie recipes in Chapter 10). Foods that are especially cleansing and terrific for this program are spinach, lettuce, collard greens, parsley, broccoli, summer squash, tomatoes, red bell peppers, bananas, papayas, blueberries, citrus, apples, and grapes.

If you get hungry and need more food, add a little avocado to your smoothie. This fatty fruit slows down the cleansing process a bit, but it may help you to stick with your cleanse.

Here's a one-day menu idea for a green smoothie cleanse:

- ✔ **Morning:** 12 ounces filtered water with lemon and 1 quart (4 cups) green smoothie with papaya, banana, grapes, spinach, kale, and lemon

- ✔ **Mid-morning:** 1 quart coconut water with 1 tablespoon Spirulina or other green powder or 2 cups water and 2 cups grape juice with Spirulina or other green powder

- ✔ **Afternoon:** 1 quart green smoothie with lettuce, apple, cucumber, celery, tomato, lemon, and dulse

- ✔ **Late afternoon:** 1 quart green smoothie with broccoli, summer squash, collards, papaya, orange, garlic, and ginger

- ✔ **Evening:** 1 quart green smoothie with papaya, parsley, lettuce, and orange

Figuring out fasting

Most fasting programs are designed for cleansing, healing, and/or weight loss. If you're new to fasting, we recommend starting with a juice fast. But the specific fasting program that's best for you depends on your lifestyle, health issues, goals, availability, physical activity, and emotional state. Different methods of fasting are appropriate for different people and at different times in an individual's life.

No matter what fasting program you choose to do, be sure to prepare for it by cleansing your body at least a week before starting. Cleanse your body by consuming light raw foods, smoothies, and juices instead of heartier foods. Also try to relax your mind by spending some time meditating, walking in nature, or doing whatever other activities that put you in a peaceful state.

Fasts vary in duration and intensity. The appropriate length of your fast depends on how you feel, what kind of fast you choose to do, and how much time you can allow yourself to stick with the program. But don't get too hung up on a goal that's time-specific. Rather, give yourself a range of time to do the fast and see how you progress. Let your body decide when to stop.

Here are some of the many benefits that most quickly follow a fast:

✔ Increased energy

✔ Increased mental clarity

✔ Reduced addiction to nutritionally deficient foods

✔ Weight loss

✔ Enhanced enjoyment of fresh foods

✔ Change of attitude toward food

✔ Brighter eyes and improved vision

✔ Clearer skin

✔ Improved sense of overall well-being

If you have a weakened immune system, cancer, or another disease, conduct a fast only under the care of a doctor.

Fasting with juice

Fasting with juice nourishes your body while cleansing it of toxins. Juice fasts are the most gentle and tend to cause the least discomfort. And it's possible to stick with this fast for long periods of time — as long as a month in some cases. To get started with a juice fast, you need a juicer and organic fruits and vegetables.

Here are the three types of juice fasts:

✔ **Fruit juice:** Any kind of juicy fruit, including citrus, pineapple, grape, or apple, belongs in this program. This program is not recommended for anyone with sugar metabolic disorders, because fruit juice is very high in sugar. Fast with fruit juice (on its own) for no more than a week. Dilute one part juice with three parts water to reduce the amount of sugar you consume. Always rinse your mouth with filtered water after drinking juice to reduce tooth decay associated with sugar.

✔ **Vegetable juice:** This fast includes juices made from high-water content, nonsweet fruits such as cucumbers, zucchini, and tomatoes as well as leafy greens (parsley, romaine, and kale), celery, and root vegetables. This program offers quick weight loss and detoxification results, and in most cases you can safely stay on this fast for a month or more.

✔ **Combination:** In this program, ripe organic fruits and vegetable juices can be combined or consumed separately. Typically, a person on a combination fruit and vegetable juice fast drinks fruit juices in the morning and vegetable juices near the end of the day. Always rinse your mouth with water or brush your teeth after drinking juice to avoid dental decay from sugar and acidic fruits.

This juice fast is the easiest because it's the most delicious and provides an abundance of energy. Most people on this fast say they feel like they could stay on it forever, but most usually stop after three to six weeks.

Check out the To-Live-For Green Juice recipe in Chapter 10 to see a typical combination juice. Use it as a guide and vary it based on your own preferences and the produce that's in season at the time of your fast. Add fresh herbs such as basil, parsley, cilantro, and even garlic to your lunch and dinner drinks to give them more zip. In the morning, include orange juice, pineapple juice, and even a little fresh gingerroot. Papaya is also a great detoxifier and wonderful in morning green juice.

Don't gulp! Sip and chew your juice so the digestive juices in your mouth have an opportunity to do their work.

Here's a one-day menu idea for a juice fast:

✔ **Morning:** 12 ounces filtered water with lemon and 1 quart green juice

✔ **Mid-morning:** 1 quart coconut water with 1 tablespoon Spirulina or other green powder or 2 cups water and 2 cups grape juice with Spirulina or other green powder

✔ **Afternoon:** 1 quart green juice

✔ **Late afternoon:** 1 quart green juice

✔ **Evening:** 1 quart green juice

Getting started

When you're ready to schedule a fast, use these tips to prepare yourself and plan for the program:

✔ Drink plenty of fluids, including pure, unchlorinated water, to keep the toxins moving out of your body.

✔ Rest and get lots of sleep. Naps are especially great when cleansing.

✔ If you're a heavy coffee drinker or smoker, don't jump into a fast without preparation. Consider doing an intense green smoothie cleanse until you feel sustained all day without withdrawal symptoms.

✔ Carefully choose the timeframe for your fast. Set yourself up for success by choosing a time when you're not overly stressed or responsible for cooking for others. Fast when you can take time to relax as needed.

✔ Make time for a walk each day. This gentle exercise helps with detox as oxygen moves in and carbon dioxide is eliminated from the lungs. But don't overdo exercise.

✔ Tell your friends and family about your fast; otherwise they may make it difficult for you by pressuring you to eat.

✔ Feeling grouchy or emotional is normal when you're detoxifying because you're cleansing emotionally as well as physically. Seek opportunities to laugh and pamper yourself.

✔ Remember to congratulate yourself each day for making it through another day of fasting!

If you simply cannot continue a fast, stop. But don't get down on yourself. Reschedule it for another time in the near future rather than give up altogether. Timing is an important element of a successful fast.

If you're considering a radical water-only fast, do so only with the support of a cleansing clinic that's well equipped to monitor your daily progress. Water fasts are extreme and often require intense preparation and complete bed rest. This program is not something to toy with; it's very serious detox that can cause your body to become dangerously depleted of minerals and electrolytes and create other serious side effects and outcomes.

Chapter 5

Gear and Gadgets: Setting Up Your Raw Food Kitchen

In This Chapter

▶ Finding and using nifty equipment to make quick and easy raw meals
▶ Gathering ingredients for your pantry and fridge
▶ Keeping raw foods fresh and safe

For some people who are thinking about incorporating raw foods into an existing meal plan or transitioning to an all-raw diet, the scariest part of the process is properly setting up their kitchen. But it really doesn't need to be frightening. For the most part, preparing raw foods is simpler than traditional cooking. (And by purchasing this book, you already made the process easier!)

In this chapter, we list everything you need to prepare raw foods, and we offer tips for finding the right ingredients and equipment to get started. We also suggest ways to set up your kitchen and store ingredients to make it easier to incorporate more raw foods into your daily routines.

Equipping a Raw Kitchen

When food is raw and unadulterated, it's naturally delicious. It's not wilted from heat or diluted with fillers, and it doesn't need a wide variety of equipment to make it delicious. Still, you do need a few gadgets to prepare many of the raw recipes in this book. But if you prepare foods at all, you probably have many of these items in your home already. In this section, we list the tools and equipment that we use regularly when preparing raw meals.

Gathering essential tools

As with any new activity, getting the right tools to get the job done can seem overwhelming. But to get started with raw food preparation, this list of small, nonelectric kitchen tools is all you need:

- **Biodegradable soap:** You must remove pesticides, toxins, and other poisons from commercially grown produce. Wash fruits and vegetables, including organic produce, and do a final rinse with unchlorinated water.

- **Cafeteria-style trays:** Segmented trays are great for growing wheat grass. Get details on growing foods in a kitchen garden in Chapter 7.

- **Cheesecloth or nut-milk bags:** Use these items to make (you guessed it) raw cheese and milk — living nut, seed, and coconut cheese and milk, that is (see Chapters 9 and 11 for recipes). Cheesecloth and nut-milk bags are also handy for draining soaked nuts and seeds.

- **Colander or strainer:** Keep a few colanders or strainers around for washing and draining produce. We recommend at least one large (4 quart) and one small (1 quart) version for handling common jobs.

- **Crock or large pickle jar:** Use this container for fermenting sauerkraut. (Chapter 13 has the how-to for creating this must-have dish.)

- **Cutting boards:** We suggest using one cutting board for garlic and onions and another for fruits and vegetables to keep savories from mixing with sweet stuff. Use NSF-rated hard plastic cutting boards for easy cleaning.

  Choose different colors for each special-use cutting board — orange for fruits and veggies and blue for garlic and onions, for example. This is an easy way to keep the boards free from cross contamination.

- **Dish rack:** Select a V-shaped rack for draining soaked nuts and seeds.

- **Dish towels:** We recommend using woven towels (rather than terrycloth) to cover fermenting foods and to blot dry produce and soaked nuts.

- **Garlic press:** This tool makes quick work of mincing garlic.

- **Grater/shredder:** Most cooks use this tool to grate dairy cheese. Raw foodists use box graters, rotary graters, or hand-held models for shredding carrots and other hard vegetables.

- **Jars:** Keep lots of wide-mouth glass jars of different sizes handy for soaking seeds and nuts, sprouting seeds, rinsing and draining sprouts, and storing foods. Start with 6 pint jars, 12 quart jars, 4 half-gallon jars, and 4 gallon jars. Flip to Chapter 7 for food-preparation methods that require these jars.

- **Kitchen scale:** When perfect measurements are required or when you're following recipes that use the metric system, a scale is vital.

✔ **Knife-sharpener:** This indispensable tool puts a nice, sharp edge on your knives. You can add a knife steel to your collection as well. Just be sure to use a sharpener or steel to knock off any burrs on your knives before you use them. Take a look at Figure 5-1 to see what a roller sharpener and sharpening steel look like.

WARNING!

Sharp knives are safe knives. People are more likely to be injured in the kitchen when using dull knives rather than sharp knives, because sharp knives go where you point them. Dull knives choose the path of least resistance, which can be your fingers, your hand, or worse. Keep your knives sharp to minimize your chance for injuries.

✔ **Knives:** A selection of goods kitchen knives makes food prep much easier. If nothing else, you'll want these two knives:

- **Chef's knife:** Select a chef's knife with a 6- to 8-inch nonserrated blade. This item is an absolute must-have. You need it to slice, chop, and dice your raw foods. Don't be thrifty; buy a good quality knife and keep it sharp with a hand-held roller sharpener.

- **Paring knife:** Choose a paring knife with a nonserrated blade for peeling fruits and vegetables and making fancy cuts.

Figure 5-1: Stock your raw food kitchen with a collection of knives and sharpening tools.

CANNELLE KNIFE CHEF'S KNIFE SHARPENING STEEL PARING KNIFE SHARPENER

HAVING SHARP KNIVES ON HAND MAKES QUICK WORK OF PREPARING FRUITS AND VEGETABLES.

✔ **Mandoline:** A mandoline quickly and easily cuts foods into flat chips, tiny matchsticks, finely diced cubes, and other shapes and sizes. Just be sure to purchase a safety glove if yours doesn't come with one — and wear it every time you use your mandoline to avoid injuries.

✔ **Measuring cups and spoons:** As in all types of cuisine, you need to measure or weigh raw ingredients to ensure proper proportions. For the recipes in this book, select a set that uses standard U.S. measurements (1 cup, ½ cup, ½ teaspoon, ¼ teaspoon, and so on).

✔ **Mesh screening:** Yes, we're talking about the kind of plastic screen you purchase at the hardware store for windows. Use mesh screening to drain soaked nuts and seeds (see Chapter 7 for the how-to on soaking).

✔ **Microplaner:** These hand graters make it easy to grate garlic, ginger, citrus zest, and other foods that need to be finely shredded or minced.

✔ **Mixing bowls:** We like glass mixing bowls, and we recommend that you have three in each size: large, medium, and small.

✔ **Rubber bands:** Use rubber bands to secure mesh screening when draining jars of soaked seeds.

✔ **Salad spinner:** Use this gadget to remove rinse water from your greens and avoid watering down dressings and condiments with excess liquid. A salad spinner is also a handy storage container for clean greens.

✔ **Salad tongs:** You'll need several sets of salad tongs for tossing and serving salads and noodle dishes. They're also handy for mixing and combining ingredients for other types of dishes. We recommend having at least one set of wooden tongs in your kitchen.

✔ **Soil (organic):** Use high-quality, organic soil to grow wheat grass (see Chapter 7).

✔ **Spatulas:** Rubber spatulas and metal offset spatulas in a variety of sizes are handy for a variety of tasks, including spreading batter when making dehydrated crackers and breads.

✔ **Springform pan:** Even though you don't need pots and (most) pans for raw food preparation, a springform pan is perfect for molding raw lasagna and some desserts, including cheesecake! Use a 9-inch springform pan to prepare recipes in this book.

✔ **Sunlit shelf:** A well-lit shelf is an ideal space to soak your nuts and seeds, grow sprouts, and cultivate greens. Be sure that the shelf has access to adequate indirect sunlight and air circulation.

✔ **Vegetable peeler:** We use ours to, uh, peel vegetables.

You don't need a microwave, stove, or a huge collection of pots and pans in your raw kitchen. Keep them around though, just in case you need to boil some water to give yourself a steamy facial, sterilize some surgical tools, or remove old wallpaper. Better yet, give away your stove and buy a small electric hot pot to heat water. Who can't use more storage space in a kitchen?

Acquiring helpful appliances

We love spending time in the kitchen creating beautiful, delicious food, but we also like time-saving devices that free up time for us to enjoy other activities. Here are some higher-ticket appliances for your raw kitchen that you may want or need to make meals more interesting and varied and to ease certain food preparation tasks:

✔ **Blender:** A good high-performance blender is a must-have for making smoothies, soups, juices, dressings, and sauces — staples of raw food meals. Most recipes can be made using a standard blender, but a high-performance blender with 2 or 3 horsepower is a worthy investment.

✔ **Dehydrator:** A dehydrator takes raw food to the next level. Use it to make raw versions of crackers, wraps, and breads; reduce sauces to make them seem cooked; and marinate foods quickly. You can also use a dehydrator to dry raw foods for away-from-home meals, travel, and other occasions. (Find out how to use a dehydrator in Chapter 7.)

✔ **Food processor:** Some raw foodists have a food processor and a high-performance blender. The two appliances are great for different jobs. The bowl on a food processor is wider than a blender's, making this appliance better for making pie crusts and bread dough. Food processors also have a wide variety of blades that can make chopping, dicing, and shredding vegetables and fruits a breeze (see Figure 5-2).

✔ **Juicer:** A juicer makes quick work of extracting juice from fruits and vegetables.

✔ **Spiral slicer or spirooli:** Create pasta from zucchini and other vegetables with this handy tool (see Figure 5-3).

✔ **Water filter:** Use a filter to remove unhealthful chemicals, metals, and bacteria from your tap water before using it in recipes or rinsing sprouts.

Clean water is important no matter what kind of food you eat, and almost all public water contains chlorine to kill unwanted bacteria. Sadly, chlorine also kills the friendly bacteria necessary for good digestion.

Here are some system suggestions for filtering your water:

- Carbon-based filters that connect to your water system are the least-expensive option, and they remove chlorine and some other chemicals. These filters can be placed on your counter or mounted under your sink for around $100.

- Reverse osmosis (RO) systems remove chlorine and many more chemicals. RO systems (which are typically a few hundred dollars) are normally installed under your sink. More-expensive systems also raise the PH (alkalinity) of the water while filtering it.

- A whole-house filtration system takes care of your food-prep water, drinking water, and your shower and bath water, too. This system can cost anywhere from $1,000 to $3,000.

✔ **Wheat-grass juicer:** If you want to juice wheat grass and your general juicer isn't designed for this job, get ahold of a manual (crank) or electric wheat-grass juicer.

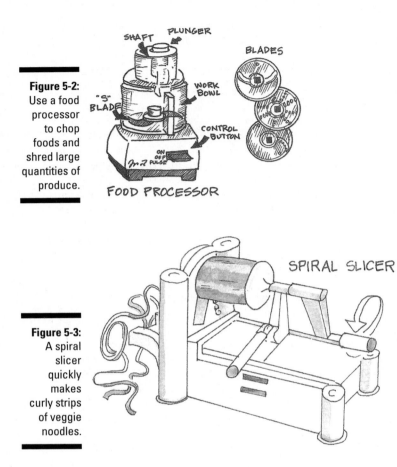

Figure 5-2:
Use a food
processor
to chop
foods and
shred large
quantities of
produce.

Figure 5-3:
A spiral
slicer
quickly
makes
curly strips
of veggie
noodles.

Stocking Your Pantry

The pantry is the heart and soul of any kitchen. It's where you keep all the dry goods that make your meals interesting and tasty. Unlike a traditional pantry, you won't find canned goods, fried items (like chips), or baked goods in a raw kitchen. Instead, you'll find naturally dried grains and fruits, raw nuts, natural sweeteners, and a variety of unprocessed ingredients.

In this section, we describe what we consider to be the staple ingredients for a raw pantry. Then we introduce you to some of our favorite specialty ingredients that can make your raw meals even more exciting.

Choosing staple ingredients

As with other types of cuisine, raw food meals feature staple ingredients that appear in many different dishes. Keep these staples stocked so you can whip up delicious raw meals whenever you want.

Finding some of these ingredients may feel like a treasure hunt, but ask around or special order foods that offer the variety and unique flavors you enjoy in your meals. Take a look at Chapter 6 for guidance on where to find foods that may not be available at your local grocery store.

Here's a list of foods to keep on hand in your kitchen. Don't be intimidated by the length of the list. You don't have to toss out your current pantry staples and start over immediately; buy what you need when you need it. We recommend that you ease into your raw food lifestyle, so you can also ease into creating your raw food pantry, one recipe at a time. (See Chapter 2 for help in deciding how raw to go.)

- ✔ **Acidophilus powder or capsules:** A powerful probiotic, acidophilus can be purchased at most health-food stores. It helps restore the balance of good bacteria that's found naturally in your body but is often destroyed by chlorine, antibiotics, and other harmful substances. Use acidophilus for making nut and seed cheeses (see Chapter 9).

- ✔ **Brown sesame seeds:** These flavorful seeds are a terrific addition to sushi rolls, dressings, sauces, and pâtés.

- ✔ **Coconut oil:** Oil from coconuts (a type of vegetable oil) is naturally saturated (as opposed to the hydrogenated saturated variety of oil) and is considered by many experts to be a good fat. Nevertheless, we don't recommend using a lot of any oil, especially saturated oils. Coconut oil is great in desserts and candies because it becomes solid at room temperature and adds a wonderful mild coconut flavor. Just be sure to buy the virgin-pressed coconut oil because it hasn't been heated at high temperatures that destroy some of its nutritional benefits.

- ✔ **Dried fruit:** Dried fruits such as raisins, apricots, goji berries, dates, figs, pineapple, mango, coconut, and papaya provide a delicious treat. If you can't find these fruits sun dried, then you can dry them yourself by slicing them thin and putting them in the sun or dehydrator. Just be sure to cover your sun-drying fruit with a screen to keep out pests.

Purchase unsulfured, unsweetened dried fruits and vegetables only if they're labeled "sun dried" or "low-temp dried." Otherwise it's possible that they've been heat dried, a process that kills many of the vital nutrients, and include added sugar or other sweeteners.

✔ **Dried spices/herbs:** Purchase dried spices and herbs in small quantities so they remain fresh and pest-free. Store them in a dark, cool environment and replace them at least twice a year. Better yet, dry your own herbs and spices to be sure that they meet your raw food standards.

Here's a list of the dried herbs and spices we use most often in our own kitchen and in the recipes in this book:

- Basil
- Black pepper
- Cardamom
- Cayenne pepper
- Cinnamon
- Cumin
- Curry powder
- Dill weed
- Garlic powder
- Italian herb seasoning
- Mexican chili powder
- Mint
- Mustard powder
- Nutmeg
- Onion powder
- Oregano
- Paprika
- Rosemary
- Sage
- Smoked paprika
- Thyme
- White pepper

✔ **Extra-virgin olive oil:** Extra-virgin olive oil is made from the first cold press of the olives. Later rounds of pressing involve heating to remove every bit of oil (along with nutrients) from the olives. Olive oil that has undergone more than the initial cold press is labeled *virgin olive oil* or just *olive oil,* so avoid those products. Keep a small amount of extra-virgin olive oil (a pint or so) in the pantry, and store the rest in the refrigerator to keep it from turning rancid. ***Note:*** It's normal for olive oil to appear thick and cloudy when stored in the refrigerator.

✔ **Fresh fruit:** When ripening, some fresh fruits (especially avocados, bananas, and tomatoes) best reach their peak when stored in the pantry (or on the counter).

✔ **Fresh onions and garlic:** Store these items in a cool, dark place, like the pantry, rather than the refrigerator.

✔ **Salt:** One of the oldest and most prevalent seasonings, salt — no matter what type — should be used sparingly. We recommend that you use a good quality salt that's full of natural minerals, such as Celtic sea salt or Himalayan crystal salt, rather than regular table salt (sodium chloride), which is not raw and has been treated with chemicals.

✔ **Sea vegetables and algae:** Sea vegetables and algae are high in protein, vitamins, and minerals. Look for these different varieties:

- *Agar agar,* a sea vegetable, is used as a vegan gelling agent in place of bovine (animal-based) gelatin. Agar agar is available in bar, flaked, or powdered form.

- *Dulse* is coarse, reddish-brown edible seaweed (available as flakes and whole dried leaves) that's very high in iron and iodine. We use it as a salty flavoring in salads.

- *Irish moss* is a sea vegetable that's used as a vegan gelling agent to thicken soups, gravies, jellies, and creams and to bind cakes.

- *Kelp* is large, brown seaweed with fluted leathery fronds that contains high amounts of trace minerals and iodine. One to two teaspoons of kelp per day is adequate for most people looking to increase their vitality. Add kelp to soups and salads.

Kelp noodles are not always raw, so be sure to read the label.

- *Nori* (dried seaweed), also known as *laver,* is ideal for making sushi rolls and can be cut into slivers and used as a garnish on Asian-inspired salads.

- *Sea palm* is a perfect base for mild seaweed salads. Yum! Remember to soak and rinse sea palm prior to using it.

- *Spirulina* is a freshwater micro-algae that's well known for its high protein (a whopping 70-plus percent!). Spirulina is also high in essential fatty acids.

- *Wild blue-green algae* is harvested in the pure waters of Klamath Lake, Oregon. It's very high in protein and essential fatty acids.

✔ **Seeds and grains for sprouting:** If you want to be a kitchen gardener and grow your own sprouts (see Chapter 7), be sure to buy organic seeds for sprouting (see Chapter 6). Try sprouting the following foods:

- Azuki beans

- Alfalfa seeds

- Broccoli seeds

- Buckwheat groats
- Clover seeds
- Flax seeds
- Garbanzo beans
- Kale seeds
- Lentils
- Mung beans
- Oat groats
- Quinoa
- Radish seeds
- Rye groats
- Whole peas
- Winter wheat berries (for growing wheat grass)

✔ **Sun-dried tomatoes:** You can find sun-dried tomatoes in many specialty markets and the international food section of some supermarkets. But you can always just purchase them online or dry tomatoes yourself.

Enhancing your meals with specialty ingredients

When you're just getting started with raw foods, you may want to stick to the staples. But when you're ready to expand your creativity and skills and vary your menus, consider stocking some nonessential ingredients. We think these specialty ingredients are great additions to the raw foods kitchen:

✔ **Cacao butter:** Fat from the cacao bean is a healthful medium-chain saturated fat, similar to coconut oil. We use cacao butter in white-chocolate-themed desserts and to replace dairy butter and shortening in candies.

✔ **Carob powder:** Used as a substitute for cocoa, carob powder comes from the carob pod, a naturally sweet fruit that's low in fat and high in calcium, potassium, iron, and magnesium. The dark brown powder contains no caffeine. Carob has a berry-like flavor and lacks the characteristic bitterness of chocolate, so when using it in place of cacao, reduce the amount of overall sweetener by 25 percent.

✔ **Chia seeds:** These tiny seeds are rich in protein and omega-3 fatty acids. Use them in whole or ground form as you would use flax seeds. Chia is nearly flavorless, making it an excellent gelling and thickening agent in smoothies, fillings, and even sauces.

✔ **Coconut:** Organic, unsweetened, shredded raw coconut is a tasty ingredient in many dishes. Packages don't typically indicate raw, but it usually is, provided that it's unsweetened and unsulfured.

✔ **Flax seeds:** Rich in omega-3 fatty acids, these tiny seeds can be used as a supplement and thickener in shakes and smoothies or as a binder in crackers, crusts, and burgers. Be certain to buy raw flax seed, as many are toasted, especially if you're purchasing ground flax seed. Always store flax meal in the fridge to avoid rancidity.

✔ **Maca powder:** Made from the Peruvian maca root, this ingredient is rich in calcium and potassium and reputed to increase energy, strengthen the adrenal glands, heighten libido, and enhance stamina. Maca has a slightly sweet yet nutty taste and can be used to thicken smoothies and shakes and to replace flour in cakes and cookies.

✔ **Mesquite powder:** This flour-like product comes from mesquite-tree seed pods and is rich in protein and calcium. It has a sweet caramel-like flavor (a cross between cinnamon and chocolate), but it doesn't elevate blood sugar levels. Mesquite meal can be used to thicken and sweeten shakes and smoothies. It can also replace flour in cakes, cookies, and pie crusts. Try adding it to recipes that call for chocolate or carob.

✔ **Psyllium:** This plant-derived soluble fiber is available as coarse husks or finely ground. You can use psyllium in a similar way to eggs — to thicken fillings, puddings, and sauces and to bind wraps and crepes.

✔ **Shiitake mushrooms:** These edible East Asian mushrooms have a golden or dark brown to blackish cap. Put dried shiitake mushrooms in a high-performance blender to create shiitake powder, which is a great addition to soups, dressings, and sauces.

✔ **Tamarind:** This pulp comes from the pod-like fruit of a tropical tree that's common in India, Asia, and Latin America. Tamarind is both sour and mildly sweet and can be used in raw ketchup, soups, and dressings; it also makes a delicious, refreshing beverage.

✔ **Wasabi:** This Japanese horseradish is easy to find in powdered form. Add a little water to form a pale green paste. Wasabi has a sharp, pungent, extremely potent flavor that's similar to mustard or horseradish.

✔ **Xanthan gum:** Produced through the fermentation of corn sugar, xanthan gum is commonly used in the food industry as a natural thickener and stabilizing agent. It adds creaminess and helps carry the flavor in sauces, soups, and dressings. If you're avoiding corn, guar gum is a suitable substitute.

TIP

Don't try to mix in xanthan gum to a recipe by hand; it gums almost instantly and form clumps. To achieve a smooth texture, keep xanthan gum in constant motion from the moment it is incorporated into liquid. For best results, put the liquid into a blender and add the xanthan gum through the chute while the blender is on.

Using select not-raw ingredients for extra appeal

In addition to the raw food staples we list in this section, most raw foodists also include a few not-raw ingredients in certain recipes to improve taste, consistency, and overall enjoyment. It's up to you to decide how raw you want to be, but the vast majority of raw foodists are willing to consume minute amounts of specific cooked ingredients.

The raw food lifestyle isn't radical (at least it doesn't have to be); rather, this cuisine preference is about feeling good and being healthy. For many, that includes consuming limited amounts of certain not-raw ingredients. In most cases, these foods can be omitted from the recipes in Part III, but the flavor of the dish will differ from what's described.

- ✔ **Agave nectar:** This mild-tasting, concentrated sweet syrup is made from the juice of the agave plant. Agave nectar is 90 percent fructose and has a much lower glycemic index than honey, maple syrup, or cane sugar (though diabetics should still use caution); but it's sweeter than pure cane sugar, so use it sparingly. Choose light agave nectar if you want a mild flavor and dark agave syrup for a heavier, molasses-like taste.

- ✔ **Coconut nectar:** This mild sweetener, the sap from the coconut palm tree, is tasty alone or used as syrup or to replace any liquid sweetener. Coconut nectar has a low glycemic index, and some people think it's a nutritionally superior sweetener to agave nectar because it has more amino acids, many B vitamins, and a neutral pH.

- ✔ **Coconut palm sugar:** Made from the sap of the coconut palm tree, this mild, low-glycemic sweetener has a light caramel color. It dissolves like brown sugar in recipes but lacks the strong flavor of molasses. Coconut palm sugar has less impact on blood sugar than white sugar.

- ✔ **Evaporated cane juice:** This granulated sweetener (also known as *Sucanat, Panela, Tapa Dulse,* and *Rapadura*) is high in iron and other minerals and is often used to replace white or brown sugar in desserts. Even though it's not raw, evaporated cane juice is a healthy alternative to sugar because it's a whole food. However, it's a high-glycemic concentrated sweetener, so use it sparingly.

- ✔ **Extracts:** Extracts provide the essential flavors of certain whole foods. Keep pure vanilla and almond extracts on hand to enhance taste in some recipes.

✔ **Maple syrup:** Made from the boiled sap of the maple tree, this sweetener is not raw, but it has a unique flavor and is often used as an alternative to refined sugar in natural desserts. Maple sugar is made from maple syrup and may be used to replace cane sugar in desserts.

✔ **Miso:** A thick paste used to flavor soups and sauces, miso is a common non-raw ingredient used by raw foodists. It needs to stay cold, so we include miso in the following section, "Stocking the Refrigerator."

✔ **Nutritional yeast:** This inactive yeast is grown on a nutrient-rich culture. Red Star Vegetarian Support Formula Nutritional Yeast powder contains vitamin B12 and high amounts of protein, and it has a cheesy flavor that's similar to parmesan cheese. Sprinkle it on salads and other foods to give them a cheesy taste and boost the nutritional value of food.

✔ **Soy lecithin:** This versatile product contains phospholipids (phosphorus-rich oils) extracted from soybean oil and is thought to have health benefits that include improving memory and supporting cardiovascular health; use it to emulsify fats and liquids in raw desserts that require stabilizers to produce a creamy consistency. Always choose GMO-free soy lecithin powder over oils and other forms.

If you're looking to reduce the amount of soy in your diet or want to avoid any amount of cooked food, substitute 1½ teaspoons of sunflower lecithin for each teaspoon of soy lecithin. This raw alternative alters the color of the resulting food and imparts a sunflower taste, but it's definitely a suitable alternative to soy lecithin.

✔ **Stevia (in liquid or powder form):** Derived from the leaf of the naturally sweet stevia plant, stevia sweetens food but doesn't elevate blood-sugar levels. Plus, it has zero calories. Stevia may be used alone to sweeten teas, beverages, and shakes, or you can combine it with other sweeteners to decrease the total amount of other sweetener needed for a recipe. Fresh stevia leaves and low-heat-dehydrated stevia leaves are raw, but liquid and powdered stevia is not raw.

Use stevia sparingly; it's extremely sweet (200 times sweeter than sugar) and can leave a bitter, licorice-like aftertaste.

✔ **Tamari:** Similar in flavor to soy sauce, tamari is naturally fermented and made from soy with little or no wheat. Tamari is not technically a raw product, but it does contain live bacteria and adds a nice salty flavor to dressings, sauces, and Asian-inspired foods. We always use unpasteurized tamari. If you have a gluten intolerance, look for gluten-free or wheat-free tamari in your local health-food store, the Asian section of your grocery store, or Asian market.

✔ **Toasted sesame oil:** This oil is great for seasoning Asian-style dressings and sauces. Even though it's not a raw product, we use it to add a cooked flavor to some dishes. Use it in drops, not teaspoons!

Stocking the Refrigerator

The refrigerator is a key part of food storage, and we suggest keeping the following foods on hand and in your refrigerator for easy snacking and simple raw meal preparation. (Foods marked with an asterisk are not raw.)

- **Avocados (ripe):** A heart-healthy fat containing vitamin E, folate, and potassium as well as other important nutrients, avocados are a great addition to many different recipes — from appetizers to desserts! Store avocados in the pantry until they're ripe and then move them to the fridge to extend their life.

- **Cabbage:** A natural diuretic, cabbage is a great crispy addition to salads.

- **Carrots:** We use these root vegetables daily in recipes and on their own as quick snacks.

- **Celery:** Sliced or whole, celery is a great addition to many raw meals. The slightly bitter flavor pairs well with dips and dressings.

- **Cucumbers:** Great in gazpacho, sliced in a salad, or on their own, cucumbers are especially delicious with a drizzle of sesame oil.

- **Dijon mustard*:** You can find this tangy staple in the pantry aisle of the grocery, but keep it in the fridge after you open it. Store-bought dijon is not a raw product. To make a raw mustard, see Chapter 9.

- **Fruit (seasonal):** Whether it's summer strawberries, fall apples, or winter squash, when in doubt, refrigerate your fruit. A few exceptions to the refrigeration rule are tomatoes and bananas. Keep these goodies out on the counter for best results.

- **Ginger (fresh):** This knobby root adds an astringent note to foods. Keep it whole and in the refrigerator until you're ready to use it.

- **Green onions:** Choose onions of this type with firm green fronds; don't buy limp ones.

- **Herbs (fresh):** Keep fresh herbs, such as basil, dill, cilantro, and parsley, on hand and in the refrigerator.

- **Kale:** This hardy leafy green is available year-round and is high in protein and calcium. Store it in a sealed plastic bag wrapped in a damp paper towel in the fridge for a week or longer.

- **Lemons:** Keep lemons on hand to add a subtle tartness to dressings and sauces. Lemons and other citrus fruits can be stored on the kitchen counter for a week or kept in the fridge for up to a month.

- **Lettuce:** Whether it's romaine, spinach, bibb, or butter, lettuce should be refrigerated in a sealed plastic bag with a damp paper towel. Handle lettuce gently when washing, and spin dry or towel blot before using.

- **Miso***: A thick paste made from fermented legumes or grains (including chickpeas, soybeans, rice, and barley), miso is a traditional staple of Japanese cuisine. Light or dark miso is used to flavor soups and sauces. (We use light miso throughout this book; for a deeper, saltier flavor, choose dark miso.) Find organic unpasteurized miso in your grocer's refrigerator case and keep it refrigerated. Miso is never raw, but it's probiotic-rich and considered a living food.

- **Nuts:** Look for raw (not roasted) almonds, walnuts, macadamia nuts, pine nuts, and cashews and use them in pie crusts, cookies, candy, and other desserts as well as sweet or savory sauces and dressings. You can also use nuts to make milk (see Chapter 11), cream, and cheese (see Chapter 9).

   Store all nuts in the refrigerator or freezer to extend their shelf life and keep their great healthy oils from becoming rancid.

- **Oranges:** Keep oranges on hand and use them in smoothies, blended soups, dressings, and sauces to add a sweet and tangy flavor. Oranges can be stored on the kitchen counter for a week or kept in the fridge for up to a month.

- **Sweet bell peppers:** Keep these delicious peppers whole and in the fridge until you're ready to use them so they stay as fresh and firm as possible. Make sure to choose red, gold, or yellow bell peppers; green bell peppers are unripe, making them more difficult to digest.

- **Rejuvelac:** This fermented, probiotic-rich liquid is prepared using wheat berries, rye, or other grains (find our recipe in Chapter 10). It improves digestion and can be used as a starter for other fermented foods such as raw nut cheeses. Purchase Rejuvelac in your health specialty market or make your own. Either way, keep it refrigerated.

   If you want to make Rejuvelac, plan ahead. It takes five days to make this health-promoting elixir.

- **Seeds:** Keep these protein powerhouses, including sunflower, sesame, pumpkin, and flax seeds, in the refrigerator to extend their shelf life and keep their healthy oils from going rancid. The exceptions are sprouting seeds and chia, which are high in antioxidants and don't become rancid.

- **Tahini:** This paste is made from ground sesame seeds. Tahini is a major component of hummus, falafels, and other Middle Eastern foods. We use it in sauces, dressings, and as a base for milk. We also sweeten it to use in desserts and as dips for fruits. Be sure to purchase raw, not roasted, tahini and refrigerate this seed butter after opening.

- **Zucchini:** This is the most versatile fruit. (That's right; zucchini contains seeds and is therefore a fruit.) Use it to make raw pasta, rice, rolls, and wraps; add it to sauces and dressings; and eat it in 101 other ways, too!

A raw food lifestyle centers on fresh living foods that aren't contaminated by chemical preservatives or cooking and therefore more susceptible to spoiling. If you smell an off odor, see brown spots, or notice a slimy texture in your produce, consider composting the food instead of consuming it.

For most people, the freezer is an extension of their refrigerator, so here are a few things you may want to keep in your freezer:

- **Bananas:** Ripened and peeled bananas stored in resealable plastic bags are a terrific go-to snack and handy for a quick and refreshing smoothie.

- **Other frozen fruits:** Other fruits, such as berries, are great for smoothies, sorbet, and ice cream as well as dressings and sauces.

- **Frozen sauces:** Sauces stored in glass jars make for quick meals. Just be sure to leave an inch of space in your container to allow for liquids to expand when freezing, or the bottle may rupture.

- **Raw desserts:** Keep a sweet or two in the freezer for a special treat. (See Chapter 17 for recipes.)

Chapter 6

Buying Organic Essentials

• •

• •

*O*ne perceived drawback of buying organically grown foods is cost; organics can be more pricey than conventional foods, whose true costs — which include health and environmental destruction due in part to the use of harmful chemicals — are less obvious. When you're shopping for food, keep in mind that the higher cost of organics is a result of the relatively small scale of organic farming compared to conventional operations, which are heavily subsidized by governments. Organic farmers receive little or no financial support from the government for their efforts.

Are organic foods worth the money? An increasing number of people now says yes, especially for the most vulnerable groups: children, the elderly, and pregnant women. But even organically grown dog food is gaining popularity. In fact, organic living has become so popular that many people even choose their vacation destinations based on availability of organic produce, organic restaurant offerings, and eco-friendly lodging.

Whether you eat a raw plant-based diet, a standard American diet, or a cuisine in between, there are plenty of reasons to choose organic foods:

✔ **Better taste:** Most organic farmers care deeply about the land, so they work to build well-balanced soils that grow strong, healthy plants that taste naturally great. If you compare a juicy organic orange or vine-ripened organic tomato to one that's conventionally grown, you'll notice a dramatic difference in taste. Raw foodists depend on the delicious natural flavors of fruits and vegetables.

✔ **Superior nutrition:** Organic fruits and vegetables contain more antioxidants than nonorganically grown produce, and on almost every other nutritional metric, organic produce is equal to or better than its conventional counterpart.

✔ **Enhanced safety:** Organic farmers keep harmful chemicals and pesticides — herbicides (weed killers), fungicides (mold killers), and insecticides (insect killers) — out of the foods they produce.

✔ **Sustainability:** Organic agriculture respects the balance of life. Organic soils contain a variety of enzyme activity, micronutrients, and other biological properties that spares the insects needed to pollinate trees and create a healthy ecosystem. Organic farming also protects topsoil and avoids toxic pollutants that contaminate water, soil, and air.

We definitely think that buying organic food is a worthy investment. In this chapter, we point out where to buy essential foods as well as the nice-to-have items for preparing delicious and organic raw meals. We offer tips for finding wholesome foods no matter where you live — urban, suburban, rural, or remote.

Buying Seasonally

Buying food in season, when it's freshest, most flavorful, and least expensive, is always a good idea. With a dehydrator or a freezer, you can preserve foods at the height of their nutrient content and use them at any time of the year.

For example, if you purchase summer corn by the case, just slice the kernels off the cobs and then freeze them. Sure, you can buy commercially frozen corn any time of the year, but this corn is always blanched before it's packaged, which destroys many of the food's nutrients. When you buy fresh produce and preserve it yourself, you know that you're getting the whole food and exactly how it's been handled and processed.

Fresh fruits freeze well, too, and frozen fruit is especially great in smoothies. You can also dehydrate fruits and enjoy them as a sweet and chewy snack or rehydrate them to sweeten desserts.

To freeze most produce and ensure it's ready for your raw recipes all year long, follow these easy steps:

1. **Wash fruits thoroughly and allow to dry.**

2. **Cut large fruits.** Mango, papaya, cherimoya, pineapple, and other large fruit is best if cut into pieces that fit easily in a blender. Depending on the type/quality of your blender, go for about ½-inch pieces.

3. **Place individual pieces of fruit on a tray or cookie sheet and then place the tray in the freezer.** This step ensures that the pieces freeze separately and not into a big clump.

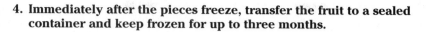

4. Immediately after the pieces freeze, transfer the fruit to a sealed container and keep frozen for up to three months.

Plastic resealable bags are okay for freezing, but we think Tupperware or Rubbermaid sealed storage containers or high-quality vacuum-sealed bags are best.

You can also use your fresh bounty to make recipes that you can freeze (or dry) for later use. This advance work can seriously cut down your prep time for meals that you enjoy weeks or months later. Check out Chapter 18 for the lowdown on menu planning and food-prep strategies.

Here's a list of our favorite make-now-and-eat-later recipes in this book:

✓ **Nacho-Cheese Kale Chips (Chapter 16):** Because it takes a day or two to make a batch of these chips, buy only as much kale as you can dry at a time; this depends on the size of your dehydrator. Ours can dry about 3 bunches of kale.

✓ **Basil Pesto (Chapter 8, see Zucchini Pasta recipe):** Buy 5 pounds of fresh basil when in season, make the pesto, and freeze it in ice-cube trays. Put the cubes in an airtight jar and store them in the freezer for up to four months. When you're ready to use some pesto, put the number of cubes you need in a glass container with a tight-fitting lid. Place the sealed container in warm water for about 30 minutes to thaw your pesto.

✓ **Sweet Red Pepper and Zucchini Hummus (Chapter 12) and Chili Colorado Sauce (Chapter 15):** These foods are especially tasty when you use in-season red bell peppers and chili peppers. Just prepare the recipes and freeze the food in pint jars for up to six months. Thaw the frozen jars in the refrigerator overnight or sit them in warm water for about 30 minutes. Ten pounds of red bell peppers goes a long way toward filling your freezer with these tasty extras.

✓ **Marinara Sauce (Chapter 8, see Zucchini Pasta recipe):** This delicious sauce sings like summer with in-season tomatoes and basil. Buy about 10 pounds of tomatoes and make the sauce in double batches (or more). Fill pint jars with the finished sauce and freeze for up to six months. Thaw a jar of sauce in the refrigerator overnight when you're ready to use it. Or whip up Zucchini Pasta in a flash by placing the frozen jar in warm (not hot) water for 30 minutes. If the sauce separates, put it in a blender and blend with a tablespoon or two of ground chia seed to bind it.

Consult a seasonal produce calendar for your region to plan your strategy for freezing and dehydrating your favorite foods. The calendar that's available online at www.epicurious.com is nice. Look for the link "seasonal food map" on the Epicurious home page.

If you purchase produce by the case, you can sometimes get a discount on the retail price. Don't be afraid to buy flats of berries or figs, even if you don't want to freeze or dehydrate them. It isn't difficult for a family to eat a flat of ripe berries within a few days. Of course we're not recommending that you eat the entire flat by yourself in one sitting, but getting your fill of your favorite foods is so satisfying — and when they're in season, why not?

Looking at Locally Produced Foods

Local produce retains most of its vitality and nutrients if it's purchased soon after it's harvested. A quick pick-to-plate turnaround seems to matter. Various studies indicate that some fruits and vegetables lose as much as half their nutrients within three to five days after harvest. Buying fresh, local produce is one of the best ways to ensure you're getting the most out of the produce you eat.

Plus, local food doesn't require as much fuel for transportation. No matter what your budget, you benefit by keeping your food money local, supporting local jobs, local farms, and local people with dollars you're already spending. The alternative is to benefit a superstore and its stockholders.

In this section, we describe ways for you to support your local community while maintaining a raw food lifestyle. We show you how to work with farmers at your local farmers' market to make sure you're buying foods that meet your dietary goals and also how to find a local farm that can keep you stocked all season with delicious, nutritious food grown nearby.

Visiting a farmers' market

These days, only a fortunate few have time to grow their own produce. The rest of us must rely on someone else's green thumb. Especially for people who are interested in knowing how and where their food is grown, a good — and fun — place to shop for fruits and vegetables is a local farmers' market. Not only is produce often reasonably priced in this venue; it's also usually grown by people who love being farmers. That is, unlike big commercial farmers, most of the vendors at farmers' markets actually spend time in the fields tending their crops.

Foods at farmers' markets is also usually far fresher than the stuff you find at grocery stores, because farmers generally harvest their produce early in the morning and bring it to market the same day. For this reason, top chefs often shop here; they that know fresh, ripe produce is the most flavorful!

Some savvy shoppers arrive at the farmers' market early in the morning to get the best quality and selection. Others, who are looking for bargain prices, shop just before the market closes or when vendors start to pack up. Most vendors prefer to sell their produce at a discount rather than haul it back home. Even after being out all day, most farmers' market produce is still fresher than grocery-store fare. Whichever group best describes you, if you see something tempting but have no clue what to do with it, ask the vendor for suggestions on how to prepare it.

When you shop at farmers' markets, be sure to talk to the vendors and ask about their growing practices. Some farmers, including small family farms, use organic (or better) methods and uphold guidelines that keep dangerous chemicals out of the food supply. But some cannot afford the steep certification fees and personnel to maintain the paperwork; therefore, they're legally prohibited from advertising their foods as organically grown. If their practices are truly organic, try to support them with your dollars.

Most vendors are honest and will tell you the truth, but you have to ask the right questions to confirm that you're getting truly organic produce:

- Is your produce certified organic?
- Do you use organic growing and farming practices?
- Do you use pesticides?
- Do you use chemical or synthetic fertilizers?
- Are you working on your organic certification (known as *transitional*)?

Not all vendors at farmers' markets are farmers, and some do not produce the foods they sell. Some people buy blemished or misshapen produce from commercial food processors and sell it at farmers' markets. Nothing is actually wrong with this produce, but it may not be of the same high quality as freshly harvested premium produce from "backyard farmers." Also watch out for produce that looks a little too perfect and shiny or out of season; these are red flags that the food was not grown by the vendor and may not be organic. If the vendor running the booth isn't also the farmer, ask for proof that the produce is certified or transitional.

Most importantly, speak up for organics. If vendors say they use chemicals, then (politely) let them know that you're committed to supporting sustainable agriculture and that you buy only organically grown produce. And move on to a booth selling organics.

Interpreting talk about farming practices

If you take our advice and ask farmers if their food is organically grown, they may tell you that they don't spray. Spraying pesticides, however, is not the only issue to worry about. Also ask vendors if they use chemical fertilizers. Organic growers use slow-release products such as compost, green manures, and colloidal rock phosphate (sometimes called *rock dust*), which have positive effects on the soil's biological community and nutrient concentration. But chemical fertilizers are highly soluble and disrupt the carbon cycle and soil ecosystems that include microorganisms, nematodes, and worms — all essential to good soil health. Organic fertilizers and natural nutrients like nitrogen are less likely than chemical fertilizers to leach into groundwater, making these options safer for the environment.

Finding and joining CSAs

Another option for enjoying locally grown food is to go directly to the farmer. *Community-supported agriculture* farms, commonly referred to as *CSAs,* provide a weekly delivery of sustainably grown produce during a growing season to people who pay an upfront membership fee to purchase a share of the farmer's bounty. This upfront payment enables the CSA farmer to prepare for the season — that is, pay for seeds, make equipment repairs, and plan crop-size needs based on how many members are in the CSA.

Some CSAs have payment plans to give members flexibility in paying for their shares. Some allow payments in installments, accept food stamps, offer sliding-scale fees based on income, and provide scholarship memberships. *Volunteer shares,* which require no cash from the member but require a certain number of hours of work each week, are offered by some CSAs. Depending on your situation, one of these arrangements may be an ideal way to gain access to high-quality produce with minimal monetary investment.

Typically, the farmer delivers the shares of produce to a convenient drop-off location near the home or workplace of members. A large share can usually feed a family of four people who supplement their diet with additional foods or a family of two who eats primarily produce.

When you become a member of a CSA, you share in the risks of farming, which include poor harvests due to unfavorable weather or pests. If you grow your own garden, you're the one who invests in the seeds, labor, equipment, and so on, and you alone absorb risks of poor weather and crop loss. As part of a CSA, you share the risk with other members. And when the farm does well, you receive extra produce to enjoy or save for the off-season.

The CSA system also offers an opportunity for you to try new foods. If you tend to get stuck in a habit of buying the same produce over and over again, you're far from alone; but a CSA can help you venture out of your culinary comfort zone and discover new favorites.

Here's a brief list of things to consider when choosing a CSA:

- ✔ **Types of produce available:** Most CSA farms offer a wide variety of seasonal fruits and vegetables. Many farms grow unusual and heirloom varieties that are otherwise unavailable. These are local farms, so they tend to grow varieties of produce that do well in your local growing conditions. So don't expect pineapple if you live in Minnesota.

- ✔ **Other items available:** Many farms also produce items such as eggs, cheese, and meat. At some locations, you may even have the opportunity to add fruit to your share. And some farms give members the first option to buy honey, flowers, wool, yarn, or other specialties from other local farmers at an additional cost.

- ✔ **Delivery location:** Factor in the driving distance you need to cover to pick up your produce. Consider carpooling or get your neighbors to buy shares as well. Often, CSAs will add additional pick-up sites if enough people participate in a particular area.

- ✔ **Length of season:** The length of season and number of deliveries offered varies by farm. Most begin in May or June and run through September or October. Some have a shorter spring schedule (5 to 8 weeks) and a longer summer season (22 weeks). Some farms also have an optional winter delivery. Look for a CSA that matches your needs.

- ✔ **Opportunities or requirements for involvement:** Community-building is an important part of the CSA approach, and most farms encourage you to become involved. Some farms expect you to help at the farm as part of membership; others organize seasonal festivals and special events. Many CSAs encourage their members to drop by any time, but it's always a good idea to call in advance to make sure you know the policies.

Shopping for Organics at the Grocery

Organic markets are becoming fixtures in neighborhoods throughout the U.S., and several major grocers are carrying an increasing number of organic products. Organics represent one of the fastest-growing industries in the world; the demand for organic products is now mainstream. Yet only a small percentage of all produce grown in the U.S. is organic. As a result, organically grown fruits and vegetables can be difficult to find and expensive.

In this section, we help you navigate your local market to find organic produce. We also give you tips on reading labels for packaged foods so you have enough information to make good-for-you food choices.

Navigating the produce section

Typically the fresh organic produce, such as leafy greens, cucumbers, bell peppers, and fresh berries, are grouped together along one wall of the store that provides moisture and refrigeration. Organic dry produce, such as onions, sweet potatoes, avocados, apples, and bananas, is often grouped together across from the perishables or near their nonorganic counterparts.

If no farmers markets are operating in your area and you must rely solely on local grocery stores, get to know your produce manager; he or she is likely your best resource for information about the freshest, most seasonal produce available. Find out when the next shipment of produce is expected and if the specific items you're looking for are coming in. If your grocery store doesn't carry the foods you want, ask the produce manager if it can be ordered. Smaller markets may even be willing to call you when special items arrive.

Ask how long the store keeps produce in the holding areas and which foods are *harvest fresh,* or shelved immediately. Often, grocery store produce is stored in holding facilities for a period ranging from several days to several months, so many stores now package fruits and vegetables in plastic wrap to extend shelf life. Unfortunately, nutrients begin waning at the moment of harvest, so neither of these grocery practices is optimal for consumers. Harvest-fresh produce is always best.

Making the best choices available

In the real world, you sometimes have to make tough choices, and you may need to carefully choose only certain organic groceries due to your budget. In Table 6-1, find out how to prioritize the foods to buy organic.

The Dirty Dozen-Plus list shows fruits and vegetables that tend to contain the highest level of pesticides and toxins, including *organophosphate* insecticides, which affect the nervous system and have been gradually removed from agriculture over the past decade. Buy organic when shopping for these foods or consider choosing a different fruit or vegetable. The Clean Fifteen foods seem to absorb fewer harmful chemicals, so consuming the nonorganic version of them is probably fine in a pinch.

Table 6-1	Guide to Choosing Organic Produce
The Dirty Dozen-Plus	*The Clean Fifteen*
Apples	Asparagus
Bell peppers	Avocados
Blueberries	Cabbage
Celery	Cantaloupe
Collard greens	Eggplant
Cucumbers	Grapefruit
Grapes	Kiwi
Green beans	Mangoes
Kale	Mushrooms
Lettuce	Onions
Nectarines	Pineapples
Peaches	Sweet corn
Potatoes	Sweet peas
Spinach	Sweet potatoes
Strawberries	Watermelon

*Source: The Environment Working Group (*www.ewg.org*)*

If you absolutely cannot find organic fruits and vegetables in your area, then be sure to wash your produce well, using a mild biodegradable soap, and rinse it thoroughly. Peel vegetables that have been waxed or coated as well as root vegetables that have been sprayed with chemicals or grown in fungicide-treated soil. Thin-skinned fruits and vegetables, such as strawberries and tomatoes, are high in pesticides — and often less flavorful — than those with thicker skins when not organic.

Reading labels

Some markets have a section for packaged organic and even raw food selections; in other markets, these items are integrated into the section with that particular type of foodstuff. Be sure to read the labels carefully to determine if packaged goods are truly raw, vegan, and organic.

What does *certified organic* mean?

Organic refers to the way agricultural products are grown and processed. Organically produced foods must comply with strict regulations governing all aspects of production. Organic farming maintains and replenishes soil fertility without using toxic and persistent pesticides and fertilizers.

Certified organic means the item was grown in accordance with strict uniform standards that are verified by independent organizations. Certification typically includes inspections of fields and processing facilities, detailed record keeping, and periodic testing of soil and water to ensure that growers and handlers are complying with the standards. Buying certified organically grown produce (or growing your own using untreated organic seeds) is the safest way to ensure that you ingest the fewest toxic residues.

A label indicating *100% Organic* ensures that only organic ingredients and organic processing methods are used. A label that says simply says *Organic* requires at least 95 percent organic ingredients while allowing a limited number of strictly regulated nonorganic ingredients. And products labeled *Made with organic* must contain at least 70 percent organic ingredients.

When you see the word *Natural* on food packaging, it can mean any number of different things; *All natural* doesn't have a strictly defined or regulated definition like organic does. In fact, you may be surprised to learn what can be considered "natural." Food companies get away with using all sorts of unhealthy processes and ingredients in a food product that they claim is all natural. This term is fairly useless to health-conscious shoppers.

When reading a food label, look at nutritional tables for levels of fiber, calories, and fat and check out the list of ingredients. Also look for these desirable terms on labels:

- *Sun dried* or *low-heat dehydrated* (dehydrated at a temperature lower than 118 degrees) indicates that the food is technically raw.

- *Organic* foods were grown under regulations that, among other things, prohibit the use of certain fertilizers or pesticides. Check out the nearby sidebar "What does *certified organic* mean?" for information on the many distinctions of the word *organic*.

- *GMO-free* or *non-GMO* means that the food hasn't been genetically modified. See the nearby sidebar "What are GMOs?" to find out why modification is a problem.

Avoid buying food with labels that list the following ingredients or terms:

✔ **Non-foods:** Chemicals don't belong in foods. After all, how healthy and delicious can butylated hydroxyanisole be?

✔ **Words you can't pronounce:** If you can't pronounce it, it's probably not food.

✔ **Saturated fats:** This ingredient directly raises total and LDL (bad) cholesterol levels.

✔ **Partially hydrogenated fats:** Hydrogenated and trans fats have been manipulated to become solid at room temperature and can raise total and LDL (bad) cholesterol levels while lowering HDL (good) cholesterol levels.

✔ **Oils:** Not all oils are created equal. Some, like flax or hempseed oil, contain good, essential fatty acids and can be consumed safely in small amounts (about 2 teaspoons a day). Even small amounts of olive oil, which has some health benefits, can be used safely in salad dressings. But polyunsaturated oils from soybeans, corn, and cottonseed can lower your (good) HDL levels, so try to avoid them.

All in all, it's better to eat whole food fats (like avocados and nuts) than oils, because these sources contain nutrients and fiber and less fat than the concentrated oils, which are often devoid of all nutrients and cause or exacerbate fat-related problems like heart disease.

✔ **Corn sugar and corn syrup:** Corn sugar is just the latest consumer-friendly marketing term for high-fructose corn syrup, a cheap concentrated sugar found in everything from sodas to baked goods. This product has been linked to a variety of health issues, including diabetes, obesity, and premature aging.

✔ **Enriched or fortified:** If a food has been enriched or fortified, it's only because something important was processed out of it. Avoid food with these terms on the label.

✔ **Bleached:** Bleach is toxic to humans. We don't recommend drinking chlorinated water, and we definitely don't suggest eating bleached food.

Watch out for what a label *doesn't* tell you, too. For example, if a label includes the ingredients soy or corn and *doesn't* indicate that either item is organic or non-GMO, then it probably isn't. Stay away.

What are GMOs?

The term *GMO*, or *genetically modified organism*, refers to organisms whose genetic material is altered in a way that does not occur by mating or natural recombination. Instead, the organism's genes are changed by *mutagenic* breeding, which occurs by radiating DNA to deliberately mutate genes to produce more desirable characteristics.

In some cases, an additional step called *transgenic* breeding (breeding across completely unrelated species by modifying the DNA) occurs. For example, a company may conduct transgenic breeding with a tomato and a peanut to make the tomato more pest-resistant. This makes the resulting tomato unsafe (and potentially life threatening) for people who are allergic to peanuts, especially if they have no idea that the tomato has peanut-like properties.

The more widespread and persistent danger is in introducing GMOs into the environment. Science cannot predict the long-term effects of genetic modification because these organisms — and the Frankenfoods they produce — have not been around long enough to compile data on their potential impact. One very real risk that some agricultural scientists fear is widespread crop failure as a result of some unforeseen genetic flaw. Given that all varieties of GMO seeds have identical genetic makeups, a blight affecting one type of GMO could wipe out an entire crop of that plant. And because pollen from GMO varieties of a species can easily crossbreed with non-GMO varieties of another, GMOs contaminate nearby fields of non-GMO crops, resulting in yet new varieties of produce and increasing confusion among consumers about what foods are safe.

Shopping Online

The Internet is good for leveling the nutritional playing field. Just because you live in a small town or a remote area with limited access to robust markets and whole food grocery stores doesn't mean you can't enjoy nutritious and delicious raw meals every day.

In fact, some items, like dried fruits and sprouting seeds, are better from online sources than other vendors no matter where you live and how easily you can access different types of food. For example, dried fruits in supermarket bulk food sections are often high-heat dehydrated, so you may want to buy these items from online raw food specialty stores that indicate these foods are low-heat dehydrated. Get the scoop on sprouting seeds in the section "Stocking up on sprouting seeds" later in this chapter.

Here are a few websites that specialize in organic foods and carry many raw products:

- **Green Polka Dot Box:** All GMO-free, organic, staple pantry items and fresh organic produce (www.greenpolkadotbox.com/rawfood)

- **Raw Food Chef Marketplace:** All organic raw vegan specialty foods, raw vegan snacks, seeds for sprouting, sea vegetables, and more (https://shop.rawfoodchef.com)

- **Sun Organic Farm:** Bulk seeds for spouting, nuts, grains, oils, dried fruits, and olives (www.sunorganicfarm.com)

- **The Date People:** One of our favorite sources for high quality raw dates at affordable prices (www.datepeople.net)

The shelf life of raw foods is shorter than conventional products that are loaded with preservatives, and the nutrients in food begin to diminish the moment it's harvested, so try to buy fresh food from online companies that ship within 24 hours of ordering and from as close to you as possible.

This section provides tips for shopping for raw products online, no matter what websites you use.

Making your money go farther

Organic products can be expensive. Yet opting for organically grown food is one of the most important choices you can make on a daily basis to support your health and the health of the planet. In making the choice to invest in organic products, you get high-quality nutritious food, and you send a strong message to governments and food companies about the foods you want to consume. That said, we definitely recommend that you make smart purchasing decisions.

Here are some tips for making the most of your organic food budget:

- **Get together with friends to order in bulk.** Online sites sometimes offer a discount on full cases or larger quantities of items. Almost all have free shipping when you spend a certain dollar amount, so even if you don't split actual cases of products, you may be able to save a few shipping dollars by pooling your resources.

 ✔ **Join membership sites that offer "at cost" or deeply discounted products.** Some sites require an annual fee but offset it with members-only discounts. If you regularly order, you can typically recoup your membership costs in a few shipments.

 ✔ **Look at the total you're paying for your order, not simply the cost of each item.** Some sites charge a per-item shipping fee; others have a sliding shipping rate that increases or decreases depending on how much you buy. Shipping charges can really drive up your costs.

 ✔ **Buy produce and staples by the case when they're on special.** As long as the products can be stored to retain quality nutrition, stockpile away.

Stocking up on sprouting seeds

Often, the seeds you buy at your local garden center are chemically treated and packaged in such small quantities that they make sprouting impractical (and quite expensive). But even if you can find organic bulk sprouting seeds, most bulk foods don't stay fresh in the grocery store — not even in a progressive organic grocery store. This is particularly true for foods that contain fat, such as nuts and seeds.

Seeds for sprouting at a store are often old, too, because avid sprouters know to buy them fresh, online. Even wheat berries in bulk can be too old to sprout well, though they may be fine for making flour. Therefore, we recommend buying organic seeds that are specifically identified for sprouting from online retailers.

If you're buying seeds from an organic sprouting supply retailer, you can rest assured that your seeds are sproutable. Otherwise, look for the words *sproutable* or *sprouting* on the package or in the item's description.

Here are some of our favorite sources for buying seeds and grains online:

 ✔ **Sun Organic Farm:** www.sunorganicfarm.com

 ✔ **Raw Food Chef Marketplace:** http://shop.rawfoodchef.com

 ✔ **Sproutman:** http://sproutman.com

Flip to Chapter 7 for details on sprouting seeds and growing your own garden kitchen. It's easier than you may think and extremely satisfying.

Chapter 7

Discovering Raw Food Preparation Techniques

reating gourmet raw cuisine is arguably the most exciting of all the culinary arts today. People who can create nutrient-packed raw foods that mimic the flavor, texture, and appearance of popular cooked foods are truly in a league of their own. The tricks of their trade require the right ingredients and specialty equipment along with innovative food-preparation techniques that are not taught in traditional cooking schools or found in ordinary cookbooks.

In this chapter, we describe the best techniques and food-preparation methods, including how to use your juicer and other appliances such as a high-performance blender and food processor in ways you may not have considered. We even help you get to know your dehydrator and all the wonderful things it can do to make your raw life even more comforting and delicious.

Here, too, are pointers for starting a kitchen garden to grow your very own sprouts and greens, a true necessity for many raw foodists. I also offer tips for converting many of your favorite dishes into healthful raw delights.

Using a Juicer

Fresh raw juices are a delicious way to satisfy your appetite while reducing the amount of energy your body needs to digest and assimilate your food. We drink juices between meals as a beverage or snack. But juicing removes most of the fiber from foods — and fiber is an essential part of a healthful diet and your long-term well-being — so we don't recommend replacing regular meals with juices except for short-term weight loss or cleansing programs conducted with the supervision of a health professional (see Chapter 4).

Raw juices have high amounts of antioxidants, enzymes, vitamins, minerals, and phytonutrients and contain medicinal properties such as antimicrobials, diuretics, chlorophyll, and most likely other near-magical substances yet to be discovered. These components work together to enable your body to function properly and efficiently.

Juicing takes very little time compared to preparing other types of meals and offers great benefits, especially if you use organic fruits and vegetables. Shop for organic produce on sale and organize your juicing menu around in-season offerings (see Chapter 6).

Washing fruits and veggies

Even if you use seemingly clean, organic produce, bacteria can be present on fruits and vegetables. That bacteria can cause illness, especially in small children, the elderly, and people with compromised immune systems. To ensure your safety and the safety of others, follow these steps when you bring home produce:

1. Wash your hands before handling any food.

2. Remove any stickers from fruits and vegetables and trim bad ends and roots.

3. Place the produce in a sink with lukewarm or cool water and agitate the water well to remove any dirt or debris.

   If insects may be hiding inside the produce (in a bunch of kale, for example), add one or two teaspoons of salt to the soaking water and let the produce sit in it for 5 minutes before rinsing with warm water.

4. Drain the sink of water, and then run fresh water over your foods. If you have a potato or vegetable brush, use it to scrub foods that grow under the soil, such as carrots and beets. Just be careful not to bruise your produce with a rough brush.

5. Towel or spin dry, and then refrigerate immediately.

The FDA does not recommend using soap, cleaning agents, or detergent to wash produce, but veggie washes are available at many markets. These washes can be helpful when trying to remove oil-based residues such as pesticides and waxy preservatives. But recent reports indicate that these products are not necessarily better for cleaning produce than clean water.

Here's how to get started with juicing:

1. **Thoroughly wash all fruits and vegetables.**

2. **Cut fruits and veggies into chunks small enough to accommodate the feeding chute of the juicer.** Carrots, celery, kale, and most other produce will probably fit without cutting, but less expensive juicers may require smaller pieces of produce to do the job.

3. **Select the right plate for the type of juice you're making.** Most *masticating* juicers (which make a paste from the vegetables and then squeeze juice from the paste) come with three different plates:

   • **A fine screen:** Recommended for most types of vegetable juice, this screen filters the most pulp, making the clearest juice.

   • **A screen with large holes:** This option is best for juices made with melon, which contains a lot of pulp that would clog a fine screen.

   • **A blank plate with no holes:** Use this plate to homogenize juice and pulp and to make sorbets, nut butters, and pâtés.

4. **Insert pieces of produce through the chute.** Alternate the types of produce so soft fruits such as cucumbers and apples and hard items such as carrots and beets are mixed up. This process helps keep pulp from the softer produce from backing up.

5. **Drink your juice immediately.** Juices are live foods; if not ingested immediately, they begin to lose their enzymatic and antioxidant value due to exposure to air.

   Chew your juice! When drinking juice, chewing activates the digestive elements in your mouth, which helps to assimilate the juice in your body.

6. **Save the fiber.** Reserve your juice pulp for other recipes, including Beefy Barbeque Sandwiches (recipe in Chapter 15). Or put it in your compost and build nutrient-rich earth for your garden.

Try making To-Live-For Green Juice (recipe in Chapter 10) and using it for your daily "green insurance." And help your kids make apple and carrot juice — a perfect after-school snack. Juicers are also great for making natural ice creams from frozen fruits (see recipes in Chapter 17) and creamy pâtés from soaked nuts and seeds (see Chapter 15).

A good quality juicer can run from $100 to $500 and comes with a solid warranty. But if you aren't quite ready to invest in a shiny new juicer, you can often find them at yard sales or online. Or you can use a blender or food processor to puree or liquefy produce with a little water. After blending or processing, just pour the juice though a juice bag or nut-milk bag to separate the pulp from the juice. Then gently squeeze the bag over the container to catch the remaining juice.

Checking out types of juicers

Juicing has taken the United States by storm. Since TV hosts like Dr. Oz began juicing and made it mainstream, the popularity of juicing has soared. Everyone from busy executives to athletes and even bartenders are embracing the health, weight-loss, and taste benefits of fresh and natural-state juice. Juicing is a quick and easy way to get nutrients from whole raw foods.

Juicers come in several different styles. What's the best juicer for you? It depends on how you plan to use it. Some juicers are better suited for certain kinds of produce than others. If you want juice greens, for example, you need a high-quality juicer to extract juice from this type of food. The same is true if you want to juice wheat grass; a particular type of juicer is required.

Here's some insight about different types of juicers:

Centrifugal juicers *masticate,* or chop, fruits and vegetables and spin produce in a stainless steel or plastic basket at a high speed to separate the juice from the pulp. This type is a good choice for most fruit and vegetable juices; but it's not good for leafy green or wheat-grass juice, and it cannot be used to make sorbet.

Centrifugal juicers with a pulp ejector operate the same as centrifugal juicers but also eject the pulp through a side opening. This type of juicer makes great carrot and apple juice, but it does not handle leafy greens and cannot be used for sorbets or pâtés.

Masticating, extruder-type juicers masticate fruits and vegetables into a paste at high speed and then squeeze the juice through a screen at the bottom. A homogenizing plate may be used to make sorbets, nut butters, and pâtés, but it's not the best choice if you want to juice greens or wheat grass.

Single or double auger juicers have slow-turning auger(s) that basically crush produce into the walls (or screen) of the juicer to extract the juice. A double auger, as the name implies, has one more gear than a single, so the gears interlock to very efficiently press juice from the produce. The double auger is our favorite all-around juicer. It juices leafy greens and wheat grass as well as other types of produce, and it can be used to make sorbet.

Juice press juicers are the most expensive kind of juicer and take the most time to use. The upside is that the juice retains more nutrients than other types of juicers, but this appliance is very heavy and bulky and requires a two-step process (pressing and straining) for getting juice.

Powering Up High-Performance Blenders and Food Processors

High-performance blenders and food processors are the best friends of a raw food chef! These machines take most of the work out of creating smoothies, soups, pâtés, dips, sauces, dressings, puddings, cookies, pie crusts, crackers, and many other delectable raw creations. Fortunately, you don't need to invest in a pricey model; most recipes in this book can be accomplished with relatively inexpensive equipment. Just keep in mind that less-expensive equipment may require you to make smaller batches of food to accomplish the right texture. Certainly don't let money stop you; use whatever equipment you have and get started now; buy the expensive equipment later if you decide you need it.

Using a high-performance blender

High-performance blenders, such as Vitamix or Blendtec, are regarded as heroes of the raw food kitchen. They can blend just about anything in large quantities quickly and efficiently. And when we say they can blend about anything, it's no joke. On Blendtec's website (www.willitblend.com), you can see testers blend a broom, a bunch of golf balls, and more! Certainly these appliances will have no trouble with your raw foods.

A high-performance blender is great for making sauces, smoothies, and soups. This appliance can also crush ice and produce flour from whole grains, flax seeds, sun-dried tomatoes, and dried shiitake mushrooms. One of the best things about this appliance is that you can skip the peeling process when blending fruits and vegetables, if desired. The whole food, which includes the peel, is incredibly high in nutrients and can be liquefied by these machines. Use organically grown produce, wash items well, and toss them in. Even garlic and ginger don't need to be peeled before going into a high-performance blender!

Not *all* peels should be used though. Some taste bitter, and some are inedible. For example, don't use the peel of avocado (although you can use the pit), pineapple, banana, melon (except watermelon), papaya, mango, or guava. Also skip the peels on onions, sweet potatoes, yams, and eggplant (when eating raw). For citrus fruits, peel off the outer zest and leave some of the white pith, which is high in riboflavin.

A drawback of using this powerful appliance for soups and sauces is that it can whip more air into your food than desireable. Another pitfall of using a high-performance blender, especially the Vitamix, is that food can become hot during extended processing, meaning the blender can actually cook your food. So don't process food for more than one or two minutes at a time. If food is frozen, it can handle a longer processing time than food at room temperature, but we suggest that you watch your blender work until it finishes its task.

Here are some general recommendations for helping your high-performance blender get the job done right:

- ✔ Set the blender on a clean, dry, flat surface before running it.

- ✔ Always put the juiciest foods in first so the blades can move easily and the juices can wash the other ingredients into the mixture.

  Ingredients that need to be pre-chopped before going in a regular blender do not require any advanced preparation for a high-performance blender. But you'll always get better results if you cut up a few pieces of an item and place them in the bottom of the pitcher to allow the blades to create juices that wash the remaining ingredients into the blades.

✔ Be sure the lid is firmly in place before turning on the machine. Put your hand on top of the lid when blending to ensure that the pitcher stays seated on the motor.

✔ Start the machine on low so your mixture doesn't jump up and hit the lid or cause food to stick to the walls of the pitcher. Starting slowly and keeping the food near the blades as you increase the speed reduces the need to stop the blender, open the lid, and scrape the sides with a spatula.

When a *vortex,* or whirlpool, forms in the center of the mixture, you may slowly increase the speed as the food becomes thicker and more manageable until the blender is on high without the mixture jumping to the top.

✔ If you're mixing hard foods (like almonds) with liquid to form a puree, cream, or milk, start with the hard item and a small amount of liquid and add more as needed to produce a thick and smooth texture. Gradually add the remaining liquid to achieve the desired consistency. The idea is to keep the hard material close to the blades to be completely pulverized.

To avoid damaging your high-performance blender or injuring yourself, heed these dangers:

✔ Never stick a spoon, spatula, or hand in the blender blades while the machine is on.

✔ Be careful when adding hot food to your blender. Hot liquids increase in pressure, sometimes causing the lid to blow off, so keep your towel on top of the lid, secured by your hand during use.

✔ Don't lift the pitcher off the blender until the motor has stopped. Doing so can strip the gear in the base of the blender.

✔ Always add liquid when crushing ice. If you crush ice dry, you may damage the container and blades.

✔ If your blender has a plastic pitcher, don't use a scrub brush to clean it. High-performance blenders act as their own dishwashers, which makes for quick and easy cleanup! Simply add hot water and a few drops of dish soap, and then blend away. Rinse thoroughly and dry; you're ready to use it again.

For videos demonstrating how to use a high-performance blender, visit `http://rawfoodchef.com/culinaryarts/freerawfoodsvideos.html`.

Using a food processor

A food processor is one of the most commonly used pieces of equipment in raw food preparation. Use it to chop vegetables, smooth sauces, puree foods, and make raw candies, breads, pie crusts, and even ice cream.

Many food processors come with several types of blades that are designed for specific functions. The most frequently used is the S blade. Named because of its shape, the S blade is most useful for chopping and homogenizing foods. When using the S blade, be sure to have an appropriate amount of food in the processor bowl. Too much food will not move well and can overburden the motor. Too little food causes the food to spray and stick to the sides of the bowl rather than circulating with the blade. In most cases, the ideal amount of food is somewhere just above the top of the plastic centerpiece.

Most food processors have a safety switch that prevents operation when the lid is not properly closed. If you can't turn on your food processor, and you're sure it's plugged in, check the lid to make sure it's properly closed. This safety feature varies between brands, so read the owner's manual to familiarize yourself with the specifics of your food processor.

Here are the basics for operating a food processor:

1. **Set the food processor on a clean, dry, flat surface.**

2. **Place the bowl on top of the machine and rotate it into the locked position.**

3. **Select the blade you wish to use and put it in place.**

   If you're using the S blade, drop it onto the middle shaft and put the food inside the bowl. Fill the bowl only up to the recommended level (usually marked on the bowl) to avoid leaks. Then place the lid on the bowl and latch it into place.

   If using the slicing/shredding blades, attach the preferred disk to the stem, drop it into place, put the lid on the bowl, and latch it into place.

4. **Trim leaves and other unwanted parts from the food you wish to chop and then drop them (or stack them) into the feed tube.**

5. **Push the On or Pulse button and use the plastic pusher to plunge food through the tube.** The On button is generally used for homogenizing and blending and can be used for several seconds or longer. To chop food without pureeing it, use the S blade and hit the Pulse button several times, watching for the ideal consistency.

Be very careful when handling food processor blades; they're extremely sharp.

Using a Dehydrator

You can prepare lots of great raw foods without a dehydrator, but when you're ready to make the investment — and enjoy homemade, raw, and crispy crackers and chips as well as wraps, breads, and cookies — you'll wonder what took you so long! A new, high-quality dehydrator can run from $125 to $250, but this appliance will last for many years. You can also look for used dehydrators at yard sales or online to cut your costs. Check out Figure 7-1 to see a dehydrator.

Our favorite dehydrator is the Excalibur dehydrator with 9-inch trays. It has removable and adjustable sliding shelves, which means you can make room for large casserole dishes and jars or anything that requires more space. Another benefit of a sliding-tray-style dehydrator like the Excalibur is that it's square; its trays don't have a hole in the center, like some models do.

Figure 7-1:
A dehydrator can help you simulate the texture of cooked foods.

When you choose a dehydrator, consider the temperature-control features. Thermostats vary in temperature by several degrees above and below the desired settings, and keeping temperatures well below 118 degrees — the highest allowable food temperature for retaining nutrients and meeting the raw standard — is important.

That said, during the first two hours of dehydrating foods with a high level of moisture, you may turn up the temperature as high as 135 degrees as long as the food is placed on a moisture barrier such as a nonstick dehydrator sheet, which traps some of the moisture inside. Even at this setting, the internal temperature of the food remains relatively low as the moisture evaporates.

Leaving food in a dehydrator at a too-low temperature for too long can create a bacteria-prone environment, especially if the food has a high degree of moisture. Even food that's free of animal products can harbor bacteria. Using a higher temperature, like 125 to 135 degrees, to warm food for one to two hours (max) can minimize this risk. Just remember to reduce the temperature before your food reaches 118 degrees.

If you're interested in using the dehydrator to warm food that's cold, you must start with a high temperature (125 to 135 degrees), turn the food over, and then reduce the temperature to 105 for another hour at most. Serve the food as soon as it's ready.

Don't leave your dehydrator set higher than 105 degrees for more than two hours, and always follow the preparation directions given in a reputable raw recipe, especially those related to temperature settings and dehydration times.

If you're concerned about temperature during the dehydrating process, touch your food to make sure it feels cool. Your body temperature is 98.6 degrees, so food feels warm to the touch when it exceeds 100 degrees. If it feels hot, turn down the dehydrator and check the temperature setting. Hot indicates that the food may have surpassed the safe temperature and lost some of its antioxidants and other nutrients. To be certain that the internal temperature of your food remains below 118 degrees, insert a calibrated food thermometer into it.

Here are some food-preparation tasks for a dehydrator:

- **Marinating vegetables:** Using a dehydrator to marinate vegetables intensifies the flavor of the food and gives the vegetables a cooked flavor and appearance.

- **Thickening sauces:** When sauces are placed in an open, glass container in a dehydrator for two to three hours, some of the liquid evaporates. It's similar to the reduction technique in traditional cooking, but gentler.

- **Warming foods:** Foods at slightly higher temperatures than your body have a comforting and warming effect you as you eat them, yet they still retain enzymatic integrity, vitamins, and antioxidants.

- **Creating crunchy snacks:** Many different raw snack foods, including trail mix, chips, and seasoned seeds and nuts get their crunch from time in a dehydrator. Fully dehydrated foods do not require refrigeration.

- **Incubating fermenting foods:** Yogurt, cheese, and other probiotic-rich foods made with young coconut, nuts, and seeds ferment well at controlled, warm temps in a dehydrator.

Growing a Kitchen Garden

A kitchen garden requires very little time and space to deliver a bounty of rewards. Seeds take as little as six hours of soaking to germinate; then they're ready to eat! Growing wheat grass takes about a week, and young sunflower greens go from soaking to harvest in only ten days.

Plus, the kitchen garden we're talking about here doesn't require you to pull weeds or contend with pests or predators. It's mobile, too. Sprouts, wheat grass, and sunflower greens can easily be grown in a hotel room or roving motor home. We know because we've done it!

Sprouts and young greens are *living foods* that provide a concentration of nutrients that's unsurpassed by most other produce. During the short period of their transformation from seed to vegetable, sprouts and young greens are more nutrient-dense, enzyme-rich, and life-generating than at any other time in their lifecycle. They promote cellular renewal to rejuvenate your body.

Soaking and sprouting seeds and nuts

In a nutshell (are you groaning?), you soak seeds and nuts to allow them to germinate. Why? Nuts, seeds, and grains, especially those with dark skins, contain *enzyme inhibitors,* which protect these foods from sprouting prematurely. Enzyme inhibitors give nuts and seeds a bitter flavor and make digesting them difficult. By soaking nuts and seeds for a few hours, you can remove the enzyme inhibitors (see Chapter 3).

Gather these supplies for soaking seeds and nuts:

- ✔ Nuts, sprouting seeds, grains, or legumes. See Figure 7-2 for ideas on what to sprout, and check out Chapter 6 for tips on where to buy sprouting seeds.
- ✔ A few jars, ranging from 1 quart to 1 gallon in size.
- ✔ Filtered water.
- ✔ Mesh screening. Pick up plastic screens from the hardware store or buy special sprouting screens designed to fit canning jars.
- ✔ Rubber bands to hold the screen around the mouth of the jar.

Follow these steps when you're ready to get started:

1. **Choose a wide-mouth soaking jar that's large enough to allow the seeds or nuts to at least double in volume.** Legumes, grains, and wild rice quadruple in size, and sprouting seeds like clover and alfalfa, which grow for six to eight days, expand to about ten times their original size.

2. **Measure the mouth of the jar to determine the screen size, allowing a couple of inches to drape over the sides, and cut the screen with ordinary scissors.** Even though the mouth of the jar is round, cut the screen square.

3. **Measure the seeds (or whatever you're using), put them in the jar, and fill the remaining space in the jar with filtered water.**

4. **Place the screen evenly over the mouth of the jar to completely cover the opening.** Secure it with a rubber band, making sure the band is placed under the lip of the jar. Carefully gather the screen evenly so there are no big gaps for the seeds to get caught in.

5. **Place the jar away from direct light to soak the seeds for the appropriate amount of time.** See Figure 7-2 for guidelines.

6. **After the required amount of time has passed, turn the jar upside down to drain. Fill the jar (without removing the screen) with fresh water to rinse the seeds, and drain again.** Continue rinsing and draining until the drained water is clear.

7. **To sprout the seeds, grains, or legumes, set the well-drained jar upside down but on an angle so the seeds don't block the screen and clog the airflow.** Rinse and drain according to the instructions in Figure 7-2 until the sprouts are the appropriate length.

To develop chlorophyll in seeds such as alfalfa and clover, place the damp sprouts in indirect light (not a sunny window) for two to three days prior to harvest. Rinse and drain every 8 to 12 hours.

Keep soaked nuts in the refrigerator for up to a week in a glass jar with water and remember to rinse them every couple of days to keep them fresh. You'll love having soaked nuts handy for recipes or to eat as a snack.

Some recipes in this book call for dehydrated nuts. If a recipe requires soaked and/or dehydrated nuts, a Plan Ahead icon tells you right away that the dish requires some advance prep.

Growing greens indoors

Growing your own greens can be a wonderful experience that allows you to tune into nature. By nurturing your plants, they nurture you — within about ten days! Yet the benefits go beyond feeling good. Growing wheat grass for juicing and young greens for salads is economical, too. You spend less money on greens when you grow your own versus buying grown ones.

To begin kitchen gardening, gather some soaked and sprouted seeds (see the earlier section "Soaking and sprouting seeds and nuts"), good organic soil, and a few cafeteria trays or garden flats. Use your own composted soil or purchase organic soil by the bag. You need about 1½ to 2 quarts of soil per 14-x-18-inch tray.

Growing wheat grass

Wheat-grass juice is a high-chlorophyll drink that helps to cleanse the blood and fortify it through oxygenation. For the best wheat grass, buy organic, hard, red winter wheat berries from your health food store or online seed suppler. After you soak and sprout the wheat berries, they're ready for planting (see Figure 7-3):

Seeds	Method	Amount per jar 1 qt	Soak Hours	Temp. (degreesF)	Number times rinse per day	Total number of days	Green on last day?	Height (in.) when mature	Uses
Alfalfa, clover, cabbage	Jar	2 tablespoons	6–8	60–85	2–3	4–6	Yes	1½–2	Salads, drinks, wraps, rolls, sandwiches, sushi
Broccoli, kale, chive, onion, garlic	Jar	3 tablespoons	4–8	60–85	2–3	4–6	Yes	1–1½	Salads, soups, wraps, rolls, sushi
Almonds, other hard nuts	Jar	2 cups	8–12	60–85	1	1–2	No	0	Salads, main dishes, sauces, dressings, desserts, breads, crackers, pâtés, drinks, cheeses
Hulled buckwheat, chia, flax, basil	Jar or bowl	2 cups	4–6	60–85	0 Rinse before soaking	1	No	0–1/4	Salads, granola, crackers, cookies
Unhulled buckwheat, sunflower, wheat berries	Jar and soil	1½ cups	6–8	60–85	2–3	2 days in jar 5 days in soil	Yes	Jar ¼–½ Soil 5½–7	Salads, soups, juice
Mung, lentil, whole pea, azuki	Jar	½ cup	5–10	65–85	2–3	2–4	No	¼–½	Salads, main dishes, sandwiches
Sunflower, sesame, and pumpkin seeds; cashews and other soft nuts and seeds	Jar	1½ cups	4–6	60–85	2	6 hours	No	0–1/4	Salads, main dishes, sauces, crackers, pâtés, drinks, cheeses

Figure 7-2:
Soaking and sprouting information for seeds and nuts.

1. **Spread 6 cups of soil evenly on a cafeteria tray that's ¾-inch deep.**

2. **Distribute the sprouted wheat berries evenly over the soil, ½ inch from the edges, and moisten with 2 to 3 cups of water.**

3. **Invert another cafeteria tray and place it on top of the planted one; set aside for a couple of days.**

4. **When the grass has pushed up the top tray, remove it. Place the grass in the light and water it daily.**

5. **Harvest your grass as you need it, using scissors or a serrated knife.**
   Cut close to the soil and discard or compost the remaining root bed.

Figure 7-3:
Growing and harvesting wheat grass.

Dehydrated wheat-grass juice is fine in a pinch or while traveling, but nothing compares to the chlorophyll in fresh wheat grass. Drink a ½-ounce shot to start and gradually increase your intake to 2 ounces. If you drink too much too soon, wheat-grass juice can make you nauseous, because it accelerates detox (see Chapter 4). If you dislike the taste of this nutritious juice, enjoy a slice of fresh orange or lemon after drinking it.

Growing sunflower greens

Sunflower greens — an excellent source of vitamins and minerals and rich in enzymes — are great in salads and other dishes that call for leafy greens. Buy organic, raw sunflower seeds in the shell. After you soak and sprout the seeds, they're ready for planting:

1. **Spread 1 quart of soil evenly in a cafeteria tray, ½-inch deep.**

2. **Distribute the sprouted seeds over the top and lay another quart of soil evenly over the first. Water the soil with 2 to 3 cups of water so it is wet but not flooded.**

3. **Invert another cafeteria tray and place it on top, and then set the trays aside for several days.**

4. **When the young sunflowers begin to push up on the top tray, remove it. Put the sunflowers in ample sunlight and water daily.**

5. **Harvest your greens as you need them or all at once, using scissors or a serrated knife.** Cut stalks close to the soil and place them in a sink of water. Swirl them around to allow the outer shells to become free of the sprout; then remove the sprouts and discard the inedible outer shells.

Sunflowers provide a second harvest from the slower-growing seeds, so continue watering the plants until they mature.

Growing buckwheat lettuce

Buckwheat lettuce is a terrific, nutrient-dense leafy green for salads and other dishes. Purchase organic buckwheat in the shell. After you soak and sprout the seeds, they're ready for planting:

1. **Spread 1½ quarts of soil evenly in a cafeteria tray, ¾-inch deep.**

2. **Distribute the soaked, sprouted buckwheat over the soil and moisten with 2 to 3 cups of water.**

3. **Invert another cafeteria tray and place it on top, and then put it aside for several days.**

4. **When the buckwheat begins to push up on the top tray, remove it. Place the buckwheat under good light and water daily.**

5. **Harvest your greens as you need them or all at once, using scissors or a serrated knife.** Cut stalks close to the soil and place them in a sink of water. Swirl them around to allow the outer shells to become free of the sprout; then remove the sprouts and discard the inedible outer shells.

Buckwheat lettuce provides a second harvest from the slower growing seeds, so continue watering for a second harvest.

Fermenting foods

Humans have been eating fermented foods for centuries, and many of the longest-surviving groups in the world continue to eat them as a staple of their diet, crediting these foods for everything from improving digestion to protecting them from cancer and heart disease. What may have started as a way to preserve foods has proven to be beneficial in many other ways as well.

Fermentation creates probiotics, the good bacteria, on which the body relies for immunity, digestion, and the assimilation of nutrients. (See Chapter 3 for the nutritional details on probiotics.) Popular fermented products include yogurt, kefir, cheese (dairy and dairy-free), sauerkraut, pickled and sour vegetables, kimchi, kambucha, miso, tamari, natto, and tempeh.

A small serving of fermented foods is ample and powerful. If you eat too much before you become accustomed to it, you may feel bloated. Start with a few tablespoons and add more as you acclimate to the detoxifying effects.

Sauerkraut

Preparing sauerkraut at home is one of the easiest ways for you to start adding probiotic-rich fermented foods to your diet. You can find a basic recipe in Chapter 13, but when you get the hang of making your own kraut, vary your batches according to your personal taste preferences. You can use any kind of cabbage (purple, green, Napa, Chinese), throw in your favorite herbs and spices (try onion, leek, garlic, and gingerroot as well as spices like caraway seeds, cayenne pepper, juniper seeds, and coriander), and even add other firm vegetables if you like; carrots, beets, and broccoli stems are great. No special starters are required for making sauerkraut; it happens like magic!

Be sure to massage the cabbage for your kraut until it's extremely juicy. (See Chapter 8 for some massaging how-to.) If the cabbage isn't massaged well enough to create a pool of liquid that rises to the top, the kraut may develop mold, so make sure you break it down enough to release plenty of juice.

Don't be discouraged if you see a cloud of white fluffy mold around the sides of your fermenting jar after a couple of days; just throw the batch away and start over. It may take one or two attempts to get it right; but the effort to learn this technique is worth it!

Nut cheese

Making some fermented nut and seed cheeses is a terrific way to eat nuts, because it makes them far more digestible. Plus, nut cheese is great on all kinds of raw foods, including enchiladas, pizza, and other foods that just aren't the same without cheese. In fact, many avowed cheese-a-holics who couldn't give up cheese to go vegan find it easy to veganize when they learn how to make nut cheese (see Chapter 9).

Any kind of nut or seed can be used to make cheese, and each has its own distinctive flavor and texture. Macadamias, peeled almonds, cashews, and pine nuts are especially good for cheese because they produce a visually attractive product that's similar to cream cheese. Pumpkin seeds make a green cheese with a delicious cheddar-like flavor.

Try partially dehydrating your nut cheese after fermenting to produce a concentrated flavor and thick texture similar to sliced cheese, or dehydrate completely to make a nut cheese that resembles a shaved Parmesan.

The amount of time it takes to ferment nut cheese depends on the temperature of the air around it. The warmer the air, the faster your cheese will ferment. Timing also depends on your taste preferences. Ferment longer for a stronger, more cheesy taste.

Creating Flavorful Foods

You can prepare and enjoy a limitless variety of raw and flavorful salad dressings, sauces, soups, and more with a little insight on a few basic principles. For starters, know that one of the most important aspects of satisfying food is taste. Luckily, remembering the principles of taste isn't hard because there are only a handful. In this section, we describe the basic elements of flavor and point out how to combine and balance flavors and use a healthy amount of fats to create raw dishes with appealing taste.

Understanding the five basic flavors

Here are the five basic flavors:

- **Sweet** flavors are pleasant and agreeable to the palate and mind. Sweet fruits and condensed sweeteners fall into the category.

- **Sour/acid** flavors produce a sharp sensation of taste and smell; they're expressive and stimulating. Acid fruits, vinegar, and some fermented foods such as yogurt fall into this category.

- **Salty** flavors increase the intensity of other flavors. Table salt, miso, tamari, and some seaweeds belong in this category.

- **Bitter** flavors are seldom enjoyed on their own. Bitter is an acquired taste that's not appreciated in all cultures. Leafy greens as well as most herbs and spices fit into this group.

- **Umami** is a Japanese term that refers to the craveable, savory element of foods. It's found in naturally occurring glutamate in foods such as tomatoes, mushrooms, cheese, and fermented and aged foods, including tamari and miso.

What differentiates so-so and great food is how these five flavors combine. Does one sing too loudly and drown out the rest, or do they harmonize to create a delicious symphony of flavors? The presence of these flavor components affects the experience of taste:

✔ **Pungent/spicy** accents complement and add drama and zest to foods. Even though pungent is not generally considered a flavor, the strong and often dramatic impact of pungent foods like onions and garlic needs to be tempered in raw foods because they're not tamed by cooking. Mustard, chili peppers, and ginger are other pungent foods.

✔ **Fatty/creamy** elements unite and harmonize various flavor components, adding richness and a velvety mouthfeel. Fat is used in so many foods because it unites flavors and tames them. Fat also helps to hold flavors on the palate longer so you continue to enjoy foods longer.

Balancing flavor in raw cuisine

Learning to put flavors together to make a great dish is essential to being a great chef — of raw or cooked food. Understanding how to balance flavors is what frees you to create your own masterpieces rather than staying dependent on other people's recipes and flavor choices.

Many ingredients satisfy two or more of the five elements of taste so you can create a simple yet delicious dressing or sauce with fewer than four ingredients. For example

✔ **Sweet and sour:** Pineapples, oranges, and tamarind contain a natural balance of these two important flavor components, which makes them ideal as a base for salad dressings and soups.

✔ **Sour and bitter:** Limes are both sour and bitter. So if the base for a sauce is sesame tahini (a bitter flavor), limes aren't a good sour ingredient to use because they may contribute too much additional bitterness. In this case, a lemon may be a better choice.

✔ **Salty and umami:** Tamari, soy sauce, dark miso, and seaweed are salty flavors that contain umami, so when a recipe calls for salt, these foods are good options because they intensify the other flavors much more than ordinary salt can and adds the "deliciousness" that umami is known for.

✔ **Sweet, salty, and umami:** Light miso is an excellent seasoning when you want both sweet and salty flavor enhancements as well as the other element of umami deliciousness.

You can also use several different ingredients from the same category of flavors to add complexity to the flavor profile of the dish. For example

✔ Garlic, ginger, and hot chile peppers all fall into the pungent category and, when combined with ingredients from the basic five tastes, they add the oomph to make a dressing, sauce, soup, or just about any savory food extraordinary.

✔ Tamari, sea vegetables, and miso belong to the salty category, yet they can be used together in one recipe to infuse a dish with different types of salty flavors. When using more than one salt ingredient, be prudent with each one. Salt is terrific if used sparingly.

✔ Orange, pineapple, tamarind, and tomato are all fruits that add a sweet quality to foods like salad dressings and dipping sauces and also provide a slightly tart element. These foods can be used alone or in combination to provide a nice layering of flavors.

Take a look at Table 7-1 for help using flavors to balance a dish.

Table 7-1	Balancing Flavors in Raw Food
If the flavor is too . . .	*Then balance it with . . .*
Sour/tart/acid	Sweet, salty, fatty, or bitter
Salty	Sweet, fatty, or sour
Spicy/pungent	Sweet, fatty, or sour
Sweet	Sour, salty, bitter, spicy, or fatty
Bitter	Sweet, salty, or sour
Fatty/rich	Sour or liquid/fat-free bulk
Bland	Aromatic herbs, sweet, salty, sour, or spicy

Understanding how fat influences flavor

Fat, oh, glorious fat! A small amount of healthy fat, especially whole-food fat (such as avocado, young coconut, cashews, and sesame tahini) can be part of a healthy diet. There's virtually no limit to the number of dressings and sauces you can make by combining whole-food fats with nonsweet fruits (such as tomatoes, bell peppers, zucchini, and cucumbers) and even sweet fruits (like mangoes and peaches).

Each of the flavors you use in a recipe is influenced by other flavors, and all are influenced by the inclusion of fats. Fats subdue flavor and add a place for others to gather. Fats also provide depth, adding contrast and balance to sour and spicy (or pungent) flavors.

For example, we think the fat from avocados in Guacamole (Chapter 12) can tame even the spiciest Pico de Gallo (Chapter 12). And the cashew cream in Creamy Red Bell Pepper–Chipotle Soup (Chapter 13) carries the smoky flavor of chipotle peppers delicately throughout.

Many whole-food fats contain essential fatty acids, which are necessary for good health. But that doesn't mean that more is better. A few whole, soaked raw nuts and seeds or nut butter can achieve the thick, creamy texture people enjoy so much in their dressings and soups. Don't overdo it.

Developing Cooked Textures

Our attachment to cooked food goes way beyond its actual temperature. The heat from cooking changes the texture of foods. It creates softness and crunch, enhances sweetness, and intensifies flavor. In this section, we show you how to deliver many of the most satisfying food experiences without overheating and thereby killing the nutrients in your foods.

Thickening the raw way

In traditional food preparation, cooks use heat to thicken sauces, soups, and fillings. They may boil a sauce to make a reduction or simmer a combination of cooked fat (often butter) and flour to serve as the base for a thick, creamy sauce. Other recipes rely on the natural thickening properties of dairy cream or butter to pull together a sauce at the end of the cooking process.

In raw food preparation, you can create delicious sauces that have a thick and satisfying mouth feel without resorting to these methods; you just need to be creative. Take a peek at Table 7-2 for recommendations on raw binders and thickening agents.

Table 7-2	Recommended Binders and Thickeners
Type of Food	*Binder, Thickener, Gelling Agent*
Bouillon, broth, consommé, sauces	Miso; dried mushroom powder; sun-dried tomato powder; Irish moss gel; ground flax; chia powder; nut, seed, or coconut cream; or pureed vegetables or fruits
Breads, chips, crackers, tortillas	Ground flax or chia seed, ground nuts or seeds, ground sprouted nuts, or nut pulp
Burgers, corn cakes, nut or mushroom loaf	Ground flax or chia seed, ground nuts or seeds, or nut pulp

(continued)

Table 7-2 *(continued)*

Type of Food	Binder, Thickener, Gelling Agent
Cakes	Irish moss gel, ground flax or chia seed, dried (soaked or moistened) fruit or dates, coconut oil or coconut butter, or cacao butter
Cookies and bars	Ground nuts or seeds, ground dried (soaked) fruit, or dates
Cream sauce	Nuts, seeds, or coconut cream
Custard, eggs, cream filling	Avocado, nut or seed cream, coconut oil, psyllium powder, lecithin powder, Irish moss gel, or blended young coconut
Dairy cheese, roasted tahini, soy tofu	Raw sesame cashew tofu, raw tahini, blended soaked sesame seeds, or nut cheese
Mayonnaise	Blended young coconut, blended cashews, pine nuts, tahini, or avocado
Tortillas, pita bread, crackers, flat bread	Dehydrated vegetable wraps and tortillas, flax crackers, romaine leaves, cabbage leaves, or dehydrated flatbreads

Here are our favorite ingredients for thickening sauces without cooking:

✔ **Chia and flax seeds:** These seeds exude a gooey substance when soaked and can be used as binders, thickeners, and emulsifiers. Use chia and flax either whole (soaked) or converted to powder or meal. Soak whole seeds in water or pulverize them using a coffee grinder or blender. Blend the powder form directly into soups and dressings or use it as a binder in cakes, burgers, nut and vegetable loafs, crackers, and crusts.

A good ratio for crackers and flatbreads is 1 cup of seed meal for each 6 cups of processed vegetables, or you can use equal parts soaked chia and/or flax seeds and ground vegetables. To use ground chia or flax as a binder or thickener, try 1 tablespoon per cup and add more as needed.

✔ **Avocado:** This fatty fruit has a creamy consistency. It acts as a thickener and emulsifier, replacing butter, cream, eggs, and mayonnaise in raw sauces, soups, dressings, dips, puddings, and dessert fillings. Use citrus juice, sweeteners, extracts, and cacao powder to mask the flavor and/or color of avocado in desserts.

Use anywhere from ¼ to ½ of an avocado to emulsify a light creamy dressing, sauce, or soup.

✔ **Cacao butter:** This fat, which is extracted from cacao beans, can replace butter and shortening in candies. Gently melt cacao butter by putting it in a sealed glass jar and placing it in a warm water bath or a warm dehydrator. The more cacao butter, the more brittle the final product will be, so use it in conjunction with gentler binders and thickeners such as lecithin for tender desserts.

Use ½ cup melted cacao butter for every 1 to 2 cups of mixture.

✔ **Coconut oil or butter:** These coconut fats are made from cold-pressed mature coconut meat, which liquefies at 78 degrees. Use coconut oil to replace shortening and create a firm consistency and rich flavor in desserts. When chilled, it solidifies nicely.

Use 1 cup of coconut oil to 1 to 3 cups of other ingredients, depending on their water content. Water and other thin liquids require more coconut oil in the recipe than foods with fattier ingredients such as nuts.

✔ **Dried fruits and dates:** Blend dates, apricots, and figs with a little water, and use the fruit paste to bind and sweeten foods. These fruits are good binders due to their high concentration of pectin, a natural gelling agent. Ground dried fruits swell to about three times their volume.

✔ **Fresh fruit and vegetables:** When pureed, these fresh foods can be used as thickeners in dressings, sauces, and soups or as binders in crackers, cookies, and fruit leathers. Use agar agar, Irish moss, or coconut meat to further thicken or solidify a puree.

✔ **Irish moss:** Rinse Irish moss, a raw sea vegetable, and then soak it for four to eight hours before rinsing it well again. Remove and discard any brown pieces before blending the moss in a high-performance blender with a small amount of water to form a gel. Check out Figure 7-4 to see this process.

Irish moss gel can be used as a binder and thickener for soups, gravies, jellies, creams, cakes, and pie fillings. For best results, blend 1 to 5 tablespoons of Irish moss gel to 1 cup of product, depending on the viscosity and flavor of the dish you're thickening. Chill the food at least two hours to set. Store extra gel in the refrigerator.

✔ **Psyllium:** This plant-derived soluble fiber is available as coarse husks or finely ground powder. Use it to thicken fillings, puddings, and sauces and to bind wraps, crepes, and quiches.

For best results, use a maximum of 1 teaspoon of psyllium powder per 2 cups of total recipe volume. Whisk or blend the psyllium into the recipe briefly, as the final blended item, and be careful to not overblend. For cream fillings, chill for at least two hours to set; for wraps and crepes, spread the mixture on dehydrator trays lined with nonstick sheets and dehydrate.

✓ **Soy lecithin:** Although not a raw food, soy lecithin is a good thickener that contains phospholipids (phosphorus-rich oils) extracted from soybean oil. Use organic, GMO-free soy lecithin powder to produce a creamy consistency while binding and emulsifying fats and liquids in raw cheesecakes and puddings. Soy lecithin can be used with young coconut meat, coconut oil, Irish moss, or agar agar.

Use about 1 teaspoon of powder per cup of total recipe volume.

✓ **Young coconut meat or raw soaked nutmeats:** Blend these foods to a cream and use to thicken soups, dressings, sauces, and desserts.

To make 1 cup of heavy coconut cream from young coconuts, blend 3 cups of young coconut flesh in a blender without any liquid until it becomes a thick, smooth cream. For nut cream, blend 1 cup of soaked nuts in 1 cup of water. To solidify the nut cream, add coconut oil, Irish moss, or agar agar.

MAKING IRISH MOSS GEL

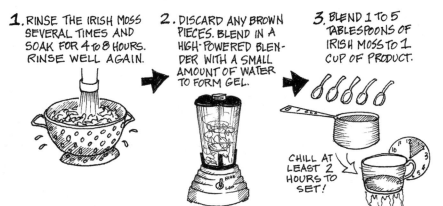

1. RINSE THE IRISH MOSS SEVERAL TIMES AND SOAK FOR 4 to 8 HOURS. RINSE WELL AGAIN.

2. DISCARD ANY BROWN PIECES. BLEND IN A HIGH-POWERED BLENDER WITH A SMALL AMOUNT OF WATER TO FORM GEL.

3. BLEND 1 TO 5 TABLESPOONS OF IRISH MOSS TO 1 CUP OF PRODUCT.

CHILL AT LEAST 2 HOURS TO SET!

Figure 7-4:
Making Irish moss gel.

One of our go-to nonfood techniques for thickening and intensifying flavors of purees, glazes, sauces, gravies, and soups is a dehydrator. See the section "Using a Dehydrator" earlier in this chapter for tips.

Substituting raw ingredients for cooked

Another simple way to transform your favorite traditional foods into raw delights is to simply substitute a raw ingredient for a cooked one of similar flavor, texture, and appearance. Use the raw counterparts listed in Table 7-3 to replace popular cooked foods.

Table 7-3	Raw Substitutions for Cooked Ingredients
Traditional Product	*Substitution Options*
Binders, thickeners, and emulsifiers that require cooking	Psyllium powder, flax seed, chia seed, Irish moss, coconut flour, avocado, dates, sprouted and dehydrated seeds and butters, or xanthan gum
Bouillon, consommé, broth, and stock	Tamari, shiitake mushroom powder, vegetable juice, blended vegetables/fruits, or thickeners
Breads, crackers, tortillas, crepes, flatbreads, and wraps	Nut, seed, and vegetable breads/tortillas/crackers; lettuce, collard, or cabbage leaves; flax-vegetable or psyllium-vegetable wraps/tortillas/crepes; or nori
Butter and shortening	Coconut butter, avocado, nut butter, or cacao butter
Canned coconut milk	Fresh or desiccated coconut blended with water or blended fresh young coconut meat
Chocolate	Carob, cacao nibs, or cacao powder
Chips and crackers	Dehydrated crackers and chips made from flax or other seeds, vegetables, and/or sprouted grains
Cooked onion and garlic	Dried onion or garlic, or rinsed and marinated onion

(continued)

Table 7-3 *(continued)*

Traditional Product	Substitution Options
Cooked tomatoes	Soaked or ground sun-dried tomatoes or peeled, seeded, slightly dehydrated tomatoes
Cooked vegetables	Diced, julienned, or chiffonaded vegetables marinated in salt/acid brine and warmed in dehydrator
Cream and eggs	Avocado, nut/coconut cream, or psyllium powder
Dairy cheese and yogurt	Nuts, seeds, or fresh coconut blended with probiotics or rejuvelac and allowed to ferment (or add lemon)
Dairy milk and cream	Soaked nuts or seeds, blended with water and strained or young coconut blended with a little water
Flour	Ground nuts or seeds, dried ground vegetable matter, mesquite powder, ground buckwheat, coconut flour, almond flour
Ice cream	Frozen nut or coconut cream, frozen bananas, or other frozen fruit made into sorbet using a juicer or food processer
Mayonnaise	Blended young coconut, nuts, or seeds; tahini; or avocado blended with spices
Meat	Ground nuts or seeds, marinated mushrooms, or ground seasoned root vegetables/root vegetable pulp
Pasta or rice	Spiralized or shredded zucchini, squash, celery root, parsnips, or minced vegetables
Peanut butter	Raw nut butters, raw tahini, or pureed wild peanuts
Roasted nuts and seeds	Soaked, seasoned, and dehydrated nuts or seeds
Salt	Sun-dried sea salt, Celtic salt, Himalayan crystal salt, tamari, sea vegetables, or celery powder
Vinegar	Citrus juice, tamarind, berries, or tart pineapple juice
White sugar	Agave nectar, dates, dried or fresh fruit, maca, stevia*, Lacanto*, coconut sugar or syrup*, evaporated cane juice*, or maple syrup*

*Not raw

Part III

Enjoying Raw and Revitalizing Meals: The Recipes

The 5th Wave   By Rich Tennant

"Bananas always lift my spirits. Especially when I hide the overripe hunks in my husband's running shoes."

In this part . . .

These chapters feature the heart of the raw lifestyle: the recipes! Find out how to prepare raw dishes that you can make today, no matter how skilled or new you are to raw cuisine. We include recipes for raw staples (such as nut milk and no-bake bread) and yummy extras, including nut cheese, condiments, and crackers, that make meals special. Certain types of foods — such as soups and salads, smoothies, and (oh, yes) desserts — are grouped for easy reference. The recipes in this part can keep you powered up and satisfied all day long.

Chapter 8

Getting Started —
No Experience Required

*I*f you're ready to jump in and start making at least some of your meals the raw way, you're in the right place! In this chapter, we give you our most basic recipes: delicious and satisfying raw foods that require almost no food-prep know-how. These recipes are easy to follow and give you a quick start to enjoying the vitality of raw food.

We describe how to make easy smoothies and soups and a refreshingly different salad. Then we move on to wraps, our take on pasta, and — everyone's favorite — desserts! You may be happy to know that chocolatey goodness is not off-limits if you're a raw foodist. After you taste our chocolate pudding, you'll never look at cacao powder the same way again.

Whipping Up Easy Smoothies, Soups, and Salads

Most raw foodists start their day with a smoothie. If you do some of the prep work ahead of time (as we recommend in Chapter 18), then you can go from blender to tasty beverage in less than five minutes. Yet blenders aren't just for smoothies. You can also use this handy appliance to make quick and flavorful soups, tangy salad dressings, and simple sauces that keep your foods interesting.

Blending vegetables and fruits is a great way to sneak nutrient-packed plants into your diet. You probably don't have time to chew 10 ounces of whole spinach, but you can definitely blend it up in a soup or smoothie and enjoy every last one of the 8 grams of protein that this amount of spinach provides. The blending process breaks down the cells of dietary fiber, allowing you to quickly absorb the nutrient-dense juice. And when you're on the go, drinking a smoothie is much easier than munching on a salad in the car.

Here are some tips to make your blending a breeze:

- ✔ Always put liquids and high-water-content foods in the blender first so the mixture starts blending right away.

- ✔ Cut firm fruits and vegetables like apples, carrots, and celery into smallish pieces so the blades can do their job more easily.

- ✔ Add fats, such as avocado and oil, at the end of the blending cycle, when the mixture is well blended. This step ensures that the fat isn't overprocessed, which can make the mixture too thick and fluffy.

- ✔ To make clean-up quick, put water and a drop of soap in the blender when you're finished with food prep. Put on the lid, blend for a few seconds, and then rinse. Voilà! No dishwasher needed!

Find more blender tips in Chapter 7. And if you want more smoothie recipes than we provide in this section, stop by Chapter 10.

Green Smoothie

Prep time: 10 min • **Yield:** 2 servings

Ingredients	*Directions*
2 pounds peeled and chopped mango, peach, or other high-water-content fruit	***1*** Blend the fruit and greens in a high-powered blender, adding water as needed. Blend until smooth and creamy, about 2 to 3 minutes.
4 cups packed, stemmed, and chopped kale or other dark leafy greens	
Filtered water as needed to thin	

Per serving: *Calories 244 (From Fat 19); Fat 2g (Saturated .2g); Cholesterol 0mg; Sodium 58mg; Carbohydrate 57g (Dietary Fiber 9g); Protein 9g.*

Note: For best results, serve this smoothie immediately. In a pinch, it can last up to 24 hours if stored in an airtight container in the refrigerator. Reblend it just before serving.

Vary It! Change the types of fruits in this smoothie to suit your mood. Great combinations include blueberry-apricot, peach-raspberry, papaya-kiwi, and orange-pineapple. Add mint, lemongrass, or basil in addition to other dark leafy greens to give the smoothie an extra burst of flavor!

Tip: For help peeling and chopping mangoes, check out Figure 8-1.

Tip: For kids who don't like raw greens, blend this up and call it a Shrek smoothie. Each time, you can add more greens, making it even more Shrek-y.

Figure 8-1:
Peeling and chopping a mango.

Strawberry Fields Smoothie

Prep time: 5 min • **Yield:** 2 servings

Ingredients	*Directions*
2 oranges, peeled and segmented	*1* Blend the oranges, bananas, and strawberries in a high-powered blender, adding water or juice to thin as needed. Blend until smooth and creamy, about 2 minutes.
2 fresh or frozen bananas, peeled and sliced	
1 pint fresh or frozen strawberries	
6 ounces filtered water or fruit juice	

Per serving: Calories 213 (From Fat 9); Fat 1g (Saturated 0.2g); Cholesterol 0mg; Sodium 6mg; Carbohydrate 53g (Dietary Fiber 9g); Protein 3g.

Note: For best results, serve this smoothie immediately. In a pinch, it can last up to 24 hours if stored in an airtight container in the refrigerator. Reblend it just before serving.

Tip: Using frozen fruit in this smoothie gives it a thick, milkshake-like consistency. If you choose to use frozen bananas, we strongly encourage you to peel the banana before freezing. Frozen bananas are very difficult to peel. Plus, the peel turns a very unappetizing color in the freezer.

Tip: If your blender isn't quite up to the task of tearing through all the fiber in the pith of the orange segments, use a sharp knife to remove the membranes from the oranges before blending. Take a look at Figure 8-2 for help.

Sectioning an Orange to Eliminate Membranes

Figure 8-2:
Make blend-
ing citrus
easier by
removing
the white
membranes.

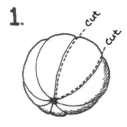

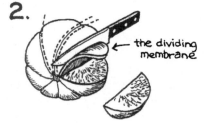

Massaged Kale Salad

Prep time: 25 min • **Waiting time:** 2–4 hr • **Yield:** 2 servings

Ingredients	*Directions*
2 tablespoons unsulfured raisins	***1*** Place raisins in ½ cup hot water. Allow to soak for 2 to 4 hours or overnight. Drain. (Discard the soaking water or save it for smoothies or dressings.)
4 cups kale, stemmed and cut into chiffonade	
¼ teaspoon salt	***2*** Combine kale, salt, lemon juice, and oil. Massage until the kale is reduced in volume by at least half.
1 tablespoon lemon juice	
1 tablespoon extra-virgin olive oil	***3*** Toss the massaged kale with bell peppers, green onion, and Cashew Mayonnaise and adjust the seasoning with salt and pepper.
½ cup seeded and diced red bell peppers	
1 tablespoon thinly sliced green onion	
½ cup favorite dressing or Cashew Mayonnaise	
Freshly ground black pepper to taste	

Per serving: Calories 339 (From Fat 220); Fat 25g (Saturated 3.5g); Cholesterol 0mg; Sodium 730mg; Carbohydrate 30g (Dietary Fiber 4g); Protein 5g.

Note: This salad lasts in the refrigerator for up to 3 days in a sealed container.

Note: To find a recipe for Cashew Mayonnaise, turn to Chapter 9.

Tip: *Chiffonade* means cut leaves into thin strips. For how-to instructions, see Chapter 11.

Massaging kale: Candles and mood music optional

Why massage kale? It's a good question, especially considering you were probably told for years not to play with your food. Now we're telling you to go ahead and use your hands. Besides being fun, all this massaging actually serves a purpose: it breaks down the fibers in the kale and makes it much easier to digest. You can actually see this process happening.

As you massage kale with an acid and a fat (lemon juice and olive oil in this recipe) and salt, the cell walls break down, and the kale's color becomes brighter. The kale wilts quite a bit during the massaging process, becoming tender and much less bitter. Another great massage combo is lime juice and avocado.

Vitality Soup

Prep time: 15 min • **Yield:** 2 servings

Ingredients	Directions
1 cup orange juice	**1** Combine the orange juice, kale, cucumber, herbs, miso, lemon juice, garlic, and green onion. Blend the mixture until smooth.
2 cups stemmed and chopped kale or other dark leafy greens	
1 small cucumber, peeled and chopped	**2** Add the avocado and blend again — no more than 1 minute — until smooth.
¼ cup fresh parsley, basil, or dill weed	
1 tablespoon light miso*	
1 tablespoon lemon juice	
½ teaspoon garlic, crushed (1 clove)	
½ green onion, chopped	
½ avocado, peeled and pitted	
Filtered water as needed for desired consistancy	

Per serving: Calories 191 (From Fat 59); Fat 6.5g (Saturated 1g); Cholesterol 0mg; Sodium 356mg; Carbohydrate 32g (Dietary Fiber 8g); Protein 6g.

Note: This soup can last 24 hours if stored in an airtight container in the refrigerator. Press plastic wrap directly on the surface of the soup inside the container. Lightly stir before serving.

Vary It! The orange juice adds sweetness to the soup. For a less sweet soup, reduce or eliminate the orange juice and replace it with lemon juice or additional water.

Tip: Figure 8-3 illustrates how best to peel and pit an avocado.

Vary It! You can use a variety of vegetables in this soup, allowing you to incorporate the season's best harvest. Great additions include chopped zucchini, tomato, bell pepper, or celery (cut crosswise to break the strings). If kale is unavailable, opt for romaine or spinach.

*Not raw

How to Pit and Peel an Avocado

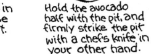

Figure 8-3: Pitting and peeling an avocado.

Slice avocado in half lengthwise and pull apart.

Hold the avocado half with the pit, and firmly strike the pit with a chef's knife in your other hand.

Lift the pit out with a gentle twist of the knife.

GENTLY scoop out the meat with a spoon.

Chop or slice according to your recipe.

Gazpacho

Prep time: 20 min • **Yield:** 2 servings

Ingredients	*Directions*
2½ cups diced tomatoes	*1* Combine tomatoes, celery, cucumber, lemon juice, oil, salt, and pepper in a bowl and toss.
¼ cup diced celery	
¼ cup seeded and diced cucumber	*2* Transfer half the mixture into a blender and blend until smooth.
1 tablespoon lemon juice	
1 tablespoon extra-virgin olive oil	*3* Return the blended mixture to the bowl and stir in the green onion and avocado.
½ teaspoon salt	
Freshly ground black pepper	*4* Serve immediately or chill until serving time.
½ small green onion, thinly sliced	
1 small avocado, peeled, pitted, and diced	

Per serving: Calories 189 (From Fat 155); Fat 17g (Saturated 2.5g); Cholesterol 0mg; Sodium 161mg; Carbohydrate 10g (Dietary Fiber 6g); Protein 2g.

Note: You can make this soup ahead of time and store it in a sealed glass jar in the refrigerator for up to 2 days. Feel free to double the recipe to save time (and an extra blender cleaning) the next day. Just wait to slice the green onions and dice the avocado until right before serving. Otherwise the onions will lose their freshness, and the avocado will oxidize, or turn an unappealing shade of brown.

Tip: For guidance on seeding and cutting up cucumber, check out Figure 8-4.

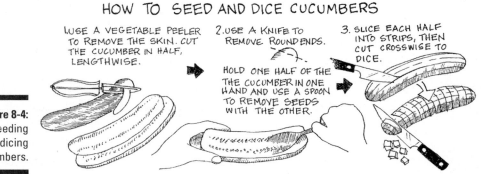

HOW TO SEED AND DICE CUCUMBERS

1.USE A VEGETABLE PEELER TO REMOVE THE SKIN. CUT THE CUCUMBER IN HALF, LENGTHWISE.

2.USE A KNIFE TO REMOVE ROUND ENDS.

HOLD ONE HALF OF THE THE CUCUMBER IN ONE HAND AND USE A SPOON TO REMOVE SEEDS WITH THE OTHER.

3. SLICE EACH HALF INTO STRIPS, THEN CUT CROSSWISE TO DICE.

Figure 8-4: Seeding and dicing cucumbers.

Staying Satisfied with Easy Snacks, Entrees, and Desserts

The distinction between types of food in raw cuisine is less clear than in traditional cooking. Raw foodists can make a wrap, salad, or soup and call it an entree as easily as a snack. Most raw foods work just as well for breakfast or lunch as a snack or dinner, or you can have all these items in a single meal.

Even better: There's no need to give up the pleasure of pasta on a raw-food diet! Spiralized zucchini looks and even tastes a lot like real pasta. After all, wheat-based pasta has little flavor of its own; the sauce is the key. In this section, we offer three different delicious sauces to try with your zucchini noodles. See for yourself: It's to live for!

Wraps are an especially easy way to incorporate raw foods into your lifestyle. You can use a variety of vegetables depending on what's in season and what you have in your refrigerator at any given time. Be creative! Use leftover pâtés, spreads, and dips as a base in your wrap and then pile on the vegetables and condiments to create delicious, portable meals and snacks. Table 8-1 reveals a system for creating many different delicious wraps. Choose one item from each column to build an easy snack or main dish.

Table 8-1	Tasty Mix-and-Match Wraps	
Wrapper	*Produce*	*Condiment*
Romaine leaves	Alfalfa or sunflower sprouts	Pesto
Raw nori seaweed sheets	Sliced tomatoes	Guacamole
Collard leaves (stems removed)	Julienned red bell peppers	Nut cheese or nut butter
Cabbage leaves (red or green)	Seeded and julienned cucumber	Cashew Mayonnaise, Sweet and Spicy Mustard, or Real Tomato Ketchup
Corn tortillas	Thinly sliced onion	Hummus
Butter lettuce leaves	Mung bean sprouts	Salsa
Kale leaves	Shredded carrots	Sauerkraut
	Thinly sliced avocado	Raw tahini

Zucchini Pasta Three Ways

Prep time: 20 min • **Waiting time:** 1 hr (optional) • **Yield:** 3 servings

Ingredients	Directions
2 firm zucchinis Marinara Sauce, Basil Pesto, or Cashew Dill Sauce (see the following recipes)	**1** With a spiral slicer, cut the zucchini into long thin ribbon noodles. **2** Place the noodles and choice of sauce together in a bowl and toss well. Allow to sit for a few minutes prior to serving to allow the sauce to soften the zucchini noodles and create an al dente (firm but tender) texture.

Marinara Sauce

Ingredients	Directions
3 cups seeded and chopped Roma tomatoes ⅓ cup sun-dried tomato powder 2 tablespoons finely minced onion 2 tablespoons minced fresh basil leaves 1 tablespoon minced fresh oregano 1 teaspoon crushed garlic (about 1 clove) ½ teaspoon salt Pinch of ground black pepper 3 tablespoons Pine Nut Parmesan Cheese (optional)	**1** Put the chopped tomatoes in a colander to allow remaining liquid to drain. When the tomatoes are thoroughly drained, put them in a food processor outfitted with the S blade and, if desired, pulse once or twice. Or simply mince them by hand. **2** Mix in the sun-dried tomato powder, onion, basil, oregano, garlic, salt, and pepper. If you are using a food processer, do not overprocess; the mixture should be slightly chunky post-processing. **3** Set the sauce aside for a few minutes before serving, or warm it slightly in a dehydrator for an hour, to allow the flavors to come together. **4** If desired, top with Pine Nut Parmesan Cheese and more freshly ground pepper.

Basil Pesto

1 cup fresh basil leaves, firmly packed

1 tablespoon extra-virgin olive oil

1½ teaspoons light miso*

1½ teaspoons nutritional yeast flakes*

1 clove garlic

Pinch of salt

¼ cup walnuts or pine nuts, chopped

Pine Nut Parmesan Cheese to taste (optional) or minced pine nuts

Black pepper to taste (optional)

1 Put the basil, oil, miso, nutritional yeast flakes, garlic, and salt in a food processor or blender. Pulse a few times to coarsely chop the basil. If using a blender, you'll need to stop the blender a few times to push the mixture down so everything chops evenly.

2 Add the walnuts and process to the desired consistency. Do not overprocess or the oil from the walnuts will separate and the mixture will become too oily. The texture should be creamy with tiny specks of walnuts throughout.

3 Serve topped with the Pine Nut Parmesan Cheese and black pepper, if desired.

Cashew Dill Sauce

¾ cup cashew cheese or thick cashew cream

1 teaspoon nutritional yeast*

1 teaspoon light miso*

½ teaspoon onion powder

¼ teaspoon garlic powder

¼ teaspoon salt

Pinch of ground nutmeg

Pinch of white or black ground pepper

2 tablespoons filtered water, plus additional water to thin as needed

1 tablespoon fresh dill weed, minced

1 Put the cashew cheese or thick cashew cream, nutritional yeast, miso, onion powder, garlic powder, salt, nutmeg, pepper, and water in a high-performance blender and blend until smooth and creamy, adding more water if necessary.

2 Add the dill and pulse blend briefly to mix.

With Marinara Sauce, per serving: Calories 57 (From Fat 6); Fat 0.5g (Saturated 0.1g); Cholesterol 0mg; Sodium 120mg; Carbohydrate 13g (Dietary Fiber 4g); Protein 3g.

With Basil Pesto, per serving: Calories 124 (From Fat 111); Fat 13g (Saturated 1g); Cholesterol 0mg; Sodium 37mg; Carbohydrate 3g (Dietary Fiber 1g); Protein 2g.

With Cashew Dill Sauce, per serving: Calories 76 (From Fat 44); Fat 5g (Saturated 0g); Cholesterol 0mg; Sodium 416mg; Carbohydrate 19g (Dietary Fiber 6g); Protein 5g.

Note: Leftover Marinara Sauce will keep in a sealed glass jar in the refrigerator for up to 2 days. Basil Pesto will keep the same way for 4 days, and Cashew Dill Sauce will stay good for 1 week.

Note: Find the recipe for Pine Nut Parmesan Cheese in Chapter 9.

Note: To make sun-dried tomato powder, process 1 cup of hard sun-dried tomatoes (that aren't pliable or oil soaked) in a high-performance blender. Store powder in a sealed glass jar in the pantry.

Tip: If you don't have a spiral slicer, use a box shredder to grate the zucchini. The final result won't have the same texture as pasta, but the dish is still delicious.

*Not raw

Banana-Strawberry Sorbet

Prep time: 15 min • **Waiting time:** 12 hr • **Yield:** 4 servings

Ingredients	*Directions*
3 bananas, peeled, sliced, and frozen for 12 hours **1 pint frozen strawberries, chopped**	*1* Combine frozen bananas and strawberries in a food processor or blender. Process until thoroughly combined.
	2 Pack the mixture into ice-cube trays. Freeze for about 12 hours.
	3 Just before serving, place frozen cubes in the bowl of a food processor fitted with the S blade. Process until the ice cubes are transformed into a soft-serve sorbet. Serve immediately.

Per serving: Calories 102 (From Fat 5); Fat 0.5g (Saturated 0.1g); Cholesterol 0mg; Sodium 2mg; Carbohydrate 26g (Dietary Fiber 4g); Protein 1g.

Vary It! In Step 3, you can allow the frozen cubes to defrost for 10 minutes and then put them in a high-performance blender.

Note: You can store the frozen cubes in the freezer for up to 3 months. When they're frozen, pop them out of the ice-cube trays and place them in a resealable container. Store them in the freezer. When ready to eat, pull out 3 or 4 cubes and process them into their final state. This sweet treat tastes of summer.

Mango-Avocado Wraps

Prep time: 30 min • **Yield:** 4 servings

Ingredients	Directions
1 mango, peeled, seeded, and julienned	*1* Divide the mango, avocado, cucumber, cilantro, and green onion into four equal portions.
1 avocado, peeled, pitted, and julienned	
1 cucumber, peeled, and julienned	*2* Place one portion of mixture in each lettuce leaf. Fold the leaf over the toppings, like a soft taco.
Several cilantro springs	
1 tablespoon thinly sliced green onion	*3* Drizzle Spicy Sweet-and-Sour Mango Sauce over the top and serve extra on the side.
4 large leaves romaine lettuce	
Spicy Sweet-and-Sour Mango Sauce (see following recipe)	

Spicy Sweet-and-Sour Mango Sauce

1 cup diced mango

1 cup peeled, seeded, and diced cucumber

1 tablespoon grated fresh gingerroot

1 tablespoon lime juice

¼ teaspoon ground cayenne pepper

¼ teaspoon salt

1 Combine all the ingredients in a blender and blend until smooth.

Wraps, per serving: Calories 130 (From Fat 51); Fat 6g (Saturated 1g); Cholesterol 0mg; Sodium 42mg; Carbohydrate 20g (Dietary Fiber 5g); Protein 2g.

Spicy Sweet-and-Sour Mango sauce, per recipe: Calories 31 (From Fat 2); Fat 0.2g (Saturated 0g); Cholesterol 0mg; Sodium 35mg; Carbohydrate 7g (Dietary Fiber 1g); Protein 1g.

Vary It! Add more lime juice, cayenne, ginger, or salt if needed to suit your taste.

Note: Store any leftover sauce in a sealed glass jar in the refrigerator for up to 3 days.

Note: You don't need to remove the stems from cilantro.

Coconut Almond Joyous

Prep time: 10 min • **Waiting time:** 22–34 hr • **Yield:** 12 servings

Ingredients

¾ cup pitted and packed dates, at room temperature

¼ cup coconut oil, warmed to liquid

1½ cups dried shredded unsweetented coconut

36 raw almonds

Directions

1 Soak almonds for 8 hours or overnight. Drain them, rinse, and drain again. Place rinsed almonds on dehydrator tray. Dehydrate at 105 degrees for 12 to 24 hours, or until dry.

2 Loosely separate the dates and place them with the coconut oil in a high-powered blender or food processor outfitted with the S blade. Puree until completely smooth.

3 In a large bowl, knead the shredded coconut into the date mixture for a couple of minutes until fully incorporated. Set aside for 1 hour at room temperature to allow the coconut to soften.

4 Shape the mixture into a 6-inch square approximately ½-inch thick. Press almonds uniformly over the top of the square (6 rows tall by 6 rows wide). Chill the square for 1 hour, or until firm. Slice into 36 pieces, each with one almond.

Per serving: Calories 117 (From Fat 77); Fat 9g (Saturated 5 g); Cholesterol 0mg; Sodium 1mg; Carbohydrate 10g (Dietary Fiber 2g); Protein 2g.

Note: Store in the refrigerator in an airtight container for up to 1 month.

Note: To warm solid coconut oil to a liquid, place it in a warm dehydrator. Or place the solid oil in a sealed, watertight glass jar and immerse the jar in hot tap water.

Vary It! Shape the candy into balls and press the almonds (or pecan halves!) into the top. Embed the almonds firmly, but don't bury them.

Tip: Figure 8-5 illustrates how to remove the pit from dates and chop them.

HOW TO PIT AND CHOP DATES

USE A SHARP KNIFE TO CUT DATES IN HALF. REMOVE THE PITS.

THEN, CHOP THE DATE INTO SMALL PIECES. YOU CAN DIP YOUR KNIFE IN WARM WATER IF IT GETS TOO STICKY.

Figure 8-5: Pitting and chopping dates is quick and easy.

Chocolate Pudding

Prep time: 5 min • **Yield:** 6 servings

Ingredients

2 cups young Thai coconut meat

1 cup coconut nectar*

½ cup cacao powder

1 tablespoon vanilla extract*

¼ teaspoon salt

¼ cup filtered water or coconut water (optional, for thinning)

Directions

1 Blend coconut meat, coconut nectar, cacao powder, vanilla extract, and salt in a high-performance blender, adding water as needed, until smooth. Serve immediately.

Per serving: Calories 322 (From Fat 250); Fat 28g (Saturated 25g); Cholesterol 0mg; Sodium 61mg; Carbohydrate 18g (Dietary Fiber 3g); Protein 4g.

Vary It! For a special summertime treat, make your own pudding pops. Pour prepared pudding into ice-cube trays or ice-pop molds. Lift the trays an inch or so off the counter and gently tap the trays on the counter to knock out air bubbles. Freeze pops for 4 hours or until frozen solid.

Tip: Figure 8-6 illustrates how to open a coconut.

*Not raw

HOW TO OPEN A COCONUT

Figure 8-6: How to open a young coconut.

CUT OFF SOME OF THE WHITE HUSK WITH A CHEF'S KNIFE.

USE A CLEAVER TO HIT AROUND THE TOP IN A FEW SPOTS. THE TOP WILL WEAKEN AND POP OFF WHEN YOU INSERT THE CLEAVER AND LIFT.

Chapter 9

The Supporting Cast: Tasty Condiments, Sauces, and More

In This Chapter

▶ Making condiments the raw way

▶ Laying the foundation with crackers, tortillas, and more

▶ Crafting cheeses and tofu

Much of what makes raw food so delicious and appealing — as with pretty much all kinds of cuisine — are sauces and dips, crackers and bread, and cheese. And that's exactly what we cover in this chapter!

The raw versions of most of these foods have a long shelf life, and all are easy to make, so we like to make them in advance and keep them on hand to spruce up any dish at any time. But some items require advance preparation (think: soaking nuts, dehydrating crackers, and so forth), so make sure you read the recipe thoroughly before you start. A realistic picture of your timeline can probably save you a few swear words. To help, we tag recipes that require advance preparation with a Plan Ahead icon.

In this chapter, we provide recipes for some all-American condiments along with a few exotic wraps and delicious crackers and croutons. We also explain how to make your own cheese and tofu. So roll up your sleeves and get ready to whip up the add-ons that make raw food meals extra satisfying.

Creating Raw Condiments

What would our food be without condiments? *So primitive,* you may be saying. Indeed! You'd basically have a pile of veggies or some nuts and berries with nothing else going on. Of course, we love basic veggies and the natural, fresh flavors of whole plant foods, but no frills can get boring over time. That's where condiments come in. A slice of bread slathered with Cashew Mayonnaise and then topped with thinly sliced veggies and cheese is suddenly a meal, not just something you dragged out of the fridge.

Condiments truly are the spice of life. They can change the complexity of a meal to make it spicy or subtle, sweet or savory, and so much more. In this section we give you raw versions of condiments you probably already know: mayonnaise, mustard, and ketchup. After you see how easy and tasty — and did we mention healthy? — they are, you'll likely never go with the store-bought versions again.

One of our favorite types of condiment is nut butter. By making your own nut butters, you ensure that your nuts are organic and fresh (never roasted). Nut butters are best if made with dry nuts, preferably soaked and dehydrated in advance to remove the enzyme inhibitors and make them more digestible. However, other spreads can be made with either dry or soaked nuts and/or seeds. Dry nuts make a richer butter; wet nuts make a moister spread. Either can then be seasoned to create a sweet or savory condiment. (Flip to Chapter 7 for the story on soaking nuts.)

You can make nut butters, pâtés, and spreads using either a juicer or food processor (see Chapter 7). If using a juicer, use the homogenizing plate, which allows the puree to flow through without separation, producing a smooth paste. You may need to run the paste through the juicer a second and even third time, adding a little bit of olive oil or avocado oil each time to help make the mixture come together. If you do add oil, make sure it's cold-pressed or extra-virgin oil.

If you're making nut butter in a food processor, you don't need to add oil. Just pour raw, shelled, and soaked nuts — almonds, walnuts, pecans, cashews, and macadamia nuts are great choices — into the processor with the S blade. Watch the nuts go from chopped, to a ball shape, and then to a thick and then thinner butter. Don't give up; it takes about eight to ten minutes to make creamy nut butter in a food processor.

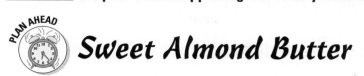

Sweet Almond Butter

Prep time: 15 minutes • **Waiting time:** 14–20 hr • **Yield:** 16 servings

Ingredients	*Directions*
3 cups raw almonds	*1* Soak the almonds in water for 6 to 8 hours and then dehydrate them for 8 to 12 hours at 105 degrees.
½ cup coconut nectar* or agave nectar*	
Pinch of salt	*2* Put the almonds, coconut nectar, and salt in a food processor fitted with the S blade and process for 10 to 15 minutes. Stop the food processor a couple of times during processing to scrape the sides with a spatula. Process until the almonds turn to smooth paste. As processing time increases, your nut butter becomes smoother and richer.

Per serving (¼ cup): Calories 184 (From Fat 117); Fat 13g (Saturated 1g); Cholesterol 0mg; Sodium 3mg; Carbohydrate 14g (Dietary Fiber 3g); Protein 6g.

Note: Store the almond butter in a sealed glass jar in the refrigerator for up to 1 month. Stir it just before using to reincorporate any separated oil.

Tip: Certain juicers, like the Champion or Green Star Juicer, are great for making nut butters. Attach the homogenizing plate and run the almonds through the chute; then stir in the coconut nectar and salt.

*Not raw

Cashew Mayonnaise

Prep time: 10 min • **Waiting time:** 4 hr • **Yield:** 6 servings

Ingredients	Directions
1 cup raw cashews	**1** Cover raw cashews with 2 cups of filtered water and allow them to soak for 4 hours to soften. After soaking, drain and rinse well.
6 tablespoons filtered water	
3 tablespoons lemon juice	
2 tablespoons coconut nectar* or agave nectar*	**2** Puree the water, lemon juice, nectar, onion powder, garlic powder, salt, and white pepper in a high-performance blender until the mixture is completely smooth. Use a rubber spatula to fold the mixture from the sides of the blender into the center of the vortex as needed.
1 teaspoon onion powder	
½ teaspoon garlic powder	
¾ teaspoon salt	
Pinch of ground white pepper	**3** With the blender running, slowly add the oil through the hole in the lid until the mixture is thoroughly combined, or *emulsified.*
¼ cup extra-virgin olive oil	

Per serving (¼ cup): Calories 233 (From Fat 174); Fat 19g (Saturated 3g); Cholesterol 0mg; Sodium 70mg; Carbohydrate 13g (Dietary Fiber 1g); Protein 4g.

Note: Store mayonnaise in an airtight container in the refrigerator for up to 2 weeks.

Tip: Try this must-have condiment anywhere you'd use traditional mayo. It's great in wraps and on veggie burgers. Mix in a little minced dill weed to make an easy dip for veggies. And add it to blended soups, dressings, and sauces to add body and creaminess.

*Not raw

What the heck does *emulsify* mean?

Emulsifying is the process of combining two liquids that normally don't mix well with each other by suspending one liquid in the other, creating a thick, creamy substance. Imagine a traditional vinaigrette salad dressing. You have to shake it up, because the liquids (vinegar and oil) don't stay combined. The addition of a third ingredient, an *emulsifier,* helps the liquids interact in a healthy way, at least until their expiration date. In the case of Cashew Mayonnaise, the lemon juice and olive oil are emulsified by adding the cashews to stabilize the mixture.

Sweet and Spicy Mustard

Prep time: 10 min • **Waiting time:** 8–12 hr • **Yield:** 8 servings

Ingredients	*Directions*
¾ **cup mustard seeds** ½ **cup lemon juice** ¾ **cup coconut nectar* or agave nectar*** **2 tablespoons unpasteurized tamari***	**1** Put mustard seeds in a glass quart jar and fill with water. Allow the seeds to soak for 8 to 12 hours to germinate. After soaking, drain and rinse well. **2** Combine soaked mustard seeds, lemon juice, nectar, and tamari in a blender and puree to form a smooth paste.

Per serving (2 tablespoons): Calories 171 (From Fat 48.6); Fat 5g (Saturated 0.5g); Cholesterol 0mg; Sodium 253mg; Carbohydrate 29g (Dietary Fiber 3g); Protein 4g.

Note: This tangy condiment lasts in the refrigerator for up to 2 months, thanks to the preservation power of lemon juice. Store it in a glass jar with an airtight lid.

Tip: This mustard mellows with age. For the first two weeks, it's pretty spicy and a little bit bitter. If you prefer to eat it immediately, consider adding a bit more lemon juice and coconut nectar.

Vary It! Mix this mustard with an equal amount of Cashew Mayonnaise for your own version of dijonaise. The mustard adds a subtle kick to the mayonnaise that makes it a perfect dip for veggies or a zippy spread for a flatbread sandwich.

*Not raw

Real Tomato Ketchup

Prep time: 10 min • **Yield:** 16 servings

Ingredients	*Directions*
2 cups seeded and chopped tomatoes	*1* Puree all the ingredients in a blender or food processor outfitted with an S blade.
⅜ cup sun-dried tomato powder	
1½ tablespoons evaporated cane juice*	
1 tablespoon lemon juice	
1 tablespoon tamarind paste, or 2 teaspoons additional lemon juice	
¾ teaspoon salt	
Pinch of white pepper	

Per serving (2 tablespoons): Calories 9 (From Fat 0); Fat 0g (Saturated 0g); Cholesterol 0mg; Sodium 29mg; Carbohydrate 2g (Dietary Fiber 0g); Protein 0g.

Note: Store the ketchup in a sealed glass jar in the refrigerator for up to 1 week.

Note: Figure 9-1 illustrates a good way to seed and dice a tomato.

Note: To make sun-dried tomato powder, put 1 cup of very hard (not pliable or oil soaked) sun-dried tomatoes in a high-performance blender and process until they're a fine powder. Store leftover powder in a sealed glass jar in the pantry.

*Not raw

HOW TO SEED AND DICE TOMATOES

Figure 9-1: Seeding and dicing tomatoes.

1. USE A CUTTING BOARD. SLICE THE TOMATO IN HALF. SLICE OFF THE ENDS.

2. SCRAPE OUT THE SEEDS WITH A SMALL TOOL OR YOUR FINGER.

3. WITH THE FLAT SIDE DOWN, SLICE THE TOMATO HALF IN ONE DIRECTION, THEN IN THE OTHER DIRECTION, TO DICE.

Cashew Sour Cream

Prep time: 10 min • **Waiting time:** 4 hr • **Yield:** 6 servings

Ingredients	*Directions*
1 cup raw cashews	*1* Cover raw cashews with 2 cups of water and allow them to soak for 4 hours to soften. After soaking, drain and rinse well.
½ cup filtered water	
¼ cup lemon juice	
1 tablespoon nutritional yeast*	*2* Combine soaked cashews, water, juice, nutritional yeast, miso, white pepper, nutmeg, and salt in a blender or food processor, and blend until the spread is smooth and creamy. The mixture should have a satin-like finish.
1 tablespoon light miso*	
Dash ground white pepper	
Dash ground nutmeg	
Dash salt	

Per serving (¼ cup): Calories 139 (From Fat 94.5); Fat 11g (Saturated 2g); Cholesterol 0mg; Sodium 123mg; Carbohydrate 9g (Dietary Fiber 1g); Protein 5g.

Note: Store this sour cream in a glass jar in the refrigerator for up to 1 month or in the freezer for up to 3 months.

Vary It! To make Cashew Pine Nut Sour Cream, replace ½ cup soaked cashews with ½ cup unsoaked pine nuts and follow the rest of the recipe. For more variation, try substituting an entire cup of pine nuts for all of the cashews. Decadent and delicious!

Vary It! This tangy dip is great with sliced veggies. Adjust the seasonings to change the flavor for a new taste every time. You can substitute 1 teaspoon curry or chili powder or 1 tablespoon Italian seasoning for the nutmeg. Or stir in 2 tablespoons of fresh dill weed for a fresh, spring-like flavor.

*Not raw

Preparing Wraps, Crackers, and Other Toppers

A common misconception about the raw food lifestyle is that you can't eat that oh-so-basic staple of the human diet: bread. The belief is that the only way to make bread is to bake it, and if it's baked, then . . . well, it's not raw. Lucky that you bought this book, because we show you how to create baked textures in foods without cooking them in the traditional sense of the word, enabling you to keep the vital life force alive and well in your food for maximum nutritional value. Find out in this section how to make raw breads and breadlike components such as wraps and crackers. (Find more how-to on mimicking cooked textures in raw foods in Chapter 7.)

All raw breads are *flatbreads,* meaning that they don't rise. These flatbreads are great for bundling whatever veggies you have on hand. Check out Chapter 8 for a table of easy wrap ingredients to assemble as you please.

One of the main tools we use to create these not-baked goodies is a dehydrator. We cover buying and using dehydrators in Chapter 7, so take a look at that chapter if you need help.

A technique that applies to many of these recipes is *scoring,* which perforates an item with an indentation and makes it easier to break off individual portions. Often we recommend that you score the slices or individual crackers after you spread batter on the dehydrator tray but before you dehydrate it. To score your batter, use a dull knife or spatula to make a linear impression. Simply press your spatula where you'll eventually cut or break the finished item.

Zucchini-Pepper Wraps

Prep time: 30 min • **Waiting time:** 9–12 hr • **Yield:** 6 servings

Ingredients	*Directions*
6 cups seeded and chopped yellow bell pepper (about 6 peppers) 6 cups chopped zucchini (about 4 to 5 zucchinis) 1 avocado, peeled, pitted, and mashed 1½ tablespoons nutritional yeast* (optional) ½ teaspoon salt 3 tablespoons psyllium powder	**1** In a high-powered blender, puree the bell peppers and zucchini until smooth. Add the avocado, nutritional yeast (if desired), and salt. Blend again. With blender running, add the psyllium powder through the hole in the lid and blend well for a few seconds. **2** Use a small offset spatula to form four flat 7-inch disks on a dehydrator tray that's lined with a nonstick sheet (½ cup of batter for each). Repeat with the remaining batter on 3 additional trays, creating 12 wraps. Spread the batter quickly. The mixture thickens within minutes and becomes difficult to spread. **3** Dehydrate the wraps at 125 degrees for about 2 hours. Then decrease the temperature to 105 degrees and dehydrate for an additional 6 to 8 hours. **4** Remove the wraps from the nonstick liners and turn the wraps over onto mesh dehydrator screens. Place an additional mesh screen on top of each tray of wraps to make the wraps flatter and easier to store. Continue dehydrating another 1 to 2 hours, until dry but still flexible.

Per serving (2 wraps): Calories 136 (From Fat 36); Fat 4g (Saturated 0.5g); Cholesterol 0mg; Sodium 58mg; Carbohydrate 24g (Dietary Fiber 10g); Protein 4g.

Note: Store wraps in an airtight container in the fridge for up to 2 weeks, or freeze them for 2 months.

Note: These wraps have high water content, so they won't reach the maximum temperature of 118 degrees for raw food during the first 2 hours of dehydrating. But don't forget to turn down the dehydrator at the 2-hour mark to avoid cooked territory.

Note: Top these wraps with veggies, a drizzle of olive oil, and a sprinkle of salt for a quick lunch. Create a pizza by spreading a bit of Marinara Sauce (Chapter 8) on a wrap, crumbling Almond Cheese (later in this chapter) on top, and warming the pizza in the dehydrator for an hour.

Tip: If your wraps feel dry when you pull them out of the fridge or freezer, mist them with water and dehydrate for a few minutes before serving.

*Not raw

Corn Tortillas

Prep time: 30 min • **Waiting time:** 7–8 hr • **Yield:** 6 servings

Ingredients	Directions
4 cups seeded and chopped yellow bell peppers (about 4 peppers) 4 cups raw corn (about 8 ears) 2 cups peeled and chopped zucchini (about 2 medium zucchinis) 2 tablespoons nutritional yeast* 1 tablespoon lemon juice ½ teaspoon salt 1 avocado, peeled, pitted, and mashed (about 1 cup) 3 tablespoons ground golden flax	*1* Place the yellow bell peppers, corn, zucchini, nutritional yeast, lemon juice, and salt in a high-performance blender and process until smooth. Add the avocado and puree again. With the blender running, add the flax through the chute and blend for a few seconds. *2* Place ½ cup of the mixture in each of four corners of a nonstick dehydrator sheet. Using a small offset spatula, quickly form four 6-inch flat disks. Spread the batter quickly. The mixture will thicken within minutes and become difficult to spread. *3* Dehydrate at 105 degrees for 4 hours, or until disks easily come off the nonstick sheets. *4* Turn over the disks onto mesh dehydrator screens. Place an additional mesh screen on top to make the tortillas flatter and easier to store. Continue dehydrating another 3 to 4 hours, until disks are dry but still flexible.

Per serving (2 tortillas): Calories 193 (From Fat 52); Fat 6g(Saturated 0.5g); Cholesterol 0mg; Sodium 53mg; Carbohydrate 35g (Dietary Fiber 7g); Protein 7g.

Note: Store tortillas in a sealed container in the fridge for up to 2 weeks, or freeze them for 2 months.

Note: Figure 9-2 shows how to use a dehydrator to make tortillas and other wraps.

*Not raw

SPREADING TORTILLAS AND WRAPS

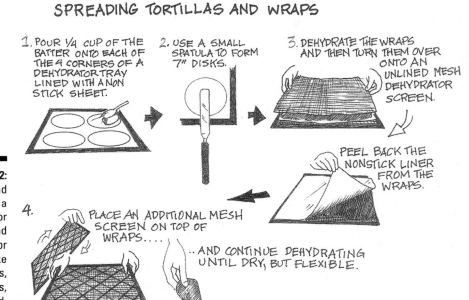

1. POUR ¼ CUP OF THE BATTER ONTO EACH OF THE 4 CORNERS OF A DEHYDRATOR TRAY LINED WITH A NON STICK SHEET.

2. USE A SMALL SPATULA TO FORM 7" DISKS.

3. DEHYDRATE THE WRAPS AND THEN TURN THEM OVER ONTO AN UNLINED MESH DEHYDRATOR SCREEN.

PEEL BACK THE NONSTICK LINER FROM THE WRAPS.

4. PLACE AN ADDITIONAL MESH SCREEN ON TOP OF WRAPS....

..AND CONTINUE DEHYDRATING UNTIL DRY, BUT FLEXIBLE.

Figure 9-2:
Spread batter on a dehydrator tray and wait for baked-like crackers, croutons, and bread.

Onion–Caraway Seed Bread

Prep time: 45 min • **Waiting time:** 28–34 hr • **Yield:** 9 servings

Ingredients	Directions
2 cups sunflower seeds	**1** Place sunflower seeds in 3 cups of filtered water for 6–8 hours. Rinse and drain.
4 medium red onions, sliced	
2 cups hot filtered water	**2** Soak onions in hot water with lemon juice for at least 30 minutes. Drain and set aside.
2 tablespoons lemon juice	
1 apple, peeled, seeded, and roughly chopped	**3** In a blender, puree all the ingredients for the onion marinade and then pour it over the drained onions. Massage onions with the marinade and set aside for 2 to 6 hours. Drain.
2 cups ground flax	
<u>**For onion marinade:**</u>	
¼ cup unpasteurized tamari*	**4** Puree soaked sunflower seeds and apple in a food processor. Put the apple mixture in a large bowl and stir in the drained marinated onions.
¼ cup extra-virgin olive oil	
2 tablespoons lemon juice	**5** Put half of the apple-onion mixture back in the food processor and pulse so onions are well combined but still visible. Place dough in a mixing bowl. Repeat with other half. Stir in flax.
2 tablespoons coconut nectar* or agave nectar*	
1 tablespoon ground caraway seeds	**6** Divide the dough in half again and spread each half evenly, about ¼-inch thick, on a dehydrator tray lined with a nonstick sheet. Use the entire tray surface.
1 teaspoon pureed garlic (about 2 cloves)	
1 teaspoon salt	**7** Dehydrate at 125 degrees for 2 hours. Reduce the temperature to 110 degrees. Flip over the batter and remove the nonstick sheet. Score bread into 9 equal squares (3 x 3). Continue dehydrating until bread is dry but still flexible, roughly 18 hours.
1 teaspoon Italian seasoning	
1 teaspoon dried thyme	
½ teaspoon ground white pepper	

Per serving: Calories 401 (From Fat 276); Fat 31g (Saturated 2.5g); Cholesterol 0mg; Sodium 512mg; Carbohydrate 26g (Dietary Fiber 12g); Protein 14g.

Note: Store this bread in a sealed container in the fridge for up to 1 month.

*Not raw

Garlic-Herb Croutons

Prep time: 30 min • **Waiting time:** 18–24 hr • **Yield:** 6 servings

Ingredients	*Directions*
1 cup fresh almond pulp	*1* Put all the ingredients into a large bowl and mix with your hands.
½ cup ground golden flax	
½ zucchini, finely diced	*2* Place the batter between two nonstick dehydrator sheets and roll it out with a rolling pin until batter is about a ½ inch thick.
1½ tablespoons extra-virgin olive oil	
½ tablespoon nutritional yeast*	
1 teaspoon minced fresh basil, oregano, and/or flat leaf parsley	*3* Cut the batter into ½-inch cubes and place them on a mesh-lined dehydrator tray with a spatula; no nonstick sheet is needed.
½ teaspoon crushed garlic (1 clove)	*4* Dehydrate at 105 degrees for 18 to 24 hours, until dry and crisp.
¼ teaspoon salt	

Per serving: Calories 145 (From Fat 108); Fat 12g (Saturated 1g); Cholesterol 0mg; Sodium 24mg; Carbohydrate 7g (Dietary Fiber 5g); Protein 6g.

Note: Store croutons in the refrigerator in an airtight container for up to 1 month.

Tip: For this recipe, use almond pulp left over from making Almond Milk (see Chapter 11).

Tip: These flavorful croutons are an excellent addition to salads. You can also toss them into Gazpacho (Chapter 8) for an extra crunch. Or crush them up and sprinkle them on pasta. Delish!

*Not raw

Sweet Pepper Sesame Chips

Prep time: 60 min • **Waiting time:** 28–36 hr • **Yield:** 60 servings

Ingredients	*Directions*
2 cups golden flaxseeds	*1* Put flaxseeds in 4 cups filtered water for 8 to 12 hours. Set aside. Do not drain.
8 cups seeded and chopped red, orange, or yellow bell peppers	*2* Combine the bell peppers, zucchini, onion, lemon juice, cane juice, garlic, and salt in a high-performance blender and blend until completely smooth.
3 cups peeled and diced zucchini	
1 cup diced red onion	*3* In a large bowl, combine the batter and soaked flaxseeds and stir. Add the sesame seeds and stir again. Sprinkle the ground flax over the top and stir well. Allow batter to sit at room temperature for 30 minutes.
2 tablespoons lemon juice	
2 tablespoons evaporated cane juice*	
5 cloves garlic	*4* Place 2½ cups of the mixture on each of the six dehydrator trays lined with a nonstick sheet. Evenly spread the mixture to the edges of the sheet, using a medium offset or flat rubber spatula.
2 teaspoons salt	
6 tablespoons black sesame seeds	*5* Score the mixture into six strips of uniform size, and then cross-score from corner to corner. Continue cutting strips parallel to the cross strip, creating five evenly spaced strips on each side of the cross-score. You'll end up with 30 parallelogram-shaped crackers and a handful of triangle crackers on each tray. See Figure 9-3 for help. Repeat with 5 more trays.
2 cups ground flax	
	6 Dehydrate for about 12 hours at 105 degrees until the top is thoroughly dry.

7 Flip over the batter onto an unlined mesh dehydrator tray and gently peel back the nonstick sheet. If the crackers resist and are too soft for the sheet to be removed, leave the sheet in place for a couple more hours until it can be peeled back easily.

8 Break the crackers at the score marks. If the score marks are no longer visible, cut the semi-dry sheets with scissors where the score marks should be. Continue dehydrating until the chips are completely crisp (8 to 12 more hours).

Per serving: Calories 63 (From Fat 31.5); Fat 3.5g (Saturated 0.5g); Cholesterol 0mg; Sodium 20mg; Carbohydrate 5g (Dietary Fiber 3g); Protein 3g.

Note: Store chips in an airtight container in the pantry or other cool dark place for up to 3 months.

Note: To grind flax seeds into meal, use a coffee grinder — ideally a grinder that's dedicated to grinding meal. If you use one that also grinds coffee, you may be a little disappointed when your cheesy chips have an aftertaste of Jamaican Blue Mountain or Costa Rican Tarrazu. Only grind as much flax as you need; it can become rancid quickly even when stored in the refrigerator. If you do have some left over, store it in a sealed glass jar in the freezer for up to 3 months.

Tip: Be sure to always use the amount of water indicated in a recipe for soaking flaxseed. Flax is a mucilaginous substance that gets a gooey texture when soaked, and it's difficult to drain excess water, and too much water affects dehydration time and thickness of the finished product.

Vary It! If you prefer to make larger crackers instead of smaller chips, cut the batter into 6-inch squares, which yields 36 crackers per sheet.

CUTTING CHIPS

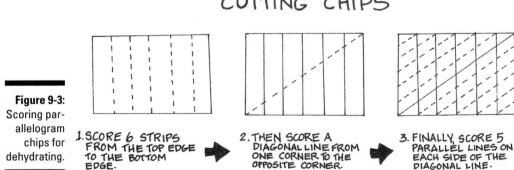

Figure 9-3: Scoring parallelogram chips for dehydrating.

1. SCORE 6 STRIPS FROM THE TOP EDGE TO THE BOTTOM EDGE.

2. THEN SCORE A DIAGONAL LINE FROM ONE CORNER TO THE OPPOSITE CORNER.

3. FINALLY SCORE 5 PARALLEL LINES ON EACH SIDE OF THE DIAGONAL LINE.

Making Your Own Tofu and Cheese

You may never have even considered making tofu or cheese in your life. In fact, the thought may seem a little intimidating at first. But honestly, people just like you have been doing it for centuries. All you need is a little know-how (which you have by virtue of simply reading this book) and a little time.

Tofu is most often made with soy. But soy beans are indigestible without cooking, so we recommend making your raw tofu with cashews. We use agar agar and Irish moss gel — two extremely nutritious sea vegetables — to thicken and coagulate the tofu so it becomes firm and sliceable after chilling in the refrigerator overnight.

Making your own cheese is only slightly more involved than the process for preparing tofu. In addition to your trusty blender, you need a strainer, cheesecloth, and a weight. Use the weight to place even pressure on the surface of the cheese. If your weight is something like a coffee cup or pint jar loaded with seeds or beans, you want to place it on top of a plate that's in direct contact with the cheese. Otherwise, you may end up with some funny dents and divots in your cheese. Take a look at Figure 9-4 to see our recommended setup.

PRESSING CHEESE

Figure 9-4:
Use a strainer, cheese-cloth, and a weight to make your own raw cheese.

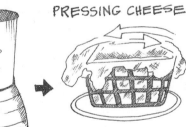

1. BLEND ALMONDS, WATER AND PROBIOTIC POWDER

2. LINE A SMALL COLANDER OR SMALL BERRY BASKET WITH DAMP CHEESECLOTH AND SET ON A DISH TO CATCH LIQUID WHEN MIXTURE IS POURED INTO CHEESECLOTH. FOLD CHEESECLOTH OVER CHEESE AND PLACE IN A WARM (NOT HOT) LOCATION TO FERMENT FOR 8 TO 12 HOURS.

3. AFTER 2 HOURS OF FERMENTING, PLACE A WEIGHT ON TOP OF THE CHEESE TO PRESS OUT EXCESS LIQUID.

The weight presses excess water from the mixture, leaving behind firm cheese. You can reserve the probiotic-rich liquid to use in dressings and smoothies in place of water. Just store it in a sealed jar in the refrigerator for up to a week.

Cashew-Sesame Tofu

Prep time: 20 min • **Waiting time:** 9–11 hr • **Yield:** 12 servings

Ingredients	Directions
1 cup raw cashews	*1* Soak cashews in 3 cups of water for 6 to 8 hours. Drain and rinse.
1 tablespoon agar agar flakes* **in ¼ cup filtered water**	
½ cup boiling filtered water	*2* Put the soaked agar agar into an electric hot pot with the boiling water and whisk constantly until the liquid is clear and very smooth, no clumps. Allow to cool slightly. Do not allow the mixture to get cold or firm.
1¼ cups filtered water (or more as needed)	
½ cup Irish moss gel	
¼ cup thick raw tahini	*3* While the agar agar is cooling, put the 1¼ cups filtered water into a high-performance blender along with the Irish moss gel, tahini, lemon juice, lecithin powder, miso, and salt. Blend until completely smooth. Add more water if needed to create a very thick cream.
1 tablespoon of lemon juice	
½ tablespoon soy lecithin powder*	
½ tablespoon light miso*	*4* While the blender is running, slowly add the cooked, slightly cooled agar agar through the hole in the lid.
½ teaspoon salt	
	5 Pour the mixture into a 9-inch square springform pan or a similar size container(s) so your tofu is about ¾-inch to 1-inch thick. Refrigerate for about 3 hours.

Per serving: Calories 102 (From Fat 76); Fat 8g (Saturated 1.5g); Cholesterol 0mg; Sodium 53mg; Carbohydrate 5g (Dietary Fiber 1g); Protein 3g.

Note: Store this tofu in a glass jar in the refrigerator for up to 1 week.

Tip: This version of tofu is so versatile. Cut it into cubes and add it to soups. Slice it into slabs and then glaze or marinate it; teriyaki sauce is especially good. Warm it briefly in the dehydrator before serving to warm and intensify the flavor.

Tip: If you can only find powdered agar agar, substitute 1 teaspoon of powder for 1 tablespoon flakes. You can find agar agar and Irish moss gel at most health foods stores or on the Internet.

*Not raw

Almond Cheese

Prep time: 10 min • **Waiting time:** 16–24 hr • **Yield:** 8 servings

Ingredients	Directions
2 cups raw almonds	**1** Plunge almonds into a bowl of boiling water and leave them immersed for 5 minutes. When the almond skins pop off easily if pressed between your fingers, add a little cool water to the bowl, making the water cool enough to handle. Peel the almonds.
1 or more cups filtered water	
¼ teaspoon probiotic powder	**2** Soak the peeled almonds in cold water for 8 to 12 hours; then rinse and drain.
	3 Blend the almonds, 1 cup water, and probiotic powder in a high-performance blender, adding more water if necessary to achieve a smooth, creamy texture.
	4 Line a small colander or plastic berry basket with damp cheesecloth, allowing several inches of the cloth to drape down the sides. (Refer to Figure 9-4.) Set the colander or basket on top of a shallow dish and pour the mixture into the cheesecloth. The dish will catch liquid that drains from the cheese.

5 Fold the excess cheesecloth over the top of the cheese and place cheese in a warm (not hot) location to ferment. After about 2 hours, place a weight on top of the cheese — set a cup of grains or seeds on top of a plate — to help press out the excess liquid.

6 Check the cheese every 2 to 3 hours and drain the excess liquid from the plate. Continue fermenting for a total of 8 to 12 hours or until the cheese reaches your desired flavor.

Per serving: Calories 206 (From Fat 159); Fat 18g (Saturated 1.5g); Cholesterol 0mg; Sodium 1mg; Carbohydrate 8g (Dietary Fiber 4g); Protein 8g.

Note: Store this cheese in a sealed glass container in the refrigerator for up to 1 week.

Vary It! Adapt this recipe to make these other kinds of cheese:

Macadamia Nut or Cashew Cheese: Replace almonds with macadamia nuts or cashews. Skip the peeling process and go straight to soaking.

Cashew Yogurt: Replace almonds with cashews and add a little lemon juice to Step 3. Put the mixture in a sealed jar and allow it to sit in a warm dark place for 6 hours. (Do not drain.)

Almond Feta Cheese: In Step 3, add in 2 teaspoons light miso*; 2 teaspoons nutritional yeast flakes*; ⅛ red onion, minced; and a pinch each of nutmeg, white pepper, and salt. After cheese ferments, put it in the refrigerator in a sealed container with the weight. For a firmer feta, increase the amount of weight. Chill for 24 hours to allow more of the liquid to drain, and continue to drain away the liquid.

*Not raw

Pine Nut Parmesan Cheese

Prep time: 10 min • **Waiting time:** 12 hr • **Yield:** 8 servings

Ingredients	*Directions*
2 cups raw pine nuts 1 or more cups filtered water ¼ teaspoon probiotic powder ½ teaspoon salt	**1** Blend all ingredients in a high-performance blender, adding water as necessary to achieve a thin creamy texture.
	2 Divide batter in half and spread each half, paper thin, on a dehydrator tray lined with a nonstick sheet. Dehydrate for 12 hours or until the cheese is completely dry and crisp.
	3 Using a pastry board scraper, scrape cheese shavings off the sheet.

Per serving: Calories 206 (From Fat 188); Fat 20g (Saturated 1.5g); Cholesterol 0mg; Sodium 31mg; Carbohydrate 4g (Dietary Fiber 1g); Protein 4g.

Note: Store this cheese in a sealed glass container in the refrigerator for up to one 1 week.

Tip: This version of Parmesan cheese is a great topper for Zucchini Pasta with sauce (Chapter 8), salads (Chapter 13), or just about any wrap. We think it will quickly become a mainstay in your raw life.

Tip: We recommend that you make this mixture thin, like light cream rather than thick and batter-like, so that it spreads paper thin on the dehydrator sheets. If it's too thick, the top dries but the center doesn't.

Chapter 10

Mixing It Up: Smoothies and Elixirs

In This Chapter

▶ Setting your sights on smoothies

▶ Enjoying energizing elixirs

Smoothies and elixirs are the lifeblood of a raw food lifestyle. For starters, they're quick to prepare. The process for most of these drinks is blend and enjoy; most take as few as five minutes to whip together. And frankly, when you're waiting a day and a half for your favorite flatbread to dehydrate and you know your cheese needs to ferment overnight, a nearly instant go-to snack that's available anytime you want it can be mighty comforting.

Aside from the quick-thrill aspect of smoothies and elixirs, they're also amazing pick-you-uppers. Loaded with nutrition, these blended staples let you enjoy even the powerhouse foods you tend to avoid. Better yet, preparation is dunce-proof and almost equipment-free. No dehydrators or fancy slicing tools needed here! Just grab your blender and that well-loved juicer and go.

In this chapter, we include some of our favorite recipes for smoothies and elixirs, along with tips for modifying them with easy substitutions. I promise that at least some of these smoothies can please even the most finicky eater or raw-resistant family member. Oh, and we also include recipes here for party-size batches of healthy and palate-pleasing beverages such as Hibiscus Rosé and Spicy Apple-Pineapple Cocktail so you can entertain the raw way, too.

Simplifying Smoothie Making

For many people, a smoothie is one of the most familiar raw foods. Most people have had some version of this popular drink. Even fast-food restaurants include smoothies on menus these days. Sadly though, commercially available smoothies are often little more than ice, high fructose corn syrup, and artificial coloring. But because you have this book, you can make your own real, fresh, and deliciously nutritious smoothies in minutes.

When you make your own smoothies, you control which ingredients are blended in and get to pick your favorite flavor combinations. You can also create a just-right texture with these tips:

- ✔ If you like smooth and creamy smoothies, blend for a few more seconds.
- ✔ If you prefer a chunky smoothie, blend yours for a few seconds less.
- ✔ If you like a milkshake-like consistency, use frozen fruits or add ice.
- ✔ If you enjoy a thin consistency, use fresh fruit in your smoothie.

Throw whatever you have handy into a blender and figure out what you like. Add a little coconut nectar to boost sweetness or some lemon or celery to tone down mixtures that are too sweet for your taste. Don't be afraid to add greens to your smoothie! The sweetness of fruit masks the bitterness of greens. Just remember to always use in-season produce for the best flavor and most nutrition. Find tips on preparing fruits for smoothies ahead of time in Chapter 7.

Just steer clear of combining melons, including watermelon and cantaloupe, with other foods in smoothies. Melons are great to enjoy as a standalone smoothie with a little citrus juice and mint, but melons digest much more quickly than other foods, so "Eat them alone or leave them alone" — as the saying goes. Pretty much any other combination of fruits and leafy greens is fair game, though, so mix it up!

Some of these recipes include nuts or seeds that require several hours of soaking. We flag these foods with a Plan Ahead icon and tell you in Chapter 7 how to soak seeds so they're ready whenever you want to use or eat them. But if you don't have time to soak nuts, don't worry about it; you can still make delicious, nutritious smoothies without them.

The smoothies in this chapter are all best when served immediately after blending. However, if you need to blend ahead of time, you can store a smoothie in an airtight container in the refrigerator for up to 24 hours.

Blueberry-Hill Smoothie

Prep time: 5 min • **Yield:** 2 servings

Ingredients	*Directions*
2 oranges, peeled and chopped	*1* Combine the oranges and blueberries and blend in a high-performance blender, adding the celery if desired. Add water to thin the smoothie to your desired consistency.
1 pint blueberries (fresh or frozen)	
1 to 2 cups filtered water to thin as needed	
1 to 2 celery ribs, sliced (optional)	

Per serving (2 cups): Calories 150 (From Fat 6); Fat 1g (Saturated 0g); Cholesterol 0mg; Sodium 37mg; Carbohydrate 38g (Dietary Fiber 7g); Protein 3g.

Note: Adding celery to your smoothie helps balance the sweetness of the fruit. It's a powerhouse of vitamins, minerals, and other nutrients, including potassium, folic acid, calcium, magnesium, iron, phosphorus, sodium, and essential amino acids, so we like to sneak it into smoothies whenever we can. Celery is also a natural diuretic to help relieve belly bloat.

Island Paradise Smoothie

Prep time: 10 min • **Yield:** 2 servings

Ingredients	*Directions*
1 orange, peeled and chopped	*1* Combine the orange, banana, pineapple, mango, and papaya in a high-performance blender and blend, adding water to thin as needed.
1 banana, fresh or frozen	
½ cup chopped pineapple, fresh or frozen	
½ cup chopped mango, fresh or frozen	
½ cup chopped papaya, fresh or frozen	
½ cup water to thin as needed	

Per serving (2 cups): Calories 144 (From Fat 4); Fat 0.5g (Saturated 0g); Cholesterol 0mg; Sodium 6mg; Carbohydrate 37g (Dietary Fiber 5g); Protein 2g.

PLAN AHEAD

Superfoods Green Smoothie

Prep time: 10 min • **Waiting time:** 8 hr • **Yield:** 2 servings

Ingredients	*Directions*
¼ **cup dried goji berries**	*1* Soak dried goji berries overnight in a little water and then drain them. Reserve the liquid and use it to thin this or other smoothies as needed.
4 oranges, peeled and chopped	
½ **pint blueberries (fresh or frozen)**	*2* Combine the soaked goji berries, oranges, blueberries, kale, chia seed, and green powder in a high-performance blender and blend, adding reserved soaking water to thin as needed.
4 large kale leaves	
1 to 2 tablespoon ground chia seed	
1 tablespoon Vitamineral Green Powder or other green powder	

Per serving (2 cups): Calories 268 (From Fat 18); Fat 2g (Saturated 0g); Cholesterol 0mg; Sodium 22mg; Carbohydrate 60g (Dietary Fiber 11g); Protein 8g.

Note: Vitamineral Green Powder is a nutritionally dense superfood supplement that supports the immune system, kidneys, and circulation; improves bone health; and helps stabilizes blood sugar. It's available at health food stores and at many online sources.

Getting to know goji berries

These large, red berries get a lot of press these days for their healthful benefits. Sometimes called *wolfberries* or *Lycium berries*, goji berries are native to China, where locals have eaten them for generations to ward off aging and to protect against diseases like diabetes and cancer. Goji berries are packed with antioxidants. Some studies indicate that they can help maintain brain function and ward off dementia.

Goji berries are most often sold dried and need to be rehydrated before use in raw foods. You can rehydrate them in warm water and drink the soaking liquid as a tea. Or simply soak the berries in filtered water overnight for plump, ready-to-use goodies in the morning.

Rise 'n' Shine Smoothie

Prep time: 10 min • **Yield:** 2 servings

Ingredients	Directions
8 ounces fresh pressed apple juice	**1** Combine and blend ingredients in a high-performance blender, adding water as needed.
1 orange, peeled and chopped	
1 cup strawberries, frozen or fresh	
1 to 2 tablespoon ground chia seeds	
10 leaves fresh mint	
1 cup filtered water to thin as needed	

Per serving (9 ounces): Calories 164 (From Fat 32); Fat 3.5g (Saturated 0.5g); Cholesterol 0mg; Sodium 14mg; Carbohydrate 32g (Dietary Fiber 7g); Protein 3g.

Note: The fresh mint leaves give this smoothie a rejuvenating freshness that's great in the morning.

Tip: To save time in the morning, assemble ingredients in a single container and store in the fridge overnight. Then simply blend them together in the morning and enjoy this smoothie immediately.

Peaches 'n' Cream Smoothie

Prep time: 10 min • **Yield:** 2 servings

Ingredients	*Directions*
1½ cups Almond Milk	**1** Blend ingredients in a high-performance blender, adding water as needed.
4 ripe peaches, pitted	
6 dates, pitted	
1 peeled banana, fresh or frozen	
½ teaspoons vanilla extract*	
Filtered water to thin as needed	

Per serving (1½ cups): Calories 248 (From Fat 14); Fat 1.5g (Saturated 0g); Cholesterol 0mg; Sodium 39mg; Carbohydrate 60g (Dietary Fiber 8g); Protein 4g.

Note: Turn to Chapter 11 to find the recipe for Almond Milk.

Tip: Don't worry about peeling the peaches; the blender can handle it, and you'll love the extra fiber.

*Not raw

Chocolate–Cherries Jubilee Smoothie

Prep time: 10 min • **Yield:** 2 servings

Ingredients	Directions
¾ cup raw cashews	**1** Blend ingredients in a high-performance blender, adding water to thin as needed.
1½ cup frozen pitted cherries	
⅓ cup coconut nectar* or agave nectar*	
¼ cup cacao nibs (or 3 tablespoons raw cacao powder)	
Pinch salt	
1½ cup filtered water, or more to thin as needed	

Per serving (9 ounces): Calories 510 (From Fat 216); Fat 24g (Saturated 4.5g); Cholesterol 0mg; Sodium 19mg; Carbohydrate 70g (Dietary Fiber 8g); Protein 12g.

Vary It! Substitute soaked and peeled almonds for the cashews for a delicious change.

*Not raw

Choconana Smoothie

Prep time: 5 min • **Yield:** 2 servings

Ingredients	Directions
1½ **cups Almond Milk**	*1* Put milk, bananas, cashews, nectar, and cacao powder in a blender and blend until smooth and creamy. Add ice and blend again. Serve immediately.
2 **peeled bananas**	
¼ **cup raw cashews**	
3 **tablespoons coconut nectar* or agave nectar***	
2 **tablespoons cacao powder**	
¾ **cup ice**	

Per serving (9 ounces): Calories 326 (From Fat 85); Fat 9g (Saturated 2g); Cholesterol 0mg; Sodium 52mg; Carbohydrate 60g (Dietary Fiber 7g); Protein 6g.

Note: See Chapter 11 for the recipe for Almond Milk.

Vary It! Try this smoothie with a frozen banana and skip the ice for a milkshake-like texture.

*Not raw

Entering the Enticing World of Raw Elixirs and Juices

When you hear the word *elixir,* you may envision a scene from *Lord of the Rings* or think of a drink that might be served in an ornate goblet by a New-Age type before he reads your aura. But an *elixir* is simply a clear, sweet liquid that's often mixed with alcohol and designed to deliver medication in a pleasing way. Our elixirs aren't alcoholic and don't deliver medication per se, but they do promote wellness and deliver health benefits. Raw foodists think of them as magical health potions.

We lump cocktails and juices into the elixir category as well. For our purposes, a *cocktail* does not contain alcohol; instead, it's simply a blend of juices from different fruits and vegetables. Find step-by-step instructions for using your juicer in Chapter 7, and take a look at Figure 10-1.

When using juice recipes, remember that flavors of produce vary with the season. Strawberries, for instance, definitely taste better in the summer. In fact, in-season produce is almost always the way to go, so substitute different kinds of fruits and vegetables in your juices based on what's in season. If fresh produce is unavailable, frozen fruits are a second-best choice because they're frozen at their peak of ripeness. Use frozen produce before using fruits that are out of season or not ripe.

When preparing green juices, use a ratio of 1 part leafy greens (such as kale or romaine lettuce) to 3 parts fruits and vegetables (such as cucumber, celery, apple, and carrots) plus flavorings, like lemon and gingerroot. For *palatability,* or general state of tastiness, add more carrots or apples or other ingredient to find the flavor you like best.

JUICER

Figure 10-1:
Juicing
fruits and
vegetables
is as simple
as pushing a
button.

Therapeutic uses of fruit and vegetable juices

We recommend including these fruits and vegetables in your juices due to their therapeutic and cleansing effects on the body:

✔ **Apple** is a good source of vitamins A and C, aids digestion, acts as laxative, and helps to detoxify the blood.

✔ **Beets** cleanse the liver, stimulate bowel movements, and are high in iron, folate, and potassium.

✔ **Cabbage** has great antioxidant properties, is a good internal cleanser, and is a good source of beta carotene, folic acid, iron, vitamin C, and potassium.

✔ **Carrots** are high in vitamins A, B, C, D, E, and K and function as a body alkalizer.

✔ **Celery** quenches thirst, is good for the nerves, contains potassium and organic sodium, and builds red blood cells.

✔ **Citrus fruits** are packed with vitamin C, beta carotene, calcium, and magnesium, and they're good for kidneys and liver.

✔ **Cucumber**, a diuretic, contains folic acid and calcium and is good for hair and nails.

✔ **Kale and other dark leafy greens** are high in chlorophyll, cleanse the kidneys, and are high in calcium and protein.

Here are some great combinations for delicious juice:

✔ Apple, cilantro, and lime

✔ Orange, carrot, and gingerroot

✔ Carrot, apple, and beets

✔ Mango, orange, and mint

✔ Apple, cranberries, and cinnamon

✔ Pineapple, lemongrass, and basil

✔ Apple, gingerroot, and fennel

✔ Pomegranate, apple, and parsley

✔ Cucumber, wheat grass, and lemon

Be creative with juices. Throw in some cayenne pepper, garlic, gingerroot, lemon, or lime to add a punch. Use a touch of cinnamon, allspice, nutmeg, cardamom, or even a pinch of salt to show off your creative side! It's actually pretty difficult to come up with a bad combination of juice.

Rejuvelac

Prep time: 10 min • **Waiting time:** 4–5 days • **Yield:** 24 servings

Ingredients	*Directions*
½ cup soft wheat or rye berries (or a mixture) 3 gallons filtered water, divided	*1* Soak the grains overnight in a half-gallon jar filled with water (see Chapter 7 for soaking how-to). The next morning, drain and rinse the grains. Then sprout the grains for 2 days, rinsing and draining with filtered water twice each day.
	2 Fill the sprouting jar with filtered water and allow the sprouts to ferment for 36 to 48 hours in a warm place, or until the desired tartness is achieved. Pour the Rejuvelac liquid into a glass jar, leaving the grains in the original jar. You can use the liquid for up to 3 days if you keep it covered and stored in the refrigerator. (It develops a scum on top and a strong odor, like well-aged cheese, so don't be alarmed!)
	3 To make the second harvest of Rejuvelac, fill the jar of sprouted grains with purified water again and ferment for 24 hours. Then pour the Rejuvelac liquid into a glass jar, cover, and store in the fridge.
	4 To prepare a third and final harvest of Rejuvelac, fill the jar with water one last time, ferment for 24 hours, and pour the Rejuvelac liquid into a glass jar. Discard the grains.

Per serving (1 cup): Calories 13 (From Fat 1); Fat 0g (Saturated 0g); Cholesterol 0mg; Sodium 14mg; Carbohydrate 3g (Dietary Fiber 1g); Protein 1g.

Note: The first harvest of Rejuvelac has a strong cheesy taste. The second and third harvest become milder in flavor, somewhat resembling the whey in yogurt or cottage cheese.

Tip: Use only filtered water without chlorine to make Rejuvelac. Chlorine is added to water to kill bacteria; yet a main benefit of Rejuvelac is that it encourages the growth of health-promoting bacteria, such as lactobacillus acidophilus and other probiotics that are vital to good digestion — and good health.

Note: You can replace water in most raw food recipes with Rejuvelac.

Wheat Grass Blast

Prep time: 5 min • **Yield:** 2 servings

Ingredients	*Directions*
1-inch piece of gingerroot	*1* Grate the ginger and, with your hands, squeeze the pulp to extract the juice (about 1 teaspoon) into a pitcher.
¾ cup apple juice	
1 tablespoon freshly squeezed lemon or lime juice	*2* Pour the apple juice, lemon juice, and wheat-grass juice into the pitcher and stir. Drink immediately.
3 ounces wheat-grass juice	

Per serving (½ cup): Calories 54 (From Fat 2); Fat 0.5g (Saturated 0g); Cholesterol 0mg; Sodium 8mg; Carbohydrate 12g (Dietary Fiber 0g); Protein 1g.

Vary It! If you need a break from apple juice, substitute raw cranberry juice. If it's too tart for your taste, reduce or eliminate the lemon or lime juice.

To-Live-For Green Juice

Prep time: 10 min • **Yield:** 4 servings

Ingredients	Directions
12 large stalks kale	**1** Combine and juice all the ingredients.
1 cucumber, peeled and chopped	
6 stalks celery, chopped	
2 apples, peeled, seeded, and chopped	
1-inch piece gingerroot	
3 tablespoons lemon juice, or 1 lemon, peeled	

Per serving (1 cup): Calories 110 (From Fat 9); Fat 1g (Saturated 0g); Cholesterol 0mg; Sodium 87mg; Carbohydrate 25g (Dietary Fiber 5g); Protein 4g.

Note: This juice tastes best if you drink it immediately, but it will last for 4 hours or more if stored in an airtight container in the refrigerator. Stir or shake before drinking.

Tip: In addition to using the whole leaves of kale, this recipe is a great chance to use the stems of the kale leftover from the Massaged Kale Salad in Chapter 8. Raw foodists rarely waste anything.

Spicy Apple-Pineapple Cocktail

Prep time: 10 min • **Yield:** 2 servings

Ingredients	Directions
4 apples	*1* Combine and juice all of the ingredients.
5 limes, peeled	
1 cup chopped pineapple, fresh or frozen	
½-inch piece of fresh gingerroot	
Pinch cayenne	

Per serving (1½ cups): Calories 279 (From Fat 10); Fat 1g (Saturated 0g); Cholesterol 0mg; Sodium 8mg; Carbohydrate 78g (Dietary Fiber 15g); Protein 3g.

Note: Serve this drink immediately if possible, especially if you want it icy cold. If you want to juice up a big batch for a party, it will last for 4 hours or more if stored in an airtight container in the refrigerator. Stir it before serving.

Tip: A tantalizing and refreshing balance of sweet and tart flavors, this cocktail is a perfect party drink. You can add more or less ginger depending on your preference. It's also very nice with a pinch of cinnamon and can satisfy your sweet tooth when you crave dessert.

Note: Check out Figure 10-2 to see how to dice pineapple.

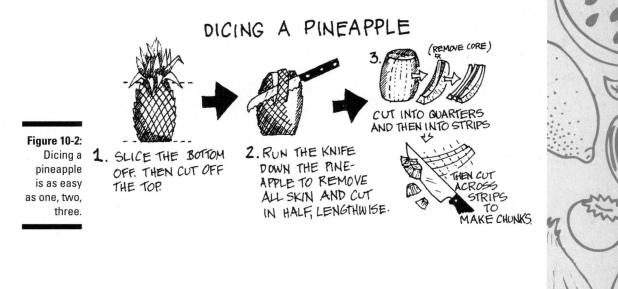

Figure 10-2: Dicing a pineapple is as easy as one, two, three.

DICING A PINEAPPLE

1. SLICE THE BOTTOM OFF. THEN CUT OFF THE TOP.

2. RUN THE KNIFE DOWN THE PINE-APPLE TO REMOVE ALL SKIN AND CUT IN HALF, LENGTHWISE.

3. (REMOVE CORE) CUT INTO QUARTERS AND THEN INTO STRIPS

THEN CUT ACROSS STRIPS TO MAKE CHUNKS.

Hibiscus Rosé

Prep time: 10 min • **Waiting time:** 24–27 hr **Yield:** 8 servings

Ingredients	*Directions*
2 quarts filtered water	**1** Combine all of the ingredients in a glass gallon jar. Cover the jar with a clean dish towel and place it in a warm place for 24 hours.
1 orange, chopped (including the peel)	
1 apple, chopped	**2** Strain out and discard the fruit and herbs.
¼ cup dried hibiscus flowers	
¼ cup coarsely chopped fresh mint	**3** If you prefer a cool beverage, refrigerate for 3 hours and serve chilled.
¼ cup coarsely chopped fresh parsley	
¼ cup sun-dried pitted cherries or unsulfured raisins	
6 dates, pitted	
6 dried prunes, pitted	

Per serving (1 cup): Calories 67 (From Fat 2); Fat 0.5g (Saturated 0g); Cholesterol 0mg; Sodium 10mg; Carbohydrate 18g (Dietary Fiber 2g); Protein 1g.

Note: Store rosé in a sealed glass gallon jar in the refrigerator for up to 3 days. Remove from the refrigerator a few hours prior to serving if you prefer to serve at room temperature.

Hibiscus, an edible flower

Hibiscus flowers have been used to make elixirs for centuries. Often, people steep the dried trumpet-shaped flowers in boiling water to make tea. Purported health benefits include reducing congestion, promoting proper kidney function, aiding digestion, and functioning as a diuretic. Rich in vitamin C, hibiscus has a tart flavor that's similar to cranberry. Luckily, you don't have to look far to find the dried variety. Dried hibiscus is available at health food stores, natural food stores (such as Trader Joe's), and most Mexican markets as well as online.

Seventh-Heaven Vegetable Cocktail

Prep time: 10 min • **Yield:** 2 servings

Ingredients	*Directions*
4 carrots	*1* Juice all the ingredients. Serve immediately or cover and chill if desired.
2 apples	
2 tomatoes	
4 cups packed kale, spinach, and/or parsley	
1 cucumber	
2 celery ribs	
1 lemon, peeled	

Per serving (2 cups): Calories 271 (From Fat 19); Fat 2g (Saturated 0.5g); Cholesterol 0mg; Sodium 185mg; Carbohydrate 64g (Dietary Fiber 14g); Protein 9g.

Tip: This cocktail has seven separate fruits and vegetables. A great afternoon pick-me-up, this juice is packed with antioxidants, protein, calcium, vitamins, and minerals. Not only that — it's delicious!

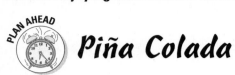

Piña Colada

Prep time: 10 min • **Yield:** 2 servings

Ingredients	*Directions*
6 ounces Coconut Milk or Almond Milk	**1** Put milk, pineapple, coconut meat, and nectar in a blender and blend until smooth.
1½ cup chopped frozen pineapple	**2** Add ice and blend again. Serve immediately.
2 ounces young coconut meat	
1 tablespoons coconut nectar* or agave nectar*	
1 cup ice	

Per serving (9 ounces): Calories 242 (From Fat 198); Fat 22g (Saturated 20g); Cholesterol 0mg; Sodium 18mg; Carbohydrate 12g (Dietary Fiber 3g); Protein 3g.

Tip: Check out Chapter 8 to find out how to open a young coconut to extract the meat.

Note: Flip to Chapter 11 to find recipes for Coconut Milk and Almond Milk.

*Not raw

Creamy Coconut-Lemongrass Cocktail

Prep time: 15 min • **Waiting time:** 3 hr • **Yield:** 2 servings

Ingredients	Directions
2 cups dried shredded unsweetened coconut 2 cups hot filtered water 6 dates, pitted 1 spear lemongrass ½ cup young Thai coconut ½ cup coconut water	**1** Combine coconut, water, dates, and lemongrass in a high-performance blender and blend for 30 to 60 seconds. **2** Pour the batter into a mesh bag and firmly squeeze to extract the cream. Discard solids. **3** Return the liquid to the blender, add the Thai coconut meat and coconut water, and blend until smooth and creamy. Chill the cocktail for about 3 hours before serving.

Per serving (1 cup): Calories 642 (From Fat 495); Fat 55g (Saturated 49g); Cholesterol 0mg; Sodium 104mg; Carbohydrate 39g (Dietary Fiber 16g); Protein 7g.

Note: Store this cocktail in a sealed glass jar for up to 2 days.

Coconut: Old or young? What's the difference?

Young coconut is a great addition to smoothies and juices, and it even makes great noodles. The meat in a young coconut is softer and sweeter than a mature coconut; its water is sweeter and more abundant, too. Coconut flesh starts as a film, becomes a gel, and becomes firmer until the coconut matures and falls from the palm. So the flesh of very immature coconuts is jelly-like and becomes firm and woody (due to reduced water content) after just a few months. When you purchase young coconuts, store them whole in the refrigerator for up to 3 weeks or remove the flesh and the water and freeze them separately in a sealed container. Freezing coconut meat and water has no discernable impact on flavor, but the water of a mature coconut may be bitter or sour. Shredded dry coconut is made from mature dried coconut. Always purchase unsweetened and unsulfured coconut.

Orange Jewels

Prep time: 10 min • **Waiting time:** 2–3 hr • **Yield:** 2 servings

Ingredients	Directions
½ **cup raw cashews**	**1** Soak cashews in water for 2 to 3 hours. Drain and rinse.
12 ounces orange juice	
2 dates, pitted	**2** Blend the soaked cashews, orange juice, dates, vanilla extract, lecithin powder, and ice until smooth and creamy.
¼ **teaspoon vanilla extract***	
¼ **teaspoon soy lecithin powder***	
1 cup ice	

Per serving (9 ounces): Calories 303 (From Fat 144); Fat 16g (Saturated 3g); Cholesterol 0mg; Sodium 6mg; Carbohydrate 35g (Dietary Fiber 2g); Protein 8g.

Note: This creamy, frothy shake is best if served immediately, but it will last for 4 hours or more if stored in an airtight container in the refrigerator.

*Not raw

Learning about lecithin

Lecithin is one of those ingredients that may sound scary and vaguely chemically. But it's actually a natural plant-based emulsifier that helps give liquids a smooth creaminess. We use soy lecithin even though it isn't raw because it adds such a wonderful creaminess to this special drink. But if you are soy intolerant or choose to eat 100 percent raw foods, just leave it out. Your drink won't be as creamy or frothy, but it'll still be delicious! Or, you can try sunflower lecithin, but this product isn't as readily available as the soy variety. Plus, sunflower lecithin has a stronger flavor and requires more of it to achieve the same effect as soy lecithin.

Chapter 11

Nourishing Breakfasts

In This Chapter

▶ Starting the day with raw versions of traditional breakfasts

▶ Going nuts for milks

▶ Feeling fresh with fruit salads

*I*f you're new to the raw foods lifestyle, you may think your breakfast choices are limited to fruit and, um, fruit. Although we love fruit (and include several recipes in this chapter for some delicious fruit salads), we know that everyone needs variety to stick with any eating plan or lifestyle. So we've packed this chapter with breakfast ideas to help you start your day the raw foods way.

This chapter includes delicious recipes to get your mornings going with the right fuel. You've heard that breakfast is the most important meal of the day; it's true. That's why we load these foods with protein from nuts and seeds, complex carbohydrates from whole sprouted grains, and healthy fats. We recommend making some of these items ahead of time, perhaps on the weekend, so you have ready-to-go meals when you need them. Find storage tips in each recipe so your foods stay fresh and tasty.

Enjoying Raw Breakfast Basics

Most raw foodists start the day with juice or a smoothie, and we dedicate Chapter 10 to those options. In addition, whole fruit is an excellent breakfast option — and to enjoy any other time of day, too. Add a little raw yogurt to your fruit to make a filling meal. That said, we understand that sometimes a morning calls for a bit more than these simple options.

Psychologically, breakfast may be the toughest meal for beginners of the raw way, especially if you're used to enjoying or entertaining at a savory weekend brunch. But committing to a raw food lifestyle doesn't mean that you need to give up elaborate and savory dishes at this time of the day.

Use the recipes in this chapter, along with delicacies in Chapters 8 and 10, to prepare a spectacular breakfast or brunch for yourself and even family and friends. Here's a sample brunch menu:

- **Buckwheat Granola:** Top it with Cashew Yogurt (see Chapter 9).

- **Cinnamon Oatmeal:** This delicious and heart-healthy recipe couldn't be easier. Just soak the oats overnight, and then blend and season them the next morning.

- **Mangoes in Lemon-Ginger Sauce:** This is an easy way to dress up fruit to make it party-perfect.

- **Tropical Fruit Ambrosia**: This colorful fruit salad will transport you guests to their favorite warm and sunny island, no matter what the temperature is outside!

- **Hibiscus Rosé:** This attractive and delicious beverage is easy to make (see Chapter 10) and elegant enough for a brunch or garden party.

This section offers great recipes for familiar breakfast fare. Who can resist warm scones? Luckily, you don't have to, even if you're a raw foodist. But because some of the foods in this chapter are dried at low temperatures in a dehydrator, they do take quite a while to prepare. So make sure you plan ahead — often a few days ahead — for meals that include them. The upside is that these recipes make several servings, so you can refrigerate or freeze extras for quick snacks.

Cinnamon Oatmeal

Prep time: 5 min • **Waiting time:** 8–12 hr • **Yield:** 2 servings

Ingredients	*Directions*
1 cup sproutable oat groats	*1* Soak oat groats for 8 to 12 hours in 3 cups of filtered water. Drain and rinse thoroughly.
2 tablespoons filtered water	
½ apple, chopped	*2* Process all the ingredients until smooth, using a food processor outfitted with an S blade. Serve immediately.
1½ tablespoons coconut nectar*, agave nectar*, or maple syrup*	
½ teaspoon ground cinnamon	
Pinch of salt	

Per serving (1 cup): *Calories 400 (From Fat 54); Fat 6g (Saturated 1g); Cholesterol 0mg; Sodium 1mg; Carbohydrate 71g (Dietary Fiber 12g); Protein 14g.*

Note: Oat groats are hulled grains of oats. The word groats refers to the hulled grains of various cereals, such as oats, buckwheat, and barley. Groats are whole grains that include the cereal germ and bran. Soaked, sprouted oat groats can be stored in a sealed container in the fridge for up to 3 days. They can quickly become rancid if not held at cool temperatures.

Tip: Try saving the cinnamon and coconut nectar for drizzling on top so these flavors don't get lost in the other ingredients in this dish.

*Not raw

Date and Walnut Wheat-Berry Scones

Prep time: 15 min • **Waiting time:** About 3 days • **Yield:** 8 servings

Ingredients	*Directions*
1½ cups winter wheat berries	*1* Place wheat berries in a ½ gallon jar and fill the jar with filtered water. Cover it with a mesh screen and attach with a rubber band. Soak the berries for 6 to 8 hours. Drain and rinse with mesh screen still attached. Drain again thoroughly. Set the jar away from direct light for 2 days to allow the berries to sprout. Rinse sprouts and drain until the drained water is clear.
¾ cup raw walnuts	
¾ cup pitted, chopped, and packed dates	
1 teaspoon ground cinnamon	
Pinch of ground nutmeg	
Pinch of salt	*2* While the wheat berries are sprouting, soak walnuts in filtered water for 8 hours. Rinse and drain. Dehydrate the soaked nuts at 105 degrees for 8 to 12 hours or until dry.
Coconut Butter (see the following recipe)	
Raspberry-Date Jam (see the following recipe)	*3* Place the sprouted wheat berries in a food processor outfitted with an S blade and process for less than a minute, until the grains are broken into 3 or more pieces each. The mixture should be sticky but not mushy.
	4 Loosely separate the dates so they aren't in a clump, and then add them along with the cinnamon, nutmeg, and salt to the food processor. Process until the dates and walnuts are mixed and broken into visible pieces but not homogenized into a smooth mixture.
	5 Remove the dough from the food processor and place it on a dehydrator tray lined with a nonstick sheet. Press the dough firmly into a round shape about 1-inch thick.
	6 Cut the round into 8 equal wedges. Separate them on the nonstick sheet and dehydrate at 125 degrees for 2 hours. (Don't worry; this recipe has high water content, so the scones won't become overheated in this amount of time.) Reduce the dehydrator temperature to 105 degrees and continue dehydrating for another 3 hours.

7 Turn the scones over onto a mesh-lined dehydrator tray (without the nonstick sheet) and dehydrate for another 2 to 3 hours, or until they're dry and crusty on the outside and tender and moist on the inside. Serve warm or cold and top with Coconut Butter and Raspberry-Date Jam (see the following recipes).

Coconut Butter

1 cup coconut oil, melted

½ cup coconut nectar* or agave nectar*

1 teaspoon ground turmeric

Pinch salt

1 Thoroughly mix all ingredients.

2 Pour the mixture into a small serving bowl and refrigerate to chill. Do not freeze.

Raspberry-Date Jam

1 pint fresh or frozen raspberries

1½ cups packed, pitted dates

1 Put the raspberries in a food processor and process until smooth.

2 Loosely separate the dates and add them to the raspberry mixture. Process until smooth.

3 Refrigerate the jam until you're ready to eat.

Scones (1 scone): Calories 167 (From Fat 72); Fat 8g (Saturated 1g); Cholesterol 0mg; Sodium 1mg; Carbohydrate 22g (Dietary Fiber 4g); Protein 2g.

Coconut Butter, per serving: Calories 295 (From Fat 243); Fat 27g (Saturated 24g); Cholesterol 0mg; Sodium 1mg; Carbohydrate 16g (Dietary Fiber 1g); Protein 0g.

Raspberry Jam, per serving: Calories 47 (From Fat 2); Fat 0.5g (Saturated 0g); Cholesterol 0mg; Sodium 1mg; Carbohydrate 12g (Dietary Fiber 3g); Protein 1g.

Note: Feel free to make these scones ahead of time. They keep well in the refrigerator in an airtight container for up to 1 week or in the freezer for up to 2 months. You can reheat scones in the dehydrator at 125 degrees for 1 hour before serving.

Note: Store Coconut Butter in an airtight container in the refrigerator for up to 1 month.

Note: Store Raspberry-Date Jam in a sealed glass jar in the refrigerator for up to 2 days or in the freezer for up to 4 months.

Note: Use a sharp knife to cut dates in half and then slice out the pits.

*Not raw

Buckwheat Granola

Prep time: 10 min • **Waiting time:** 40 hr • **Yield:** 12 servings

Ingredients	*Directions*
2½ cups raw buckwheat groats (1 pound)	**1** Put the buckwheat groats in a colander set inside a larger bowl and cover with 6 cups of filtered water. Soak for 8 hours and then rinse and drain. The groats will not drain fully because they become slightly *mucilaginous* (gooey) after soaking.
¼ cup raw sunflower seeds	
¼ cup raw pumpkin seeds	
¼ cup raw sesame seeds	
¼ cup raw flaxseeds	**2** Meanwhile, combine the sunflower seeds, pumpkin seeds, and sesame seeds in a quart jar and fill the jar with water. Allow the seed mixture to soak for 4 to 6 hours, and then rinse and drain.
1½ to 2 cups packed, pitted soft dates (¾ to 1 pound)	
½ cup filtered water	**3** At the same time, soak the flaxseeds in a jar with 1½ cup water for 8 hours. These seeds will make a gel, so the water will not drain away.
1 teaspoon cinnamon	
¾ cup dried currants or unsulfured raisins	**4** Loosely separate the dates and put them in a high-performance blender. Add the water and blend to form a thick, smooth paste, adding a bit more water if needed.
½ cup unsweetened shredded or shaved raw coconut	
	5 Combine the date paste, drained buckwheat groats, soaked sunflower-pumpkin-sesame seed mixture, flaxseeds in water, cinnamon, currants, and coconut in a large mixing bowl and stir well or mix with your hands.

6 Spread 2 cups of batter evenly onto a dehydrator tray lined with a nonstick sheet so that it's about ⅛ inch thick. Repeat on 2 additional trays until all the batter is used.

7 Dehydrate for 8 hours at 105 degrees; then flip the granola onto mesh dehydrator screens and continue dehydrating for an additional 24 hours until completely dry. Break apart the granola or crumble it into chunks.

Per serving (1 cup): Calories 213 (From Fat 63); Fat 7g (Saturated 1.5g); Cholesterol 0mg; Sodium 4mg; Carbohydrate 38g (Dietary Fiber 5g); Protein 5g.

Note: The granola will keep for up to 3 months if it's stored in sealed glass jars in the refrigerator.

Vary It! Add 4 cored and shredded apples to make Apple Cinnamon Granola. For Berry Granola, skip the cinnamon and add 1 pound of raw, unsulfured, dried berries.

Making Your Own Nut Milks

Nut milks are delicious to drink; they also go well with cereal, and they're a perfect base for raw sauces and ice cream. Making nut milks may sound scary, but it's incredibly easy. You simply blend soaked raw nuts with filtered water and a pitted date or two, strain out the pulp with a mesh bag (see Figure 11-1), and refrigerate. Just don't throw away the pulp! It's great for adding to cookies, burgers, and cakes.

STRAINING ALMOND MILK

Figure 11-1:
Use a mesh
bag to strain
nut milks.

1. PUREE ALL IN-GREDIENTS IN A HIGH-POWERED BLENDER.

2. POUR BATTER INTO MESH BAG AND SQUEEZE TO EXTRACT MILK.

3. AFTER THE MILK HAS DRAINED, RESERVE THE PULP!

Although you can purchase almond milk in many stores, in most cases, it's not raw and contains thickening agents. In addition, commercial almond milk doesn't taste nearly as good as fresh nut milk. By making your own nut milk, you know the quality of the ingredients and the production method, so you can rest assured that it meets your lifestyle and nutritional goals.

Vary your milk by changing nuts or adding extracts (which aren't raw) or sweeteners, such as raisins, dried figs, coconut or agave nectar, or stevia. Here's a list of our favorite nuts and seeds for milk:

- ✔ Almond
- ✔ Cashew
- ✔ Macadamia
- ✔ Hazelnut
- ✔ Hemp
- ✔ Sunflower-sesame
- ✔ Coconut (This isn't really a nut, but it makes delicious milk.)

After you get comfortable making nut milks, you may want to vary the standard recipes. For example, you can adjust the amount of water you use; add less to make a heavier, richer milk or cream. Or, instead of water, use Rejuvelac (see Chapter 10), a fermented, probiotic-rich elixir. After straining, place milk in a jar on the counter and allow it to ferment at room temp for 6 to 8 hours to create a delightfully refreshing and health-promoting drink that can also be used in smoothies.

Coconut Milk

Prep time: 5 min • **Yield:** 2 servings

Ingredients	*Directions*
2 cups dried shredded unsweetened coconut	**1** Combine coconut and water in a high-performance blender and blend for 30 to 60 seconds.
2 cups warm filtered water	
	2 Pour the mixture into a mesh bag and firmly squeeze to extract the milk. Discard the squeezed dry coconut and refrigerate the coconut milk.

Per serving (1 cup): Calories 552 (From Fat 513); Fat 57g (Saturated 51g); Cholesterol 0mg; Sodium 36mg; Carbohydrate 13g (Dietary Fiber 5g); Protein 5g.

Note: Store this milk in a sealed glass jar for up to 2 days, and use it as a replacement for water or juice in a smoothie.

Note: Total yield in this recipe may vary based on the strength of the person squeezing the mixture. That is, a strong person will remove more milk than one who doesn't squeeze as firmly.

Vary It! To make a thicker coconut milk, blend the strained milk with 1 cup of young coconut meat.

Vary It! To make a fermented coconut drink, replace the water with Rejuvelac (see recipe Chapter 10), and allow the coconut milk to sit on the kitchen counter for 8 hours to ferment.

Almond Milk

Prep time: 5 min • **Waiting time:** 8 hr • **Yield:** 2 servings

Ingredients	Directions
½ cup raw almonds	*1* Soak almonds in water for 8 hours. Rinse and drain.
1½ cups filtered water	
2 to 3 soft dates, pitted	*2* Put soaked almonds, water, dates, and vanilla extract (if using) in a high-performance blender and blend until smooth, approximately 60 seconds.
¼ teaspoon vanilla extract* (optional)	
	3 Pour the mixture in a cloth mesh bag, nut-milk bag, or a double layer of cheesecloth. Firmly squeeze the mixture to extract the milk. Reserve the pulp for other recipes.
	4 Serve at room temperature or chilled.

Per serving: Calories 60 (From Fat 23); Fat 2.5g (Saturated 0g); Cholesterol 0mg; Sodium 150mg; Carbohydrate 8g (Dietary Fiber 1g); Protein 1g.

Note: Store this milk in a sealed glass jar in the refrigerator for up to 4 days.

Note: Store leftover almond pulp in an airtight container in the freezer for up to 4 months. Use it in breads, cookies, croutons, cinnamon rolls, and scones.

Tip: Dates vary in their size and degree of sweetness. If using larger, sweeter dates such as medjools, you may wish to use 2 dates rather than 3.

*Not raw

Fixing Up Fabulous Fruit

Probably the least surprising raw breakfast option is the humble bowl of fruit. But with these recipes, your breakfast has nothing humble about it. Aside from the obvious choices of throwing fruit into a smoothie (delish), topping it with nut yogurt (heck yes), or simply enjoying it naked (the fruit, we mean), you can brighten the flavors of fruit by providing a bit of contrast to their natural flavors. Try adding herbs, spices, and juice from acidic fruits. Layer your fruit with Cashew Yogurt (Chapter 9) for guilt-free indulgence.

Choose unexpected accompaniments to spice up your fruit. If you're used to standard sweet fruit flavors, consider sprinkling on these favorites:

- ✔ Fresh mint
- ✔ Fresh basil
- ✔ Lemon juice
- ✔ Lime juice
- ✔ Citrus zest
- ✔ Himalayan crystal salt
- ✔ Nutmeg
- ✔ Fennel seed
- ✔ Cayenne pepper
- ✔ Cardamom
- ✔ Black pepper
- ✔ Fresh gingerroot

For another way to use fresh ginger and lemon juice with fruit, check out the following recipe for Mangoes in Lemon-Ginger Sauce. Divine — and definitely not boring.

Mangoes in Lemon-Ginger Sauce

Prep time: 15 min • **Yield:** 4 servings

Ingredients	*Directions*
2-inch piece fresh gingerroot, peeled	*1* Finely grate the ginger and, over a bowl, squeeze it in your palm or through a mesh bag to extract the juice. Discard the pulp.
4 dates, pitted	
2 tablespoons lemon juice	*2* Put 2 teaspoons of ginger juice in a blender with the dates, lemon juice, and a little water and blend until smooth and creamy.
Filtered water as needed	
4 fresh mangoes, peeled and cut into 1-inch chunks	
½ cup dried shredded unsweetened coconut	*3* Pour mixture into a bowl and gently toss in the diced mangoes. Garnish with the coconut and serve immediately.

Per serving: Calories 182 (From Fat 36); Fat 4g (Saturated 3g); Cholesterol 0mg; Sodium 4mg; Carbohydrate 39g (Dietary Fiber 5g); Protein 2g.

Ginger: Good for what ails you

The root of the ginger plant is the most common part used for food. You may recognize the concentrated spicy scent of ginger even if you don't recognize the gnarled root labeled as *gingerroot* or *ginger*. Ginger has been used medicinally for thousands of years. It's a terrific digestive aid. It helps minimize nausea of all kinds, including motion sickness, morning sickness related to pregnancy, and even side effects from chemotherapy. In recent studies, it's also showing promise in reducing inflammation, improving circulation, and minimizing symptoms of diabetes, including lowering blood sugar. Ginger is used to treat cold and flu-like symptoms as well. You can, of course, find ginger supplements on the market, but we recommend getting your ginger the old-fashioned way: in recipes like the ones in this chapter or in ginger tea.

To make ginger tea, follow these steps:

1. Peel a 2-inch piece of ginger. Slice into thin rounds.

2. Steep the sliced ginger in 4 cups of hot water for 5 minutes.

3. Remove the ginger slices, and enjoy your tea!

Tropical Fruit Ambrosia

Prep time: 20 min • **Yield:** 6 servings

Ingredients	*Directions*
3 papayas, peeled, seeded, and cut into 1-inch chunks	*1* Toss together the papayas, pineapple, bananas, grapes, oranges, lemon juice, mint, and coconut. Serve immediately.
½ pineapple, peeled, cored, and cut into 1-inch chunks	
3 bananas, peeled and sliced	
6 ounces grapes	
3 oranges, peeled and separated into sections, membranes removed	
1 cup orange juice	
¼ cup lemon juice	
3 mint leaves, cut into chiffonade	
½ cup young coconut meat in long, fine shreds (or substitute dried shredded coconut)	

Per serving: Calories 211 (From Fat 9); Fat 1g (Saturated 0.5g); Cholesterol 0mg; Sodium 15mg; Carbohydrate 53g (Dietary Fiber 7g); Protein 3g.

Note: Remove the membranes of the oranges to create supremes. Peel the orange, and then, using a sharp paring knife, cut along the inside of the membrane.

Note: To chiffonade mint, roll it first and then cut it as shown in Figure 11-2.

Figure 11-2: Chiffonade mint by rolling it and then slicing it to make strips.

CHIFFONADE

TO CHIFFONADE, ROLL SEVERAL MINT LEAVES TOGETHER TIGHTLY.

SLICE NARROW ⅛" STRIPS SIDEWAYS ACROSS STEMS.

THIS ACTION MAKES RIBBONS OF THE LEAVES CALLED CHIFFONADES.

Chapter 12

Appealing Appetizers

In This Chapter

▶ Whipping up dips and spreads

▶ Creating shareable small bites

Appetizers — also known in some circles as *hors d'oeuvres* — are small-portion menu items, perfect for starting a meal or party. Truth be told, we've been known to make an entire meal out of appetizers. Each of these little bites offers a different flavor and feel, and all are raw and delicious.

In this chapter, we get you going with great raw starters. We begin with a few popular items that are likely familiar to you: Pico de Gallo salsa and Guacamole. Then we move to a slightly more difficult level with other dips and spreads, culminating in the visually impressive Layered Herb Pesto and Almond Cheese Torte. The last section of this chapter takes you to a whole new world of hand-held appetizers with a sampling of international delights, including our take on spring rolls (Asian Fusion Salad Rolls) and Thai Miang Kom (Thai-Style Spinach Tacos).

Sound fancy? You bet. Complicated? Not at all. Most of these starters go from idea to table in 30 minutes or less, and none require extravagant food-prep technique.

Digging In: Tasty Dips and Spreads

Almost anything can be an appetizer, but dips and spreads are almost universally recognized as the pre-party elements of a rockin' meal. In traditional cuisine, you may have shied away from dips and spreads because they're often full of fat and empty calories, but to create this delicious fare, we use nutrient-rich nuts, fresh fruits, and vegetables.

You can enjoy these recipes with anything that suits your taste, but we recommend these delicious raw dippers (recipes in Chapter 9):

- **Sweet Pepper Sesame Chips:** Try these delicious chips with the Sweet Red Pepper and Zucchini Hummus or Herbed Almond Cheese Spread for a simply awesome treat.

- **Corn Tortillas:** Dry our take on corn tortillas until they're crispy, and enjoy them as chips with our Avocado-Pineapple Salsa or Pico de Gallo.

- **Cucumber slices, carrot and celery sticks:** A childhood lunchbox isn't complete without these all-purpose dippers. When in doubt, go with what you know. These make great dippers for hummus and guacamole.

Besides being delicious as stand-alone appetizers, many of the recipes in this section can be used to enhance salads and wraps, too.

Pico de Gallo

Prep time: 15 min • **Yield:** 3 servings

Ingredients	Directions
4 Roma tomatoes, seeded and diced **2 tablespoons chopped cilantro** **1 green onion, thinly sliced** **1 serrano or jalapeño pepper, seeded and minced** **½ teaspoon pureed garlic (about 1 clove)** **1 teaspoon salt**	*1* Combine all the ingredients in a bowl and toss gently. Lightly stir just before serving.

Per serving: Calories 43 (From Fat 5); Fat 0.5g (Saturated 0g); Cholesterol 0mg; Sodium 51mg; Carbohydrate 9g (Dietary Fiber 3g); Protein 2g.

Note: Store this dip in a sealed glass jar in the refrigerator for up to 2 days.

Vary It! Substitute red, white, or sweet yellow onion for the green onions, especially if that's what you have. Don't let a lack of desire to run to the market keep you from making this tasty dip.

Avocado-Pineapple Salsa

Prep time: 30 min • **Yield:** 3 servings

Ingredients	*Directions*
½ cup diced pineapple	**1** Put all the ingredients into a bowl and stir to mix.
2 Roma tomatoes, finely diced	
1 avocado, peeled, pitted, and cut into ¼-inch cubes	
½ cup peeled, seeded, and finely diced cucumber	
¼ cup packed chopped cilantro	
1 green onion, thinly sliced	
2 tablespoons minced red onion	
½ jalapeño pepper, seeded and minced	
1 ½ teaspoons lime juice	
½ teaspoon salt	

Per serving: Calories 115 (From Fat 63); Fat 7g (Saturated 1g); Cholesterol 0mg; Sodium 101mg; Carbohydrate 13g (Dietary Fiber 5g); Protein 2g.

Note: Store this delicious blend of sweet and spicy salsa in an airtight container in the refrigerator for up to 12 hours. The avocado can't hold its appealing green color much longer than that.

Note: If you want some guidance on preparing avocados and cucumbers, flip to Chapter 8.

Vary It! Try presenting this salsa in style by making a bowl from half of a whole pineapple. With the fronds intact, cut the pineapple in half lengthwise. Remove the pineapple flesh from half of the pineapple, creating a serving bowl, as shown in Figure 12-1. Reserve the bowl in the refrigerator until ready to use.

Tip: A single pineapple yields about 2 cups of tasty, juicy fruit. Because you only need ½ cup of diced pineapple for this recipe, if you start with a whole pineapple, we suggest that you save the rest for smoothies, dressings, or just snacking. Use the fruit within a day or two of dicing, though. If you need to keep it longer, freeze it.

Figure 12-1:
Make a bowl from a whole pineapple for added flair in presentation.

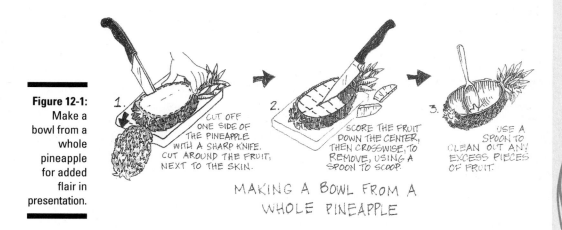

1. CUT OFF ONE SIDE OF THE PINEAPPLE WITH A SHARP KNIFE. CUT AROUND THE FRUIT, NEXT TO THE SKIN.

2. SCORE THE FRUIT DOWN THE CENTER, THEN CROSSWISE, TO REMOVE, USING A SPOON TO SCOOP.

3. USE A SPOON TO CLEAN OUT ANY EXCESS PIECES OF FRUIT.

MAKING A BOWL FROM A WHOLE PINEAPPLE

Guacamole

Prep time: 10 min • **Yield:** 3 servings

Ingredients	Directions
2 avocados, peeled and pitted	*1* Mash the avocados lightly, using a fork or potato masher. Then add the onion, lemon juice, garlic, salt, and cayenne to the mashed avocado. Stir thoroughly.
¼ cup finely minced onion	
2 tablespoons lemon juice or lime juice	
½ teaspoon crushed garlic (about 1 clove)	
¼ teaspoon salt	
Pinch of ground cayenne pepper	

Per serving: Calories 158 (From Fat 126); Fat 14g (Saturated 2g); Cholesterol 0mg; Sodium 53mg; Carbohydrate 10g (Dietary Fiber 6g); Protein 2g.

Note: This dip keeps well in the refrigerator for up to 12 hours. Place plastic wrap directly on the surface of the dip, creating an airtight seal, to keep the color bright.

Vary It! If you like spiciness, toss in a tablespoon of minced serrano pepper.

Herbed Almond Cheese Spread

Prep time: 10 min • **Yield:** 3 servings

Ingredients	*Directions*
½ cup Almond Cheese	**1** Combine all the ingredients in a medium bowl and stir well.
1 tablespoon light miso*	
1 tablespoon chopped raw pine nuts	
1 tablespoon finely minced red onion	
½ tablespoon minced fresh parsley	
1 teaspoon minced fresh dill weed	
1 teaspoon finely minced green onion	
1 teaspoon nutritional yeast* (optional)	
¼ teaspoon pureed garlic (about 1 clove)	
Pinch of ground black pepper	

Per serving (¼ cup each): Calories 153 (From Fat 117); Fat 13g (Saturated 1g); Cholesterol 0mg; Sodium 215mg; Carbohydrate 7g (Dietary Fiber 3g); Protein 6g.

Note: Store this savory spread in an airtight container in the refrigerator for up to 4 days.

Note: See Chapter 9 for the recipe for Almond Cheese. If you make it especially for this recipe, ferment it lightly so the flavors of the herbs take center stage.

Vary It! For a chili-cheese sauce for Mexican cuisine, replace the dill weed with taco seasoning or a Mexican chili powder blend and paprika. Then add a little bit of filtered water (a teaspoon at a time) to thin the spread to your desired consistency.

*Not raw

Sweet Red Pepper and Zucchini Hummus

Prep time: 10 min • **Waiting time:** 4 hr • **Yield:** 6 servings

Ingredients	*Directions*
6 tablespoons sesame seeds	*1* Soak sesame seeds in purified water for 4 hours and then rinse and drain.
1 cup packed, peeled, and chopped zucchini (about 1 fruit)	
1 cup peeled, seeded, and chopped red bell pepper	*2* Combine zucchini, bell pepper, lemon juice, olive oil, garlic, paprika, salt, cumin, and cayenne in a high-performance blender or food processor and puree until smooth.
3 tablespoons lemon juice	
3 tablespoons extra-virgin olive oil	
2 teaspoons crushed garlic (about 4 cloves)	*3* Add the soaked sesame seeds and puree until creamy. Add the tahini and blend for another minute until the tahini is thoroughly mixed in.
1 teaspoon ground paprika	
1 teaspoon salt	
¼ teaspoon ground cumin (optional)	
Pinch of ground cayenne or smoked paprika	
6 tablespoons raw tahini	

Per serving: Calories 218 (From Fat 171); Fat 19g (Saturated 3g); Cholesterol 0mg; Sodium 100mg; Carbohydrate 9g (Dietary Fiber 3g); Protein 5g.

Note: Store the hummus in a sealed glass jar in the refrigerator for up to 4 days.

Note: Figure 12-2 provides guidance on an easy way to prep bell peppers.

Tip: Spread this hummus on whole romaine leaves and make a wrap with chopped tomatoes and clover sprouts (see Chapter 7 for tips on sprouting.)

How to Core and Seed a Pepper

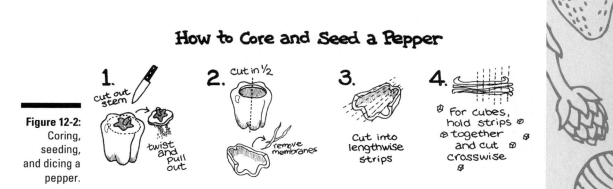

Figure 12-2:
Coring,
seeding,
and dicing a
pepper.

Layered Herb Pesto and Almond Cheese Torte

Prep time: 20 min • **Waiting time:** 1 hr • **Yield:** 6 servings

Ingredients	*Directions*
1 cup Almond Cheese **3 tablespoons light unpasteurized miso*, divided** **1 teaspoon plus 1 tablespoon nutritional yeast*, divided** **Pinch of ground nutmeg** **Pinch of salt** **3 cups chopped fresh basil** **½ cup raw pine nuts** **¼ cup chopped chives** **3 tablespoons extra-virgin olive oil** **1 tablespoon chopped fresh oregano** **1 tablespoon chopped fresh sage** **2 teaspoons pureed garlic (about 4 cloves)**	*1* Put the Almond Cheese, 1 tablespoon of the miso, 1 teaspoon of the nutritional yeast, nutmeg, and salt in a bowl and stir well to combine. Set aside. *2* Combine basil, pine nuts, chives, olive oil, oregano, sage, and garlic in a food processor and process until the pesto mixture begins to stick together but is still slightly chunky. *3* To assemble the torte, drape a 2- to 3-cup mold (you can use a small glass bowl) with damp cheesecloth. Evenly pack a third of the cheese mixture into the bottom of the mold, followed by half of the pesto. Press firmly to flatten before adding the next layer of cheese and another layer of pesto, firmly packing each layer into place. Spread the remaining cheese on top, and press firmly. *4* Fold the excess cheesecloth liner over the top and chill in the refrigerator for 1 hour. *5* To serve, fold the cheesecloth back to expose the cheese. Place the serving plate upside down on top of the torte-filled mold. Center the plate carefully. Holding the plate and the torte together, turn the plate over and remove the cheesecloth and the mold, exposing the beautiful torte, now centered on the serving plate.

Per serving: Calories 287 (From Fat 234); Fat 26g (Saturated 2.5g); Cholesterol 0mg; Sodium 323mg; Carbohydrate 11g (Dietary Fiber 5g); Protein 8g.

Note: Store the torte in the mold in an airtight container in the refrigerator for 4 to 5 days.

Note: Find the recipe for Almond Cheese in Chapter 9.

*Not raw

Sampling Small Bites

Almost every culture has some version of small bites or small plates of shareable tasty foods. In Spain, you can enjoy *tapas*. In France, ask for *canapés*. Middle Eastern cultures serve *dolmas,* which are stuffed grape leaves, and Asian cuisine has fresh and flavorful spring rolls.

Small bites can be the prelude to a meal, setting the tone and letting diners know what to expect from the other courses. But small bites can also make a nice varied meal. It's just important that small bites are packed with flavor because you only have a bite or two to enjoy each one.

The elegant Layered Herb Pesto and Almond Cheese Torte and Herbed Almond Cheese Spread are both elegant enough for any reception, and the entertaining buffet-style presentation of the Thai Miang Kom (Thai-Style Spinach Tacos) sets the mood for a night of fun.

Plates of small bites can be served sequentially to make a unique meal. Grazing has become a popular style of dining; diners sometimes enjoy eating several dishes over the course of an evening filled with playing games and chatting with friends. And one of the great benefits of entertaining with raw cuisine is that most dishes can be made in advance so you're out of the kitchen and enjoying your guests or family near mealtimes.

This section is all about the hand-held, easy-to-eat creations that make such a great start for a meal . . . or comprise a fantastic meal on their own. We've chosen our favorite raw appetizers that are both simple to prepare and visually impressive. Schedule a get-together to introduce your friends and family to the amazing flavors and textures of raw foods — one small, delicious bite at a time.

Make sure first bites are savory and packed with flavor but not too heavy on the spice, because hot and spicy starters can ruin your palate for the upcoming courses.

Asian Fusion Salad Rolls

Prep time: 20 min • **Yield:** 6 servings

Ingredients	*Directions*
6 Vietnamese dried raw, young coconut wrappers or rice wrappers	**1** Dip a wrapper in a bowl of water and put it flat on a cutting board. Place two lettuce leaves on top, with stem sides together and leaves sticking out the bottom of the wrapper.
½ head curly green leaf lettuce (like romaine or butter)	
Sweet Chili Sauce (see following recipe)	**2** Stack the remaining ingredients on top, beginning with 1 tablespoon of sauce drizzled lengthwise across the wrapper. Layer ⅙ of each remaining ingredient on top.
2 cups (½ recipe) Cashew-Sesame Tofu	
1 green onion, thinly sliced	**3** Roll up the salad roll and cut in half crosswise. Repeat until all 6 rolls are complete.
2 cups loosely packed cilantro sprigs, large stems removed	
1 cucumber, peeled and julienned	
1¼ cup shredded carrots	
6 leaves fresh mint or Thai basil, slivered	

Sweet Chili Sauce

4 cups seeded and chopped jalapeño peppers

1 cup seeded and chopped red bell pepper

½ cup coconut nectar* or agave nectar*

½ cup lemon juice

1½ tablespoons finely grated gingerroot

4 teaspoons unpasteurized tamari*

1 tablespoon onion powder

1 tablespoon dulse flakes or leaves (optional; for fishy flavor)

2 teaspoons chopped garlic (about 4 cloves)

¾ teaspoon salt

1 Blend the ingredients in a food processor or blender until smooth.

Per serving (2 rolls with sauce): Calories 274 (From Fat 81); Fat 9g (Saturated 1.5g); Cholesterol 0mg; Sodium 312mg; Carbohydrate 47g (Dietary Fiber 7g); Protein 6g.

Note: Freeze sauce in ice-cube trays. Store rolls in a sealed container in the fridge for up to a day.

Note: The recipe for Cashew-Sesame Tofu is in Chapter 9.

Note: Use 8-inch Vietnamese dried rice paper wrappers (labeled *banh trang*) to ensure raw standard.

*Not raw

Dolmas (Stuffed Grape Leaves)

Prep time: 30 min • **Waiting time:** 1 hr • **Yield:** 3 servings

Ingredients	Directions
¼ cup orange juice	*1* In a small bowl, make a marinade by combining the orange juice, ¼ cup olive oil, 1 tablespoon lemon juice, ½ teaspoon salt, nectar, and ½ teaspoon garlic. Set aside.
¼ cup plus 1 tablespoon extra-virgin olive oil	
2 tablespoons lemon juice, divided	*2* Trim the stem ends of the grape leaves and dip the leaves in the marinade so each is completely coated. Put the leaves in a glass baking dish and set aside to marinate for 30 minutes to 1 hour.
1¼ teaspoon salt, divided	
½ teaspoon coconut nectar* or agave nectar*	
1 teaspoon crushed garlic (about 2 cloves), divided	*3* Use scissors or a knife to cut the julienned zucchini into pieces the size of rice. Place the zucchini in a medium mixing bowl, sprinkle ½ teaspoon salt over the zucchini, toss it, and wait 5 minutes.
12 grape leaves from a jar of brined grape leaves*	
2 medium zucchini, finely julienned	*4* Gently squeeze out excess moisture from the zucchini using your hands. Discard the zucchini liquid or keep it to use in a salad dressing or soup.
¼ cup coarsely chopped raw pine nuts	
1½ tablespoons minced fresh parsley	*5* Combine the zucchini "rice" with the remaining 1 tablespoon olive oil, 1 tablespoon lemon juice, ¼ teaspoon salt, ½ teaspoon garlic, pine nuts, parsley, dill weed, green onion, flax oil, currants, oregano, and black pepper in a medium bowl. Toss gently to combine. (Overmixing will make the zucchini mushy.)
1½ tablespoons minced fresh dill weed	
1 tablespoon minced green onion	
1 tablespoon cold-pressed flax oil	
1 tablespoon dried currants or chopped unsulfured raisins	
½ teaspoon minced fresh oregano	
½ teaspoon ground black pepper	

6 Place a grape leaf with the stem end closest to you, stem side up, on a flat surface. Place 1 heaping tablespoon of filling inv the center and draw the two sides of the leaf over toward the center. Take hold of the edge of the leaf that is closest to you and roll it completely over the filling, tucking it under the filling slightly and pulling back gently to create a firm envelope. (Peek at Figure 12-3 to see what this technique looks like.)

7 Place the assembled dolma seam-side down in a medium glass baking dish. Continue assembling dolmas and placing them close together in the dish until all leaves are filled.

8 Serve the dolmas warmed, chilled, or at room temperature. To warm, cover the dolmas and put them in a dehydrator set at 125 degrees for 30 minutes to 2 hours, or in a warmed oven (preheated to warm and turned off) for 30 minutes.

Per serving (4 dolmas): Calories 371 (From Fat 324); Fat 36g (Saturated 4g); Cholesterol 0mg; Sodium 918mg; Carbohydrate 13g (Dietary Fiber 2g); Protein 4g.

Note: Store in an airtight container in the refrigerator for up to 2 days.

Note: Each jar of grape leaves contains about 50 leaves. To remove the tightly packed leaves from the jar, grasp them and twist gently while pulling. Drain the brine and reserve it. Separate the leaves you need, rinse them well, and place them in a cold-water bath for a few minutes. Rinse well and gently pat each leaf dry using a clean, dry towel. Place any extra leaves back in the jar with the reserved brine.

*Not raw

Figure 12-3:
Rolling a dolma is similar to rolling a burrito.

DON'T WRAP TOO TIGHTLY!

I'm stuffed!

Thai Miang Kom (Thai-Style Spinach Tacos)

Prep time: 15 min • **Waiting time:** 12 hr • **Yield:** 6 servings

Ingredients	*Directions*
36 small whole, large spinach leaves, stems removed	**1** Arrange all ingredients attractively on a platter and in small bowls.
½ cup Sweet Chili-Coconut Chips (see following recipe)	**2** Serve, allowing each person to create his own mini taco using a spinach leaf as a shell.
¼ cup Savory Cashews	
2 tablespoons finely diced gingerroot	
2 limes, peeled and finely diced	
¼ red onion, finely diced	
3 red chilies, seeded and finely diced	
1½ cups Sweet Chili Sauce	

Sweet Chili–Coconut Chips

2 cups dried unsweetened coconut flakes

½ cup Sweet Chili Sauce

1 Combine the coconut flakes and Sweet Chili Sauce in a bowl and gently mix.

2 Place mixture loosely on a dehydrator tray lined with a nonstick sheet and use a fork to separate chips on the tray. Dehydrate at 105 degrees for 12 hours or until crisp.

Per serving (6 tacos): Calories 155 (From Fat 63); Fat 7g (Saturated 3.5g); Cholesterol 0mg; Sodium 141mg; Carbohydrate 24g (Dietary Fiber 4g); Protein 4g.

Note: The instructions for Savory Cashews are in Chapter 16. The recipe for Sweet Chili Sauce appears earlier in this chapter with Asian Fusion Salad Rolls.

Note: To dice a lime, peel it and then cut off the top and bottom rind. Place one cut side down on the cutting board and cut thin rounds (about ⅛-inch thick), stack the rounds on top of each other, and cut julienne strips about ⅛-inch thick. Finally, cross-cut the strips to form small dices of roughly ⅛-inch cubes.

Vary It! Use 1½ cups large dehydrated chilies for the fresh chilies if needed. Simply seed and then soak the dehydrated chilies for 1 hour. Drain and chop the rehydrated chilies.

Tip: If you find that your coconut chips aren't drying evenly, you can stir them around a bit during the dehydrating time.

Chapter 13

Sensational Soups and Salads

Many people begin their raw food journey with soups and salads, and this fare is a mainstay of raw foodists' daily nutrition. Raw soups and salads are terrific sources of protein, calcium, fiber, antioxidants, and phytonutrients; and they're downright delicious. Plus, raw soups and salads are incredibly quick and easy to prepare, especially if you prep ingredients in advance and have them handy in your pantry and refrigerator. (Check out Chapter 18 for tips on how to plan your meals in advance and get ahead on some of the more time-consuming tasks such as soaking seeds and nuts.)

For the most part, if you have some fresh foods in the fridge and your pantry is stocked (see Chapter 5), you're likely only 20 minutes away from a soup and salad meal at all times.

Recipes that call for ingredients you need to make ahead of time are flagged with a Plan Ahead icon. Many of the salad toppings stay fresh in the refrigerator for at least four days — often longer. Just choose a salad green and a topping or two, and you're set in minutes. Add a cup of delicious raw soup, and you've created a truly satisfying meal. Most raw soups keep in an airtight glass container in the fridge for two days, but check the notes at the end of the recipes for exact times.

Oh, and you'll probably quickly see that we love citrus fruits. Many of the recipes in this chapter call for fresh juice from lemons and limes. If you need help getting the most juice with the fewest seeds, take a look at Figure 13-1 and fork over the goodness.

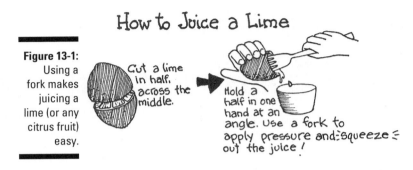

Figure 13-1:
Using a
fork makes
juicing a
lime (or any
citrus fruit)
easy.

Savoring Soups

Soups are a great part of a raw foods lifestyle. They're very comforting and — perhaps more importantly — easy and quick to prepare. Most soups don't require any dehydrating, so that saves a ton of time compared to what's involved with many other kinds of hearty raw meals.

People new to raw foods may not think about soup as an everyday menu option, but it's a standard for busy raw foodists who want easy, satisfying, and nutrient-rich foods. Of course, we aren't talking about a piping hot bowl of vegetable soup on a cold day, but raw soups aren't necessarily chilled. As long as a soup is warmer than your body temperature, it won't chill you.

An easy way to shake the nippiness from your bowl is to use warming spices, such as ginger and cayenne pepper. Or use these tricks to get your soup to a just-right temperature:

- Wash the ingredients in warm water before blending them.

- Pour your prepared soup in a sealed glass jar and submerge it in hot water until it's warm, usually about 15 minutes.

- Place your bowl of soup in a dehydrator set at 125 degrees for about a half hour to take off the chill without damaging the nutrients and enzymes.

Of course, sometimes a frosty treat is just the thing. Enjoying a chilled soup on a hot summer day can be refreshing. Check out our recipe for one of the most popular cold soups of all time, Gazpacho, in Chapter 8.

Use a high-performance blender for raw soups. It cuts through fibrous vegetables, making them smooth, and helps turn nuts into creamy, mouth-watering milks that are packed with calcium, protein, and heart-healthy fats.

Creamy Red Bell Pepper–Chipotle Soup

Prep time: 20 min • **Waiting time:** 8 hr • **Yield:** 6 servings

Ingredients	Directions
1 cup raw cashews	**1** Soak the cashews in water for 8 hours. Drain, reserving the soaking water. While cashews are soaking, cover chipotle pepper in 1 cup of warm water.
1 smoked, dried chipotle pepper	
2 cups seeded and chopped red bell pepper	**2** Put soaked cashews and 2 cups of the soaking water in a blender and blend until creamy.
1 tablespoon light miso*	
1½ teaspoons salt, plus more to taste	**3** Add soaked chipotle pepper, chopped bell peppers, miso, 1½ teaspoons salt, lemon juice, nutritional yeast, regular and smoked paprika, onion powder, garlic powder, and white pepper. Blend until silky smooth.
1 teaspoon lemon juice	
1 teaspoon nutritional yeast*	
1 teaspoon ground paprika	**4** Add the tomatoes and 2 more cups of water and blend again until smooth, about 20 seconds. Do not overblend or the mixture will become frothy. Add additional water, if needed, to achieve the desired consistency. The soup should be creamy, like sour cream, but not overly thick.
¼ teaspoon ground smoked paprika	
½ teaspoon onion powder	
¼ teaspoon garlic powder	
⅛ teaspoon ground white pepper	**5** Add salt, if needed. Top each serving with an optional dollop (roughly 1 tablespoon) of Cashew Mayonnaise.
1 cup peeled, seeded, and chopped tomatoes	
2 cups filtered water	
½ cup Cashew Mayonnaise (optional)	

Per serving (1 cup): Calories 208 (From Fat 126); Fat 14g (Saturated 2.5g); Cholesterol 0mg; Sodium 160mg; Carbohydrate 16g (Dietary Fiber 3g); Protein 7g.

Note: Check out Chapter 9 for the Cashew Mayonnaise recipe.

*Not raw

Lemony Zucchini Bisque with Shaved Fennel

Prep time: 15 min • **Yield:** 6 servings

Ingredients	Directions
5 cups peeled and chopped zucchini	*1* Put zucchini, water, olive oil, lemon juice, garlic, onion powder, nectar, garlic powder, salt, and cumin in a high-performance blender and blend until perfectly smooth.
2 cups filtered water	
½ cup extra-virgin olive oil	
⅓ cup lemon juice	*2* Serve the soup, garnishing each serving with a little shaved fennel.
¾ teaspoon crushed garlic (about 1 large clove)	
1 tablespoon onion powder	
1 tablespoon agave nectar* or coconut nectar*	
2½ teaspoons garlic powder	
2 teaspoons salt	
½ teaspoon ground cumin	
½ cup fennel bulbs, sliced paper thin	

Per serving: Calories 197 (From Fat 162); Fat 18g (Saturated 2.5g); Cholesterol 0mg; Sodium 156mg; Carbohydrate 8g (Dietary Fiber 2g); Protein 2g.

Note: This soup can be stored in an airtight container in the refrigerator for up to 2 days.

Note: This recipe offers another great opportunity to use your mandoline. Slice the fennel bulbs paper thin to enjoy the sweet flavor while retaining the delicate texture of this soup. Just remember to use your safety glove!

*Not raw

Building Sumptuous Salads

As you likely suspected when you first heard about the raw food lifestyle, raw foodists eat a lot of salads. And honestly, it never gets boring. We use a variety of greens to build the salads we recommend, which provides a wide range of nutrients as well as an adequate daily dose of protein and calcium. Plus, each kind of green offers a different flavor and texture. We love crunchy romaine and delicate butter leaf lettuce and everything in between! Take a look at these and other tasty specimens in Figure 13-2.

Greens aren't just for salads! Be sure to also use them in smoothies (such as the Green Smoothie in Chapter 8) and juices (such as To-Live-For Green Juice in Chapter 10).

Figure 13-2:
Try a new leafy green each week and see which ones you like best.

Caesar Salad

Prep time: 20 min • **Yield:** 4 servings

Ingredients	Directions
¼ cup filtered water 1 large clove garlic 1 tablespoon Sweet and Spicy Mustard or Dijon mustard* 1½ tablespoons lemon juice 2 tablespoons light unpasteurized miso* 1 tablespoon unpasteurized tamari* 1 tablespoon nutritional yeast* ½ tablespoon dulse flakes or kelp powder ¼ cup extra-virgin olive oil 2 tablespoons cold-pressed flax oil 1 large head romaine lettuce, torn or cut into pieces ¼ cup Pine Nut Parmesan Cheese ½ cup Garlic-Herb Croutons Freshly ground black pepper to taste	**1** Combine water, garlic, mustard, lemon juice, miso, tamari, nutritional yeast, and dulse in a high-performance blender and puree until creamy. While the blender is running, slowly add the oils until the mixture is emulsified. **2** Toss dressing with the lettuce and sprinkle with Pine Nut Parmesan Cheese and Garlic-Herb Croutons. Add pepper to taste and serve immediately.

Per serving: Calories 325 (From Fat 270); Fat 30g (Saturated 3g); Cholesterol 0mg; Sodium 630mg; Carbohydrate 12g (Dietary Fiber 4g); Protein 6g.

Note: The recipes for Sweet and Spicy Mustard and Garlic-Herb Croutons are in Chapter 9. Pine Nut Parmesan Cheese is a variation of the Almond Cheese recipe in Chapter 9.

Tip: If you happen to have any leftover dressing, store it in a sealed glass jar in the refrigerator for up to 4 days.

Tip: Flip to Chapter 5 for details on dulse flakes, kelp powder, and other types of sea vegetables.

*Not raw

Waldorf Salad with Dried Cranberries and Walnuts

Prep time: 15 min • **Yield:** 6 servings

Ingredients	Directions
½ cup orange juice	**1** Combine the orange juice, flax oil, mustard, orange zest, and onion powder in a large bowl and whisk to blend.
2 tablespoons cold-pressed flax oil	
1 teaspoon Dijon mustard*	**2** Add the apple, fennel, onion, and celery and toss well.
½ teaspoon orange zest	
½ teaspoon onion powder	**3** Place butter lettuce leaves attractively on a platter and heap salad on top. Garnish with walnuts and dried cranberries and serve immediately.
3 red apples, seeded and diced	
1 large fennel bulb, thinly sliced	
¼ red onion, julienned paper thin	
½ cup thinly sliced celery	
1 pound butter leaf lettuce	
½ cup raw walnuts	
¼ cup dried unsweetened cranberries	

Per serving: Calories 196 (From Fat 108); Fat 12g (Saturated 1g); Cholesterol 0mg; Sodium 52mg; Carbohydrate 22g (Dietary Fiber 6g); Protein 2g.

Tip: Use a mandoline to slice the fennel, onion, and celery for this salad.

*Not raw

Horiatiki (Greek Salad)

Prep time: 15 min • **Yield:** 4 servings

Ingredients	*Directions*
2 tablespoons extra-virgin olive oil	*1* Put the oil, lemon juice, oregano, salt, and pepper in a large bowl. Whisk to blend.
1 tablespoon lemon juice	
1 teaspoon crushed dried oregano leaves	*2* Add the remaining ingredients, except the cheese, and toss to coat.
½ teaspoon salt	
Freshly ground black pepper to taste	*3* Dot the top of each salad with cheese and serve immediately.
5 ripe Roma tomatoes (about 1 pound), cut into chunks	
1 cucumber (about ¾-pound), seeded and cut into ¼-inch half-moons	
½ cup seeded and chopped red bell pepper	
¼ red onion, julienned finely	
2 heads romaine lettuce, trimmed and cut into 1-inch pieces	
¼ cup pitted, packed Great Greek Olives	
½ cup Almond Feta Cheese, cut into ½-inch cubes	

Per serving: Calories 239 (From Fat 171); Fat 19g (Saturated 1.5g); Cholesterol 0mg; Sodium 502mg; Carbohydrate 17g (Dietary Fiber 6g); Protein 5g.

Note: This salad can be stored in an airtight container in the refrigerator for up to 24 hours, but hold the cheese until you're ready to serve so it doesn't become too soft.

Note: To crush dried herbs, use a mortar and pestle or rub the leaves between your fingers so they are partially crushed but not reduced to a fine powder. To use fresh herbs, remove the stems and mince. In general, you need three times more fresh herb than dried.

Note: We prepare Great Greek Olives later in this chapter. The recipe for Almond Feta Cheese is a variation of the Almond Cheese recipe in Chapter 9.

Salad Dressing and Toppings

If you've ever enjoyed a restaurant salad bar with friends, you know that a single bowl of mixed greens and a few dozen containers of toppings, dressings, and prepared salads results in a seemingly endless variety of possibilities. Each person goes through the same line, passing by the same ingredients, but everyone comes away with a completely different meal. That's the beauty of salad. It's so versatile!

This section is all about creating options to keep your salads interesting. We show you how to prepare delicious salad toppings to keep in your refrigerator and pantry so you can put together a nourishing meal at the spur of the moment. Who knows? Maybe you'll have a deluxe salad bar in your very own kitchen.

Although you certainly *can* put an endless number of toppings on your salad, we recommend limiting a single dish to six ingredients or fewer. This ensures that your salads don't taste the same day in and day out. So maybe you enjoy seasoned seeds on today's salad and avocados or Greek olives tomorrow.

Sweet and Spicy Dijon Dressing

Prep time: 15 min • **Yield:** 4 servings

Ingredients	Directions
¼ **cup lemon juice**	**1** In a small bowl, whisk together all ingredients.
¼ **cup extra-virgin olive oil**	
¼ **cup cold-pressed flax oil**	
2 tablespoons finely minced red onion	
2 tablespoons Sweet and Spicy Mustard	
2 teaspoons coconut nectar* or agave nectar*	
½ **teaspoon salt**	
½ **teaspoon crushed garlic (about 1 clove)**	
Pinch of ground black pepper	

Per serving (¼ cup): Calories 298 (From Fat 252); Fat 28g (Saturated 3g); Cholesterol 0mg; Sodium 130mg; Carbohydrate 12g (Dietary Fiber 1g); Protein 1g.

Note: Store this dressing in a sealed glass jar in the refrigerator for up to 4 days.

Note: Turn to Chapter 9 to find the recipe for Sweet and Spicy Mustard.

Tip: This dressing is especially delicious over spinach and bitter greens, such as arugula and kale, but it's also great as a marinade for chopped vegetable salads and slaws.

*Not raw

Pineapple Lemongrette

Prep time: 10 min • **Waiting time:** 1 hr • **Yield:** 6 servings

Ingredients	Directions
4 ounces dried, unsweetened pineapple	*1* Soak dried pineapple in warm filtered water for 1 hour. Drain, reserving the soaking water for a smoothie or other recipe.
¼ cup extra-virgin olive oil	
1 tablespoon lime juice	*2* Combine the soaked pineapple, olive oil, lime juice, Sweet and Spicy Mustard, salt, powdered mustard, black pepper, and garlic in a blender and blend.
1 teaspoon Sweet and Spicy Mustard	
½ teaspoon salt	
¼ teaspoon powdered mustard	
¼ teaspoon ground black pepper	
1 teaspoon crushed garlic (about 2 cloves)	

Per serving: Calories 95 (From Fat 90); Fat 10g (Saturated 1.5g); Cholesterol 0mg; Sodium 51mg; Carbohydrate 4g (Dietary Fiber 0g); Protein 0g.

Note: Store this salad dressing in a sealed glass jar in the refrigerator for up to 4 days.

Note: The recipe for Sweet and Spicy Mustard appears in Chapter 9.

Tip: We love this dressing over spring mix with apples. It's also great on Asian-style salads with sliced shiitake mushrooms and seasoned cashews. Actually, you can use this versatile dressing to top pretty much any kind of fruit or vegetable salad.

Vary It! If dried pineapple isn't available, substitute 1 cup fresh pineapple, adding ½ to 1 teaspoon of coconut nectar for sweetness, if needed.

Italian Herb Dressing

Prep time: 5 min • **Yield:** 6 servings

Ingredients	Directions
½ cup extra-virgin olive oil	*1* Combine all the ingredients in a blender and blend until smooth, or whisk together the ingredients by hand.
¼ cup filtered water	
3 tablespoons lemon juice	
2 teaspoons coconut nectar* or agave nectar*	
1 teaspoon dried Italian seasoning	
1 teaspoon onion powder	
½ teaspoon salt	
1 teaspoon crushed garlic (about 2 cloves)	
⅛ teaspoon powdered mustard	

Per serving: Calories 171 (From Fat 162); Fat 18g (Saturated 2.5g); Cholesterol 0mg; Sodium 264mg; Carbohydrate 3g (Dietary Fiber 0g); Protein 0g.

Note: Store this dressing in a sealed glass jar in the refrigerator for up to 4 days.

Tip: This dressing is a great addition to any Italian feast. Try marinating mushrooms caps in this for a few hours and then filling them with pesto! The dressing also works as a marinade to soften thinly sliced eggplant or zucchini so these vegetables can be used as wraps for nut-cheese fillings or layered with tomatoes, avocados, or nut cheese in a terrine-style salad. We also enjoy this dressing as a marinade for sliced mushrooms and leek salad.

*Not raw

Tahini Dressing

Prep time: 5 min • **Yield:** 7 servings

Ingredients	*Directions*
½ **cup raw tahini**	*1* Combine all the ingredients in a blender and blend until smooth.
2 tablespoons lemon juice	
2 tablespoons unpasteurized tamari*	
2 teaspoons grated fresh gingerroot	
1 tablespoon coconut nectar* or agave nectar*	
1 teaspoon crushed garlic (about 2 cloves)	
1 cup filtered water	

Per serving (¼ cup): Calories 116 (From Fat 81); Fat 9g (Saturated 1.5g); Cholesterol 0mg; Sodium 294mg; Carbohydrate 7g (Dietary Fiber 1g); Protein 4g.

Note: Store this dressing in a sealed glass jar in the refrigerator for up to 1 week.

Tip: Tahini dressing is great over a hearty cabbage salad or Asian-style slaw. We also love it over soaked wild rice or cooked grains like quinoa. It's truly wonderful over tofu*. And it makes a terrific dipping sauce for sushi or salad rolls.

*Not raw

Seasoned Seeds

Prep time: 10 min • **Waiting time:** 18–24 hr • **Yield:** 24 servings

Ingredients	*Directions*
6 cups raw pumpkin or sunflower seeds	**1** In a medium bowl, combine all the ingredients and stir to mix. Spread the seasoned seeds on four dehydrator trays lined with nonstick sheets (use a scant 2 cups per tray). Dehydrate at 105 degrees for 18 to 24 hours or until crisp.
⅓ cup unpasteurized tamari*	
1 tablespoon onion powder	
½ teaspoon garlic powder	
½ teaspoon ground cayenne pepper	

Per serving (¼ cup): Calories 197 (From Fat 153); Fat 17g (Saturated 3g); Cholesterol 0mg; Sodium 226mg; Carbohydrate 4g (Dietary Fiber 2g); Protein 11g.

Note: Store seeds in an airtight container in the refrigerator for up to 6 months.

Vary It! Season seeds with chili powder, curry powder, or even nutritional yeast flakes instead of garlic and cayenne. Or, instead of seeds, try this recipe with cashews, almonds, or pistachios.

*Not raw

Pickled Red Onions

Prep time: 45 min • **Waiting time:** 8 hr • **Yield:** 8 servings

Ingredients	Directions
1 red onion, very thinly sliced	*1* Combine all ingredients in a bowl. Put the mixture in a glass jar and allow it to sit on the kitchen counter for 8 hours before serving.
¼ cup lime juice	
¼ cup coconut nectar* or agave nectar*	
1 teaspoon salt	

Per serving (¼ cup): Calories 38 (From Fat 0); Fat 0g (Saturated 0g); Cholesterol 0mg; Sodium 50mg; Carbohydrate 10g (Dietary Fiber 1g); Protein 0g.

Note: Serve these onions at room temperature immediately after the initial 8 hours of sitting (or melding time), or you can serve them later straight from the refrigerator. They keep well in a glass jar in the refrigerator for up to 1 week.

*Not raw

Sauerkraut

Prep time: 15 min • **Waiting time:** 3–7 days • **Yield:** 12 servings

Ingredients	*Directions*
1 large head Napa cabbage (about 2 pounds or 8–9 cups shredded) 2 teaspoons salt 1 teaspoon fresh minced dill weed or fennel seed	*1* Using a knife, a fine mandoline slicing blade, or the 2-millimeter blade from a food processor, finely shred the remaining cabbage into a large bowl.
	2 Top the shredded cabbage with the salt and vigorously massage the salt into the cabbage for several minutes, until the cabbage starts to release juice. Let the cabbage rest for 10 to 15 minutes and massage it again for several minutes. Repeat as often as necessary until the cabbage is very juicy. When it's ready, you should be able to wring it out (and it should look like you're wringing out a very wet rag).
	3 Pack the massaged cabbage and dill weed firmly into a large jar or sauerkraut crock. Press the cabbage down until its liquid rises to the top and covers it by at least ⅛ inch. Put a plate on top of the shredded cabbage. Fill a glass pint jar with water and seal the glass with a firm lid to create a weight. Place the weight on top of the plate, and cover everything with a clean dish towel.
	4 Allow the kraut to ferment in a warm, dark place for at least 3 days and up to a week, depending on your desired degree of sourness and how warm your house is. The warmer your house, the faster the sauerkraut will ferment.

Per serving (¼ cup): Calories 15 (From Fat 0); Fat 0g (Saturated 0g); Cholesterol 0mg; Sodium 44mg; Carbohydrate 3g (Dietary Fiber 2g); Protein 1g.

Note: When the kraut is ready, store it in sealed glass jars in the refrigerator for up to 2 months. You'll need enough jars to hold 3 cups of finished sauerkraut.

Tip: Sauerkraut ferments more rapidly in a warm room than a cool one, so check it every day for the desired flavor and texture. Don't be alarmed when it starts to smell — usually on the second or third day of fermenting. This is normal. As the cabbage continues fermenting, the odor will change to a more acidic smell. As long as your sauerkraut doesn't develop mold on top or around the inside of the container, it's perfectly fine. If mold does develop, send your kraut to the compost heap and try again. Next time, massage the cabbage until it produces more liquid.

Vary It! Add small amounts of other root or cruciferous vegetables to your sauerkraut. Carrots, beets, and broccoli work well, or try shredded apples and gingerroot. Seasonings and herbs, such as lemon juice, garlic, chilies, or caraway seed, also provide a tasty surprise.

Great Greek Olives

Prep time: 5 min • **Waiting time:** 3–4 days • **Yield:** 16 servings

Ingredients	*Directions*
1 quart sun-dried, salt-cured olives **1½ teaspoons crushed garlic (about 3 cloves)**	*1* Separate the olives into two equal portions and place them in two 1-quart jars. Fill each jar with filtered water. Seal the jar and let the olives soak in the refrigerator for 1 day.
1 tablespoon dried oregano or Italian herb blend **¼ cup extra-virgin olive oil**	*2* After soaking the olives for 1 day, drain and rinse them and refill the jars with fresh filtered water. Add the garlic and herbs to the jars, replace the lids, and return them to the refrigerator for another 2 to 3 days.
	3 Drain the olives, rinse, and drain again — well. Toss the olives with olive oil.

Per serving (¼ cup): Calories 70 (From Fat 63); Fat 7g (Saturated 1g); Cholesterol 0mg; Sodium 247mg; Carbohydrate 3g (Dietary Fiber 1g); Protein 0g.

Note: Cover and store olives in a sealed glass jar in the refrigerator for up to 2 months.

Tip: Many people find sun-dried olives to be extremely salty and sharp in flavor. This recipe solves that problem, making them less salty while imparting a wonderful Italian flavor. These olives are delicious in salads and salad dressings or on pizza.

Vary It! Substitute 1 teaspoon of fresh rosemary and ½ teaspoon of fresh thyme for the oregano. Then add 2 tablespoons of coconut butter to olives with the olive oil. Hello, garlic butter olives!

Sun-dried olives

Olives are one of the few fruits that aren't typically consumed raw — as in fresh from the tree. Freshly picked olives are tough and contain a compound that's concentrated in their skin that makes them very bitter and unpalatable to most people. Therefore, some minor processing has to happen to make olives the delicious food that you may already know and love.

Sun-dried olives are cured in salt, usually sea salt, until they soften and mellow. Then, as the name suggests, they're sun dried, which intensifies their flavor. We suggest soaking your sun-dried olives for a couple of days with fresh herbs and garlic to add another level of flavor. Then drain and rinse them well to remove the salt before tossing in a little olive oil to coat them and increase their shelf life. Store your prepared olives in a sealed glass jar in the fridge for a month or so (if you don't eat them in a matter of days or weeks!).

Chapter 14

Sumptuous Side Dishes

A raw foods meal doesn't require side dishes and multiple courses to satisfy you, but you can have fun showing off the potential of raw culinary arts for friends and family by including these extras! Plus, you may like the familiarity of including several different menu options on a plate when first enjoying raw meals.

When eating a traditional meal, you're probably used to seeing a protein (such as a grilled chicken breast or tofu steak) as well as a starch (roasted potatoes, maybe) and a vegetable (such as steamed green beans) on your plate. Indeed, these common dishes may look healthy and appealing, but the vitality, nutrition, and energy have been prepared right out of these foods. Literally, they've been cooked to death. Fortunately, you can have both living nourishment *and* delicious meals.

If you're not ready to adopt a 100 percent raw food lifestyle, side dishes are a great way to begin introducing more raw food into your meals. Serve a raw side with a traditionally prepared entree and enjoy the burst of raw nutrition.

We include recipes for all kinds of side dishes in this chapter. Some let veggies take the starring role; others feature some of our favorite grain substitutes. So move over mashed potatoes; these raw options are too easy and energizing to ignore anymore.

Taking Veggies Beyond Salad

As you can imagine, getting your daily recommended allowance of vegetables isn't difficult when you follow a raw food lifestyle. In fact, most of what many raw foodists eat is fruits and veggies. But don't worry; you have plenty of options beyond basic salads for enjoying veggies. In this section, we offer recipes for higher-end vegetable-centered menu items that keep things raw and remarkable.

One easy way to make your transition from traditional cooking to raw is to start with familiar foods. That is, put a raw twist on the side dishes you currently make. Maybe your current fave is steamed green beans, boiled broccoli with cheese sauce, or roasted asparagus. All those dishes have a raw counterpart that's equally delicious and even more nutritious.

You don't need to be dogmatic about raw. Eating vegetables after they've been lightly blanched in hot water is better than not eating them at all. Here are some tips for making familiar veggie side dishes the nearly raw way:

1. **Cut the vegetables into bite-size pieces.**

2. **Remove woody stalks or peel away tougher outer skin on stems as necessary.** Use a peeler to trim the skin from broccoli stems or a knife to make quick work of asparagus stalks. Snap off the ends of string beans with your hands.

3. **Plunge the veggies into very hot tap water or slightly cooled boiled water for 1 to 2 minutes.** This light cooking, called *blanching,* takes away the raw taste.

4. **Drain the blanched veggies well and towel blot to dry them.**

5. **Toss the veggies with a sauce or seasoning.** Try nacho-cheese sauce (see recipe for Nacho-Cheese Kale Chips in Chapter 16), Basil Pesto (Chapter 8), or a light drizzle of flax oil and Himalayan crystal salt.

6. **Warm the dish in a dehydrator set at 125 degrees for 20 to 30 minutes to finish.**

For leafy vegetables like kale and cabbage, toss pieces in your favorite dressing and massage gently to tenderize before serving.

PLAN AHEAD

Asian Slaw

Prep time: 15 min • **Waiting time:** 5 hr • **Yield:** 4 servings

Ingredients	*Directions*
5 cups finely shredded cabbage	**1** Put the cabbage in a large bowl and toss well with the lemon juice and sesame oil. Gently massage to soften the cabbage. Allow it to sit for 5 minutes.
1½ tablespoons lemon juice	
1 tablespoon untoasted sesame oil	
½ cup Cashew Mayonnaise	**2** In a small dish, mix the mayonnaise, mustard, miso, tamari, cayenne, and toasted sesame oil. Add the dressing to the softened cabbage and toss well.
1 tablespoon Sweet and Spicy Mustard or Dijon mustard*	
1 teaspoon light miso*	**3** Chill at least 5 hours or, ideally, overnight.
1 teaspoon unpasteurized tamari*	**4** Just before serving the slaw, use scissors to cut 2 sheets of nori into ¼-inch shreds. Sprinkle the slaw with the nori pieces and sesame seeds and toss.
¼ teaspoon ground cayenne pepper	
¼ teaspoon toasted sesame oil*	
2 sheets raw nori	
¼ cup raw sesame seeds	

Per serving: Calories 253 (From Fat 171); Fat 19g (Saturated 3g); Cholesterol 0mg; Sodium 223mg; Carbohydrate 19g (Dietary Fiber 5g); Protein 6g.

Note: You can keep this slaw for up to 2 days in an airtight container in the refrigerator.

Note: The recipes for Cashew Mayonnaise and Sweet and Spicy Mustard appear in Chapter 9.

Note: Figure 14-1 shows an efficient way to slice up cabbage.

*Not raw

Preparing Cabbage for Slaw

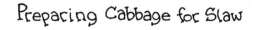

Figure 14-1:
Use a sharp
knife to
make thin
slices of
cabbage.

Cut the cabbage
in half, then
in quarters.

Remove the core
from each quarter.

Place a quarter
on a flat surface,
curved side down.
Hold with one hand
at the wedged top
and cut thin slices on the
bias with the knife in your
other hand!

Zucchini Pasta Salad

Prep time: 10 min • **Waiting time:** 40 min • **Yield:** 2 servings

Ingredients	Directions
8 cups Zucchini Pasta	**1** Put the Zucchini Pasta in a bowl and top with ½ cup of the pesto. Add the remaining ingredients except the cheese.
Sun-Dried Tomato Pesto (see following recipe)	
1 sweet ripe tomato, seeded and diced	**2** Toss the ingredients thoroughly, making sure to distribute pesto evenly. Garnish with Pine Nut Parmesan Cheese.
2 tablespoons pitted and chopped organic sun-dried black olives or raw organic olives	
2 tablespoons chopped capers	
2 tablespoons fine chopped fresh Italian flat-leaf parsley	
2 tablespoons chopped fresh basil	
½ cup Pine Nut Parmesan Cheese	

Sun-Dried Tomato Pesto

1 cup sun-dried tomatoes	**1** Soak sun-dried tomatoes in 1 quart of warm unchlorinated water for 40 minutes or until soft. Drain. Reserve water for dressings or discard.
2 tablespoons nutritional yeast*	
1 teaspoon garlic, minced	**2** Combine the soaked tomatoes with the remaining ingredients and process in a food processor to form a paste.
1 teaspoon coconut nectar* or agave nectar*	
2 fresh chilies, minced	
¼ teaspoon ground cayenne pepper	
¼ cup extra-virgin olive oil	

Pasta salad, per serving: Calories 553 (From Fat 378); Glycemic Load X (X); Fat 42g (Saturated 5g); Cholesterol 0mg; Sodium 543mg; Carbohydrate 42g (Dietary Fiber 11g); Protein 14g.

Note: Store any extra pesto in an airtight glass jar in the refrigerator for up to 1 week.

Note: You can find the recipes for Zucchini Pasta and Pine Nut Parmesan Cheese in Chapter 8.

Tip: For an Italian feast, serve this dish with Caesar Salad (Chapter 13) and Vegetable Antipasto (earlier in this chapter).

Tip: This Sun-Dried Tomato Pesto is a great spread for Onion-Caraway Seed Bread (Chapter 9). Top it with a bit of Almond Feta Cheese (Chapter 9).

Vegetable Antipasto

Prep time: 15 min • **Waiting time:** 6–8 hr **Yield:** 3 servings

Ingredients	*Directions*
½ **cup orange juice**	**1** Combine the juices, oils, Italian seasoning, onion powder, salt, garlic, and powdered mustard in a large glass bowl and stir well.
1½ **tablespoons lemon juice**	
2 tablespoons extra-virgin olive oil	
2 tablespoons cold-pressed flax oil	**2** Add the remaining ingredients and toss to mix the vegetables with the marinade.
½ **teaspoon Italian seasoning**	
½ **teaspoon onion powder**	**3** To let the flavors blend, seal the glass mixing bowl or put the vegetable mixture and the marinade into sealed glass jars and marinate in the refrigerator for 8 hours. Or put the containers of marinated vegetables in a dehydrator and warm for 6 hours at 105 degrees to help the vegetables soften and absorb the flavors of the marinade.
½ **teaspoon salt**	
½ **teaspoon crushed garlic (about 1 clove)**	
⅛ **teaspoon powdered mustard**	
¼ **pound green beans, sliced lengthwise**	
¼ **pound crimini mushrooms (about 4 large), sliced**	
½ **cup cauliflower florets**	
½ **cup broccoli florets**	
1 zucchini, cut crosswise into pieces	
½ **red bell pepper, julienned**	
¼ **leek, thinly sliced**	

Per serving: Calories 235 (From Fat 171); Fat 19g (Saturated 2g); Cholesterol 0mg; Sodium 29mg; Carbohydrate 16g (Dietary Fiber 3g); Protein 4g.

Note: Store these marinated veggies in an airtight container in the refrigerator for up to 2 days. Using a sealed glass jar ensures that your fridge doesn't take on the smells of the marinade.

Tip: Serve this versatile side dish chilled, at room temperature, or warm with the sauce on the side. It's a great addition to a raw appetizer buffet with Great Greek Olives (Chapter 13) and Sweet Red Pepper and Zucchini Hummus (Chapter 12). It's also delicious when paired with Italian dishes such as Zucchini Pasta (Chapter 8), Linguini (Chapter 15), or Spinach Manicotti (Chapter 15).

Enjoying Seeds and Grains

Since our hunting-and-gathering days, seeds and grains have been an important part of the human diet. Even before people discovered fire, they knew instinctively that seeds and grains provide essential nutrition. These powerhouse foods include essential nutrients such as protein, zinc, and magnesium.

Most grains contain gluten, which has a negative effect on some people, including those who don't consider themselves to be gluten intolerant.

Raw foodists typically eat seeds but not grains, because grains aren't easily eaten raw. Some grains can be sprouted, but most require cooking. A favorite grain substitute among raw foodists is wild rice — a seed —because it can be softened without cooking, and it provides a hearty, grain-like experience. However, wild rice requires a little preparation before using it in a recipe.

To *bloom* (soften) wild rice without cooking, put it in a gallon jar and fill the jar with unchlorinated water. Put the jar in a dehydrator set at 120 degrees for 12 to 24 hours or until the rice is soft and chewy. Then put the rice in a colander or mesh strainer, rinse well, and store in water in the refrigerator until ready to use. Soaked wild rice lasts in the refrigerator up to seven days.

The blooming process takes a day, so we recommend preparing this ingredient ahead of time and keeping it on hand so you can make the recipes in this section whenever the mood strikes. When you're ready to use your rice, just drain, rinse, drain again thoroughly, and towel dry. Presto! Ready to serve.

In this section, we describe how to make delectable rice pilaf, rice salad, corn fritters, and more. So fire up the dehydrator and start soaking some seeds!

Holiday Wild Rice Pilaf

Prep time: 20 min • **Waiting time:** 13–25 hr • **Yield:** 6 servings

Ingredients	*Directions*

Ingredients

¼ **cup wild rice (1 cup bloomed)**

3 tablespoons unsweetened dried cranberries

¼ **cup orange juice**

½ **cup shredded carrot**

½ **cup diced celery**

¼ **cup chopped raw pecans**

3 tablespoons minced fresh parsley

2 tablespoons thinly sliced green onion (about 1)

3 shiitake mushrooms, thinly sliced

1 tablespoon onion powder

1½ **teaspoons poultry seasoning***

¼ **teaspoon garlic powder**

¼ **cup extra-virgin olive oil**

1½ **teaspoons lemon juice**

1½ **tablespoons unpasteurized tamari***

1½ **teaspoons unpasteurized dark miso***

¼ **teaspoon orange zest**

Salt and pepper to taste

Directions

1 Put wild rice in a gallon jar and fill the jar with filtered water. Put the jar in a dehydrator set at 120 degrees for 12 to 24 hours or until the rice is soft and chewy. Then put the rice in a colander, rinse well, drain, rinse, and drain again thoroughly. Towel dry and transfer the rice to a large bowl.

2 While rice is blooming, soak cranberries in ¼ cup orange juice for 1 hour. Then toss the soaked cranberries along with the orange juice, carrot, celery, pecans, parsley, green onion, mushrooms, onion powder, poultry seasoning, and garlic powder with the rice. Set aside.

3 In a separate bowl, combine the olive oil, lemon juice, tamari, miso, and orange zest. Add this liquid mixture to the rice and stir thoroughly. Add salt and pepper to taste.

4 Put the pilaf in a sealed gallon jar and place it in a warm dehydrator or a warm water bath for 1 hour to enliven the flavors and take off the chill before eating.

Per serving: Calories 151 (From Fat 108); Fat 12g (Saturated 1.5g); Cholesterol 0mg; Sodium 119mg; Carbohydrate 10g (Dietary Fiber 2g); Protein 2g.

Note: Serve immediately or store in a sealed container in the refrigerator for up to 4 days.

*Not raw

Wild Rice and Corn Salad

Prep time: 20 min • **Waiting Time:** 13–25 hr • **Yield:** 6 servings

Ingredients	*Directions*
½ **cup wild rice (about 2 cups bloomed)**	*1* Put rice in a gallon jar and fill the jar with filtered water. Put the jar in a dehydrator set at 120 degrees for 12 to 24 hours or until the rice is soft and chewy. Then put the rice in a colander, rinse well, drain, rinse, and drain again thoroughly. Towel dry and transfer the rice to a large bowl.
2 cups sweet corn	
½ **cup seeded and diced tomatoes**	
½ **cup seeded and diced red bell pepper**	*2* Add all remaining ingredients to the bowl of rice, toss well, and marinate on the counter or in the dehydrator set at 105 degrees for 30 minutes to 1 hour before serving.
½ **cup seeded and diced yellow bell pepper**	
¼ **cup raw shelled pumpkin seeds**	
¼ **cup chopped fresh cilantro**	
¼ **cup finely minced red onion**	
1 green onion, thinly sliced	
2 tablespoons lemon juice	
2 tablespoons extra-virgin olive oil	
1 teaspoon minced garlic (above 2 cloves)	
1 teaspoon salt	
¼ **teaspoon ground cayenne pepper**	
1 jalapeño pepper, seeded and minced (optional)	
Ground black pepper to taste	

Per serving: *Calories 181 (From Fat 72); Glycemic Load X (X); Fat 8g (Saturated 1.5g); Cholesterol 0mg; Sodium 74mg; Carbohydrate 25g (Dietary Fiber 3g); Protein 6g.*

Note: The salad will keep for up to 3 days in a sealed container in the refrigerator.

Tip: We recommend using fresh corn or corn you've frozen yourself. Find out how to freeze your summer corn in Chapter 6. Commercially frozen corn isn't raw.

Jalapeño-Onion Corn Bread

Prep time: 10 min • **Waiting time:** 6–8 hr • **Yield:** 8 servings

Ingredients	*Directions*
4 cups fresh corn **2 cups ground raw freeze-dried corn** **2 cups raw white almond flour** **½ cup Coconut Butter** **½ cup warm filtered water** **1 tablespoon salt** **½ teaspoon ground cayenne pepper** **¼ cup minced onion** **1–2 jalapeño peppers, seeded and minced**	*1* Put fresh and ground corn, almond flour, soft Coconut Butter, warm water, and salt in a food processor and process until smooth. *2* Rinse and towel blot minced onions before adding them and the jalapeño to the food processor. Pulse briefly, just to mix. Do not puree. *3* Spread the batter about ½-inch thick on a dehydrator tray covered with a nonstick sheet. Score the batter into 4-x-4-inch squares to form 16 pieces. *4* Dehydrate at 125 degrees for 2 hours. Flip the bread and remove nonstick sheet. Reduce the temperature to 105 degrees and dehydrate for another 4 to 6 hours or until bread is pliable but easy to handle without falling apart.

Per serving (2 squares): Calories 313 (From Fat 153); Fat 17g (Saturated 2.5g); Cholesterol 0mg; Sodium 429mg; Carbohydrate 38g (Dietary Fiber 7g); Protein 10g.

Note: Serve warm with softened Coconut Butter (recipe in Chapter 11) or other favorite spread.

Note: Let the bread cool before storing it in a sealed container in the fridge for up to 1 week.

Tip: Grind freeze-dried corn with a spice grinder or a high-performance blender. Figure 14-2 shows how to prepare jalapeños and other chiles.

Seeding a Jalapeño

Figure 14-2: How to seed a jalapeño without getting burned.

Slice lengthwise... ...or in rings

Remove stem and seeds with the end of rounded table knife.

★ CAREFUL! Some say use rubber gloves or dip fingers in lemon juice and use lots of soap and water!

Hemp-Seed Tabouli

Prep time: 10 min • **Yield:** 4 servings

Ingredients	*Directions*
½ **cup hemp seeds, cracked**	*1* Put all the ingredients in a large bowl and stir well to combine.
½ **cup seeded and diced tomatoes**	
½ **cup seeded and finely diced cucumber**	
½ **cup minced fresh parsley**	
2 tablespoons extra-virgin olive oil	
2 tablespoons thinly sliced green onion	
2 tablespoons minced fresh mint leaves	
1 tablespoon lemon juice	
½ **teaspoon pureed garlic (about 1 clove)**	
½ **teaspoon salt**	
¼ **teaspoon ground black pepper**	

Per serving: Calories 239 (From Fat 189); Fat 21g (Saturated 19g); Cholesterol 0mg; Sodium 72mg; Carbohydrate 6g (Dietary Fiber 4g); Protein 11g.

Note: Store leftovers in a sealed container in the refrigerator for up to 3 days.

Vary It! Make sprouted quinoa tabouli by replacing hemp seeds with sprouted quinoa.

Tip: Serve with Dolmas (Chapter 12) and Horiatiki Salad (Chapter 13).

Corn Cakes

Prep time: 15 min • **Waiting time:** 32–52 hr • **Yield:** 4 servings

Ingredients	Directions
4½ cups fresh corn, divided	**1** Put 4 cups fresh corn in a food processor and pulse briefly to break kernels into pieces.
1 cup raw macadamia nut butter	
¾ cup ground raw freeze-dried corn	**2** Add remaining ingredients, except the remaining ½ cup corn kernels, and pulse again to blend. Do not overprocess. This mixture should be chunky — not a puree. Stir in the remaining corn.
¼ cup ground golden flax	
¼ cup minced celery	
¼ cup seeded and minced red bell pepper	**3** Put the dough between two nonstick dehydrator sheets. Using a rolling pin on top of the nonstick dehydrator sheet, roll out the dough evenly. Remove the top sheet carefully.
3 tablespoons minced onion	
½ cup almond flour	
2 tablespoons dried shiitake mushroom powder	**4** Place the rolled dough and nonstick dehydrator sheet on a tray in the dehydrator and dehydrate for 1 hour at 130 degrees. Then reduce the temperature to 115 degrees, flip the tray over, remove the nonstick sheet, and continue dehydrating for another hour.
2 tablespoons lemon juice	
1 teaspoon salt	
1 teaspoon onion powder	
1 teaspoon seeded and minced red jalapeño	**5** Cut the mixture into eight equal pieces and form each portion into small round cakes, about ½-inch thick.
1 teaspoon poultry seasoning*	
½ teaspoon smoked salt	**6** Place the cakes on a dehydrator screen (no nonstick sheet required) and dehydrate at 105 degrees for another 12 to 18 hours prior to serving (depending on desired texture).
½ teaspoon pureed garlic (about 1 clove)	
⅛ teaspoon ground white pepper	
Chimichurri Sauce (see following recipe)	**7** Serve with Chimichurri Sauce.

Chimichurri Sauce

1 cup packed fresh parsley	*1* Put the parsley, cilantro, lemon juice, cumin, garlic, crushed red pepper, and salt in a high-performance blender and blend to a coarse paste. It's the perfect texture when it has tiny pieces of crushed herbs; it should not be completely smooth.
1 cup packed fresh cilantro	
⅓ cup lemon juice	
2 teaspoons ground cumin	
2 teaspoons pureed garlic (about 4 cloves)	*2* With the blender still running, pour in the olive oil in a thin stream to thicken and emulsify the sauce.
1½–2 teaspoons dried crushed red pepper	
1 teaspoon salt	
½ cup extra-virgin olive oil	

Per serving (4 fritters): Calories 985 (From Fat 792); Glycemic Load X (X); Fat88g (Saturated 13g); Cholesterol 0mg; Sodium 783mg; Carbohydrate 51g (Dietary Fiber 15g); Protein 16g.

Note: When the desired texture is achieved, the cakes will hold in the dehydrator for up to 4 hours at 105 degrees without drying out too much. Store unused Chimichurri Sauce in a sealed glass jar in the refrigerator for up to 1 week.

Note: A spice grinder is perfect for grinding the freeze-dried corn in this recipe.

Tip: To make almond flour, soak raw almonds in unchlorinated water for 6 to 8 hours. Drain. Dehydrate at 105 degrees for12 to 24 hours, until completely dry. Grind the soaked and dehydrated almonds in a food processor or high-performance blender.

Tip: Serve this dish with Creamy Red Bell Pepper–Chipotle Soup (Chapter 13) and a green salad.

Vary It! Try these corn cakes with Tartar Sauce (Chapter 15) instead of the Chimichurri Sauce for a savory change.

*Not raw

Chapter 15

Gourmet Raw Entrees

In This Chapter

▶ Trying raw versions of traditional dinnertime favorites

▶ Using veggie noodles for easy and elegant meals

Recipes in This Chapter

↻ Soy-Ginger-Glazed Cashew-Sesame Tofu

↻ Beefy Barbeque Sandwich

↻ Barbeque Sauce

↻ Better-Than-Eggs Salad Sandwich

↻ Not-Salmon Pâté Tomato Sliders

↻ Green Burrito

↻ Vegan Bay Crab Cakes

↻ Creamy Dill Tartar Sauce

↻ Vegetable Enchiladas

↻ Chili Colorado Sauce

↻ Linguini with White Truffle Cream

↻ Spinach Manicotti

↻ Béchamel Sauce

↻ Root-Vegetable Ravioli with Basil Pesto on Tomato Concassé

*E*ating is one of the quintessential activities of daily life. You must have food several times a day to maintain a healthy body and a sharp mind. But mealtime is often a social time as well — not just a requirement for survival. An evening meal may be the only time of the day you sit down to talk with your family or partner, so why not make it special?

In this chapter we show you how to make hearty gourmet main dish fare for special events and gatherings. Think barbecue sandwiches, burritos, vegan crab cakes, veggie kabobs, sliders, and enchiladas as well as raw fruit and vegetable pastas to mimic familiar favorites such as manicotti and ravioli.

Many of these dishes take a fair amount of time to prepare; they're not your everyday raw meals. These are special dishes for festive meals or for the home cook who loves to spend time in the kitchen. Raw food meals can be as simple as salad or as complex as the most extravagant cooked spread.

Take a look at Chapter 6 to get the skinny on finding raw recipe components that may not be familiar. Chapter 7 offers help with prepping techniques that make a raw lifestyle so much more fun.

Making "Meaty" Main Dishes

Meat is the superstar of many traditional meals, so unless you're already a vegetarian or vegan, you may feel like the raw food lifestyle is just too much sacrifice of flavor and textures. Maybe you worry you'll miss your cheesy enchiladas or barbecued beef. And how can you live without your favorite deli sandwich or burger?

We encourage you to try the raw versions of some of your favorite foods. You may be surprised at how satisfying it can be. Here are some of the mouth-watering menu items you can find out how to prepare in this section:

- **Soy-Ginger-Glazed Cashew-Sesame Tofu:** The cashew tofu recipe in Chapter 9 gets a main-dish makeover with a delicious soy ginger glaze.

- **Better-Than-Eggs Salad Sandwich:** This dish may become your new go-to to-go lunch. Enjoy it with crackers, on a sandwich (as it is in our recipe), or even as a dip for veggies.

- **Beefy Barbeque Sandwich:** Always a surprise to new raw food cooks, this *beefy* sandwich is made with pulp from a variety of fresh vegetables. See how to make your own barbeque sauce as well and then customize it — make it just as sweet or hot as you like — to delight your taste buds.

- **Green Burrito:** This delicious entrée gets its name from its distinctive wrapper. Instead of a traditional tortilla, use a large collard leaf. Surprised? Trust us, you won't miss the flour at all.

- **Vegan Bay Crab Cakes with Creamy Dill Tartar Sauce:** These not-so-crabby patties are delicious in their own right. Plus you get the added bonus of finding out how to make garlic mayonnaise and dill tartar sauce. Cha-ching!

- **Vegetable Enchiladas with Chili Colorado Sauce:** Mushrooms and cabbage make a delicious filling for these zesty, Mexican-inspired enchiladas. Make your own easy enchilada sauce, the raw way.

Soy-Ginger-Glazed Cashew-Sesame Tofu

Prep time: 10 min • **Waiting time:** 9–10 hr • **Yield:** 6 servings

Ingredients	*Directions*
¼ cup unpasteurized tamari* ¼ cup sesame oil	**1** Combine all ingredients except tofu in a high-performance blender and blend until smooth.
2 tablespoons coconut palm sugar* or evaporated cane sugar* 1½ tablespoons lemon juice	**2** Place the mixture in an uncovered glass jar in the dehydrator at 105 degrees and dehydrate overnight, or at least 8 hours, to thicken and intensify the flavor.
1 tablespoon onion powder 2 teaspoons grated fresh ginger ¼ teaspoon toasted sesame oil* ¼ teaspoon ground black pepper 1½ teaspoons pureed garlic (about 3 cloves) 2 quarts Cashew-Sesame Tofu (full recipe yield)	**3** Cut firm tofu into cubes or 6 slabs. Coat with the glaze on all sides and place on a nonstick sheet in the dehydrator set at 125 degrees for 1 to 2 hours to warm and intensify the flavor.

Per serving: Calories 316 (From Fat 234); Fat 26g (Saturated 4g); Cholesterol 0mg; Sodium 777mg; Carbohydrate 17g (Dietary Fiber 2g); Protein 8g.

Note: The recipe for Cashew-Sesame Tofu is in Chapter 9. Make the tofu at least 3 hours in advance and put it in the fridge to chill and become firm. Feel free to make the tofu further ahead if needed; it will last in a sealed container in the fridge for up to 4 days. The Soy Ginger Glaze has a much longer life span. It keeps well in a sealed glass jar for up to 2 weeks or frozen for 2 months.

Tip: To serve, place a serving of Massaged Kale (Chapter 8) in the middle of the plate. Top with a serving of glazed tofu and drizzle a little of the Soy Ginger Glaze around the plate. Repeat with remaining servings to create an Asian-inspired feast.

*Not raw

Beefy Barbeque Sandwich

Prep time: 30 min • **Waiting time:** 2–3 hr • **Yield:** 3 servings

Ingredients

6 cups chopped root vegetables of choice

½ cup sun-dried tomato powder

½ cup extra-virgin olive oil

½ cup ground flax

3 teaspoons pureed garlic (about 6 cloves)

2 tablespoons unpasteurized dark miso paste*

4 teaspoons onion powder

3 teaspoons garlic powder

2 teaspoons ground fennel seed

2 teaspoons Italian seasoning

2 teaspoons dried basil

1 teaspoon dried sage

½ teaspoon dried oregano

½ teaspoon ground black pepper

1½ cups Barbeque Sauce (see following recipe)

6 slices Onion–Caraway Seed Bread

2 tomatoes, sliced

1½ cup finely shredded cabbage

½ sweet onion, thinly sliced

Directions

1 Put the root vegetables through a juicer to extract the juice. Only the pulp is used for this recipe, so set the juice aside to drink.

2 In a food processor, combine vegetable pulp from Step 1 with sun-dried tomato powder, olive oil, ground flax, garlic, miso paste, onion powder, garlic powder, fennel seed, Italian seasoning, basil, sage, oregano, and pepper. Pulse to mix. Do not overprocess.

3 Spread the mixture on two nonstick dehydrator sheets, about ½ inch deep, and dehydrate for 2 to 3 hours.

4 To assemble sandwiches, mix 1½ cups of Barbeque Sauce with the "meat" mixture and divide it among 3 pieces of bread. Top it with the cabbage, tomato, and onion, and place another piece of bread on top.

Barbeque Sauce

¼ **cup sun-dried tomatoes**

1 chipotle pepper, seeded (or substitute 2 teaspoons dry flakes)

¼ **cup tamarind paste**

¼ **cup unpasteurized tamari***

2 tablespoons extra-virgin olive oil

1 teaspoon toasted sesame oil*

1 tablespoon unpasteurized dark miso*

2 tablespoons coconut nectar* or agave nectar* (or more as needed to taste)

2 teaspoons onion powder

1 teaspoon salt

1 teaspoon ground black pepper

1 teaspoon pureed garlic (about 2 cloves)

1 tablespoon coconut palm sugar* or evaporated cane sugar*

1 tablespoon gingerroot, grated or juice

1 teaspoon Sweet and Spicy Mustard or prepared Dijon mustard*

1 Soak sun-dried tomatoes in ¾ cup filtered water for 2 hours and, in a separate bowl, the chipotle pepper in ½ cup of filtered water for 2 hours. Reserve the soaking water to use as needed.

2 Process all the ingredients together in a high-performance blender to achieve a smooth consistency. Use the soaking water from either the sun-dried tomatoes or chipotle to thin the sauce as desired.

Per serving (1 sandwich): Calories 2,151 (From Fat 1,287); Fat 143g (Saturated 15g); Cholesterol 0mg; Sodium 6,951mg; Carbohydrate 205g (Dietary Fiber 50g); Protein 54g.

Note: Store the "meat" mixture in an airtight container in the fridge for up to 3 days. Store the Barbeque Sauce in the refrigerator in a glass jar for up to 5 days.

Note: You can find the recipe for Sweet and Spicy Mustard in Chapter 9.

Tip: For best results, use any combination of three different root vegetables.

Note: To make ginger juice, grate fresh gingerroot and then use your hand to squeeze out the liquid.

Vary It! This "meat" is a great filling for tacos, lasagna, ravioli, and cannelloni. You can use it as a layer in raw shepherd's pie or form it into burger patties.

*Not raw

Better-Than-Eggs Salad Sandwich

Prep time: 20 min • **Yield:** 8 servings

Ingredients	*Directions*
1 cup finely diced young coconut meat	**1** Combine the coconut, avocado, corn, bell pepper, celery, diced onion, parsley, and mayonnaise and stir well.
1 avocado, peeled, pitted, and diced	
1 cup fresh sweet corn	**2** To assemble sandwiches, spread ½ cup of the filling on a slice of bread and top with lettuce, tomato, and sprouts. Cover with another slice of bread and enjoy!
½ cup seeded and chopped bell pepper	
¼ cup finely diced celery	
2 tablespoons finely diced red onion plus ½ red onion in thinly sliced rings	
2 tablespoons minced parsley	
½ cup Cashew Mayonnaise	
16 slices Onion–Caraway Seed Bread	
8 leaves of lettuce	
4 tomatoes, sliced	
6–8 cups clover or broccoli sprouts	

Per serving (1 sandwich): Calories 535 (From Fat 351); Fat 39g (Saturated 4g); Cholesterol 0mg; Sodium 540mg; Carbohydrate 41g (Dietary Fiber 15g); Protein 18g.

Note: Store Better-Than-Eggs Salad in a sealed glass or plastic container in the refrigerator for up to 48 hours. Don't assemble the sandwiches until you're ready to eat, or they'll get soggy.

Note: The recipes for Cashew Mayonnaise and Onion–Caraway Seed Bread are in Chapter 9.

Vary It! You can use Corn Tortillas (recipe in Chapter 9) instead of the Onion–Caraway Seed Bread. Spread the Better-Than-Eggs Salad on the wrap; top with lettuce, tomato, and sprouts; roll it up; and enjoy! Also try Better-Than-Eggs Salad as a spread on Sweet Pepper Sesame Chips (Chapter 9).

Not-Salmon Pâté Tomato Sliders

Prep time: 25 min • **Waiting time:** 8 hr • **Yield:** 6 servings

Ingredients	Directions
½ cup raw almonds	**1** Soak the almonds in water for 8 hours. Meanwhile, in a separate bowl, soak the sunflower seeds in water for 4 to 6 hours. Drain.
½ cup raw sunflower seeds	
2 tablespoons flax oil	
½ cup carrot pulp	**2** Put the soaked almonds and sunflower seeds in a food processor with the flax oil, carrot pulp, lemon juice, paprika, and both kinds of salt. Blend until smooth and creamy, adding a few drops of water, if needed, to blend well.
4 tablespoons lemon juice	
⅜ teaspoon smoked paprika*	
½ teaspoon salt	
Pinch of smoked salt*	**3** Add the celery, onion, parsley, dulse flakes, and dill weed and pulse to mix. Do not overprocess; the mixture should be slightly chunky with bits of vegetables visible.
4 tablespoons minced celery	
4 tablespoons minced red onion	
4 tablespoons minced parsley	**4** To assemble a slider, place one slice of tomato on a plate and spread about a ¼ cup of pâté on it. Place another slice of tomato on top and spread another ¼ cup of pâté on it. Top with sprouts and garnish the plate with a generous spoonful of Creamy Dill Tartar Sauce for dipping. Continue assembling, using the remaining ingredients.
1 teaspoon dulse flakes	
½ teaspoon dried dill weed or 1½ teaspoons fresh dill	
3 large ripe tomatoes, in ¼-inch-thick slices	
2 cups alfalfa sprouts	
½ cup Creamy Dill Tartar Sauce	

Per serving (1 slider): Calories 217 (From Fat 162); Fat 18g (Saturated 1.5g); Cholesterol 0mg; Sodium 106mg; Carbohydrate 11g (Dietary Fiber 4g); Protein 7g.

Note: Store pâté in an airtight container in the refrigerator for up to 5 days.

Note: Find Creamy Dill Tartar Sauce recipe earlier in this chapter with Vegan Bay Crab Cakes.

Tip: Plate like a pro! Spoon 2 to 3 tablespoons of the tartar sauce on the plate where the slider will sit. Using the spoon, make an impression for the slider and push the sauce outward so it extends slightly outside the perimeter of the slider so the sauce is visible when the slider is placed on top.

Green Burrito

Prep time: 20 min • **Waiting time:** 5–6 hr   **Yield:** 4 servings

Ingredients

1 cup raw sunflower seeds

1 medium carrot, chopped

¼ small beet, peeled and chopped

1 cup filtered water

2 tablespoons chopped red onion

2 tablespoons extra-virgin olive oil

2 tablespoons Sweet Almond Butter

1 tablespoon unpasteurized dark miso*

1 tablespoon lemon juice

½ teaspoon taco seasoning or chili powder

¼ teaspoon ground cumin

¼ teaspoon salt

½ teaspoon pureed garlic (about 1 clove)

4 cups (6 ounces) sliced romaine lettuce

½ cup seeded and julienned red bell pepper

½ cup pitted and chopped Greek or raw olives

4 large collard leaves, large stem shaved off

½ cup Pico de Gallo

½ cup Guacamole

¼ cup Cashew Sour Cream

Directions

1 Soak sunflower seeds for 2 hours, and then rinse and drain them.

2 Combine carrot, beet, and 1 cup water in a high-performance blender and blend until smooth. You may need to stop and scrape the mixture down a few times to puree it thoroughly. Add the soaked sunflower seeds, onion, olive oil, Almond Butter, miso, lemon juice, taco seasoning, cumin, salt, and garlic. Process until the mixture is a smooth paste similar to pureed refried beans.

3 Spread about one-quarter of the paste on a dehydrator tray lined with a nonstick sheet. Repeat with three more dehydrator sheets, and dehydrate at 125 degrees for 3 to 4 hours. Use a metal scraper to lift the mixture off the dehydrator tray. It should be brown on top and slightly pink underneath. Lightly stir.

4 In a medium bowl, mix lettuce, bell peppers, and olives.

5 To assemble a burrito, place 1 cup of the lettuce mixture in the center of a collard leaf. Add 2 tablespoons Pico de Gallo, 2 tablespoons Guacamole, and 2 to 3 tablespoons of the "bean" mixture. Top with 1 tablespoon Cashew Sour Cream and roll up, burrito style. Repeat with remaining collard leaves and filling.

Per serving (1 burrito): *Calories 512 (From Fat 396); Fat 44g (Saturated 4g); Cholesterol 0mg; Sodium 705mg; Carbohydrate 25g (Dietary Fiber 10g); Protein 14g.*

Note: Leftover "bean" mixture will keep in a sealed container in the refrigerator for up to 1 week.

Note: Recipes for Pico de Gallo and Guacamole are in Chapter 12, and Sweet Almond Butter and Cashew Sour Cream are in Chapter 9.

Tip: See how to make collard leaves easier to roll by shaving the stem as shown in Figure 15-1.

*Not raw

Figure 15-1:
Trim the stem on greens to make the leaf more pliable and easier to use as a wrap.

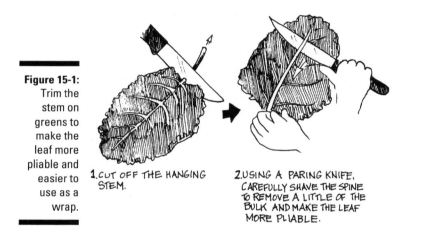

1. CUT OFF THE HANGING STEM.

2. USING A PARING KNIFE, CAREFULLY SHAVE THE SPINE TO REMOVE A LITTLE OF THE BULK AND MAKE THE LEAF MORE PLIABLE.

Talking about tamarind

The pulp of the tamarind fruit is prized for its sweetly sour flavor, and it's used extensively in cuisine throughout the world, especially Southeast Asia, Mexico, India, the Caribbean, and Africa. The fruit is the star of preserves, jams, and chutneys, and it's a popular ingredient in rice, curries, and even soft drinks and candy. The leaves can flavor teas and soups. We love it in sauces and salad dressings, too. Plus, tamarind has many health benefits. Long prized as a digestive aid, tamarind's sour taste comes from tartaric acid, which acts as a powerful antioxidant. Tamarind has also been noted as a relief for nausea, helps in liver function, and acts as a laxative. If you're not lucky enough to find fresh tamarind in your local market, don't worry; most Asian markets and some Latin American markets carry tamarind paste.

Vegan Bay Crab Cakes

Prep time: 60 min • **Waiting time:** 4–5 hr • **Yield:** 3 servings

Ingredients	*Directions*
2 zucchinis	**1** Peel the zucchini and finely julienne it using a spiral slicer or grater. Cut into pieces about ½-inch long. Using a clean towel, pat dry.
¾ cup raw almond flour (or 1 cup peeled and finely ground almonds)	
⅜ cup finely minced onion	**2** Combine the zucchini and almond flour in a large bowl. Toss to coat. Set aside.
¼ cup seeded and finely diced red bell pepper	**3** Combine onion, bell pepper, and celery in a small bowl and toss. Add the vegetables to the zucchini mixture. Add nutritional yeast and kelp powder and toss again lightly to mix. (Handle the mixture gently so it doesn't become wet.) Set aside.
¼ cup finely minced celery	
2 tablespoons nutritional yeast*	
2 teaspoons kelp powder	
½ cup finely ground macadamia nuts	**4** Combine macadamia nuts, lemon juice, salt, and garlic in a high-performance blender or food processor and process until smooth to make garlic mayonnaise. Carefully fold mayonnaise into the vegetable mixture. Handle the mixture gently so it doesn't pack together.
3 tablespoons lemon juice	
¾ teaspoon salt	
½ teaspoon pureed garlic (above 1 clove)	**5** Form the mixture into 6 cakes, each about ¾-inch thick.
1½ cups Creamy Dill Tartar Sauce (see following recipe)	**6** Place the cakes on a mesh dehydrator sheet with the smooth side facing up, and put into the dehydrator at 135 degrees for 2 hours; then reduce the temperature to 105 degrees and continue dehydrating for another 2 to 3 hours.
	7 Dollop 2 tablespoons of Creamy Dill Tartar Sauce on each cake and serve them warm.

Creamy Dill Tartar Sauce

¼ **cup raw cashews**

¼ **cup raw pine nuts**

¼ **cup lemon juice**

1½ **tablespoons coconut nectar* or agave nectar***

½ **teaspoon salt**

3 **tablespoons filtered water, as needed to thin**

3 **tablespoons minced fresh dill weed**

¼ **cup capers, drained**

¼ **cup celery, minced**

2½ **tablespoons fresh or jarred horseradish**

1½ **tablespoons minced red onion**

1 Soak cashews and pine nuts separately for 2 hours. Drain and rinse.

2 Place soaked cashews and pine nuts, lemon juice, coconut nectar, and salt in a high-performance blender and add just enough water to form a thick, smooth consistency. The mixture should be creamy with a satiny appearance.

3 Add dill, capers, celery, horseradish, and onion. Pulse just enough to mix without blending smooth. The final mixture should be slightly chunky with bits of dill, celery, onions, and capers visible.

Per serving (2 cakes): Calories 518 (From Fat 504); Fat 45g (Saturated 5g); Cholesterol 0mg; Sodium 241mg; Carbohydrate 23g (Dietary Fiber 10g); Protein 16g.

Note: The crabless cakes stay delicious for 2 days if stored in the fridge in a sealed container. Store the sauce in a sealed glass jar in the fridge for up to 1 week or freeze for up to 3 months.

Note: You may be wondering if this is a raw recipe if you're dehydrating at 135 degrees. In this particular circumstance, the high moisture content of the cakes cools the patties as they dehydrate, so they don't get hot enough to destroy the nutrients and enzymes. You're clear!

Tip: Add your favorite green salad to make this a meal. Alternately, you can top 2 cups of mixed greens with the crabless cakes and slightly thin the tartar sauce to resemble a salad dressing for your own quick and easy not-so-seafood salad. You can up the sour notes by adding more lemon or throw in additional agave nectar to sweeten the dish.

*Not raw

Vegetable Enchiladas

Prep time: 30 min • **Waiting time:** 2–5 hr • **Yield:** 4 servings

Ingredients	*Directions*
2 tablespoons orange juice	*1* Combine orange juice, olive oil, lime juice, garlic, salt, cumin, and chili powder in a large bowl and stir to make a marinade.
1 tablespoon extra-virgin olive oil	
1 teaspoon lime juice	
½ teaspoon crushed garlic (about 1 clove)	*2* Add cabbage, mushrooms, onion, corn, and bell pepper to the marinade and allow the mixture to sit for 1 to 3 hours, covered. (Or, if time is limited, put the filling in a jar and dehydrate at 115 degrees for 30 minutes.)
½ teaspoon salt	
¼ teaspoon ground cumin	
¼ teaspoon Mexican chili powder blend	*3* Drain the marinated vegetables, gently squeezing excess moisture from the filling. Reserve the marinade for use in dressings and soups.
⅛ head cabbage, very finely shredded (1 cup)	
6 crimini mushrooms, diced (1 cup)	*4* Mix half of the Chili Colorado Sauce and avocado with the marinated vegetables.
1 tablespoon diced red onion	*5* Brush each Corn Tortilla with approximately 1 tablespoon of the Chili Colorado Sauce. Spoon ¼ cup of the marinated vegetables along the middle of each tortilla; roll and place them seam-side down on a dehydrator tray lined with a nonstick sheet.
½ cup fresh corn	
½ red bell pepper, seeded and diced (about ½ cup)	
¾ cup Chili Colorado Sauce (see following recipe)	*6* Brush additional sauce over the top of the 4 enchiladas. Place enchiladas in a dehydrator at 115 degrees for 1 to 2 hours before serving.
½ avocado, peeled, pitted, and diced	
4 Corn Tortillas	

Chili Colorado Sauce

2 dried red California (or Anaheim) chilies

1 red bell pepper, seeded and chopped (1 cup)

½ tablespoon coconut palm sugar* or evaporated cane sugar*

1 teaspoon onion powder

1 teaspoon Mexican chili powder blend

½ teaspoon garlic powder

½ teaspoon salt

⅛ teaspoon ground cumin

⅛ teaspoon dried oregano

⅛ teaspoon ground black pepper

1 tablespoon extra-virgin olive oil

1 In a medium bowl, break the dried chilies into pieces, remove the stems and seeds, and pour water over the top. Set aside for 30 minutes. Drain and discard the seeds and water.

2 Place the chilies in a high-performance blender with the bell pepper, sugar, onion powder, chili powder, garlic powder, salt, cumin, oregano, and pepper, and blend until completely smooth.

3 Add the olive oil in a thin stream while the blender is running until the mixture is emulsified.

Per serving (1 enchilada): Calories 256 (From Fat 117); Fat 13g (Saturated 2g); Cholesterol 0mg; Sodium 235mg; Carbohydrate 35g (Dietary Fiber 7g); Protein 6g.

Tip: The enchiladas are best served immediately, warm from the dehydrator. However, you can make the filling a day ahead and assemble the enchiladas when ready to serve. Store leftovers covered in the fridge for up to 3 days.

Note: Turn to Chapter 9 to find a recipe for Corn Tortillas.

Note: Dried California, or Anaheim, chilies can be hot or mild, so taste-test them before using the recommended quantity.

Note: Chili powder blend is a mixture of chile peppers and other spices, including cumin, oregano, garlic powder, and salt. The chilies are usually either red chile peppers or cayenne peppers, but other types of hot peppers may be used, including ancho, jalapeño, New Mexico, and pasilla chilies. As a result, the spiciness of any given chili powder varies. Taste your sauce to determine if it needs a little more kick for your taste. And be certain to buy a non-processed spice that's free of fillers such as sulfur dioxide.

*Not raw

Noshing on Fruit and Vegetable Noodles

Noodles are a part of many different cuisines around the world, and they take the starring role in some. I mean, how many entrees on a traditional Italian dinner menu don't include a noodle?

When most people think of noodles, they envision a chewy form of pasta made from a grain — such as semolina (from durum wheat), as in Italian pasta — or processed from rice and buckwheat in Asian cuisines. But unfortunately, to make traditional pasta dough, the grain or rice is processed and refined in a way that removes many of the nutritional components.

Another issue is that most pastas contain *gluten,* a protein found in wheat, barley, rye, spelt, and kamut. Gluten, a staple of the American diet, hides in pizza, pasta, bread, wraps, rolls, and most processed foods and can cause serious health problems. One of the great benefits of a raw plant-based diet is that, in most cases, it's free of gluten as well as dairy and soy. Check out Chapter 3 for more information about the health consequences of gluten.

Thanks to the modern age in which we live, a variety of kitchen tools are available to create "noodles" from fruits and veggies that are sturdy enough to handle any sauce or raw food preparation technique. And because the nutritional benefits of the food remain intact, you get all the vitamins, minerals, fiber, and vitality of your foods, without the gluten!

In this section, find out how to make these satisfying noodles:

- ✔ **Zucchini noodles:** Find out how to make this raw staple in Chapter 8 and then use the noodles in several recipes in this chapter. A spiral slicer makes it easy to get long, skinny noodles, and a mandoline helps you create long, wide noodles.

- ✔ **Raw-violi wrappers:** Use a mandoline to make very thin slices of root vegetables, and then fill them as you would ravioli. In this chapter we fill them with pesto. Yum.

After you get started with vegetable noodles, be on the lookout for new sauces and ingredients to toss with them. The options are truly limitless.

Linguini with White Truffle Cream

Prep time: 30 min • **Waiting time:** 2 hr • **Yield:** 3 servings

Ingredients

¼ **cup raw pine nuts**

¼ **cup raw cashews**

½ **ounce dried porcini mushrooms**

2½ **cups filtered water**

4 medium zucchinis (1 pound)

1 teaspoon salt

1 tablespoon lemon juice

½ **tablespoon unpasteurized tamari***

½ **tablespoon coconut nectar* or agave nectar***

2 teaspoons white truffle oil

Pinch of ground white pepper

½ **cup seeded and finely julienned Roma tomatoes**

¼ **cup finely julienned red onion**

¼ **cup seeded and finely julienned yellow bell pepper**

2 tablespoons capers

1 tablespoon dulse flakes

½ **teaspoon kelp powder**

½ **tablespoon fresh dill weed**

1 tablespoon fresh parsley

Pinch ground black pepper

Directions

1 Combine the pine nuts and cashews in a bowl and soak in 1 cup of water for 2 hours. Rinse and drain. While the nuts are soaking, combine the dried mushrooms with ½ cup to soften for 1 hour. Then drain the mushrooms, reserving the water for use in the sauce. Dice the mushrooms and set aside.

2 Cut zucchini into noodles, place in a bowl, and toss well with the salt. Set aside.

3 Combine the soaked pine nuts and cashews, lemon juice, tamari, coconut nectar, truffle oil, and white pepper in a high-performance blender, adding a small amount of the mushroom soak water as needed to make a very thick, creamy sauce.

4 Drain the zucchini noodles thoroughly and pat dry. Toss them gently with tomatoes, onion, bell pepper, capers, dulse flakes, kelp powder, and dill. Add the truffle cream sauce and toss again gently. Garnish with minced parsley and black pepper.

Per serving: Calories 225 (From Fat 153); Fat 17g (Saturated 1.5g); Cholesterol 0mg; Sodium 542mg; Carbohydrate 17g (Dietary Fiber 3g); Protein 7g.

*Not raw

Spinach Manicotti

Prep time: 30 min • **Waiting time:** 30 min • **Yield:** 6 servings

Ingredients	*Directions*
2 large zucchinis	*1* Using a mandoline, shave the zucchini length-wise, creating long, wide strips. Cut the strips into pieces 3 inches long by 2 inches wide. You need at least 12 perfect wrappers. Lay them in a single layer on a clean towel and allow them to air dry while preparing the remaining components.
6 cups chopped spinach	
1 cup Almond Cheese	
2 tablespoons minced and rinsed red onion	
1 tablespoon extra-virgin olive oil	*2* Place spinach, Almond Cheese, onion, olive oil, garlic, onion powder, salt, and white pepper in a bowl and mix until all the cheese and spinach are integrated with the seasonings.
1 teaspoon pureed garlic (about 2 cloves)	
½ teaspoon onion powder	
½ teaspoon salt	*3* To assemble the manicotti, lay down one slice of zucchini in a glass baking dish that fits into your dehydrator and spread 2 to 3 tablespoons of the filling in the center of the zucchini, in a horizontal line, from one end to the other. At one end, begin rolling the zucchini strip over the filing and continue until the seam is down. Repeat until all the manicotti are snuggling together without overlapping.
Pinch of ground white pepper	
1 cup Béchamel Sauce (see the following recipe)	
¼ cup Pine Nut Parmesan Cheese or ground walnuts	
2 tablespoons minced fresh parsley	*4* Place the baking dish in a dehydrator set at 125 degrees for 30 minutes to warm.
	5 Spoon warm Béchamel Sauce over the manicotti and top with a sprinkle of Pine Nut Parmesan Cheese and parsley.

Béchamel Sauce

1 cup raw cashews

1 cup filtered water

2 teaspoons nutritional yeast*

4 teaspoons unpasteurized light miso*

1 teaspoon onion powder

1 teaspoon lemon juice

¼ teaspoon garlic powder

¼ teaspoon ground nutmeg

¼ teaspoon ground white pepper

¼ teaspoon salt

1 Put all the ingredients in a high-performance blender and blend until the mixture is smooth and creamy. The sauce should have a satiny finish.

2 Serve warm or chilled. To warm, put the mixture into a glass jar and place it in the dehydrator with the manicotti (for 30 minutes at 125 degrees).

Per serving (2 manicotti): Calories 202 (From Fat 135); Fat 15g (Saturated 2.5g); Cholesterol 0mg; Sodium 243mg; Carbohydrate 13g (Dietary Fiber 3g); Protein 7g.

Note: The recipes for Almond Cheese and Pine Nut Parmesan Cheese are in Chapter 9.

Note: You can make the manicotti ahead of time and store it in the refrigerator for up to two days. Don't top with sauce though until you're ready to serve it, or the noodles will weep and thin the sauce, resulting in less flavor.

*Not raw

Root-Vegetable Raw-violi with Basil Pesto on Tomato Concassé

Prep time: 30 min • **Waiting time:** 1 hr • **Yield:** 4 servings

Ingredients	*Directions*
3 large golden beets, turnips, or rutabagas	*1* Slice the beets, turnips, or rutabagas paper thin using a mandoline to form large rounds.
¼ cup extra-virgin olive oil	
1½ tablespoons salt, divided	*2* Combine the sliced root vegetables with the oil and 1 tablespoon of the salt and allow the vegetables to marinate for 1 hour.
3 cups quartered cherry tomatoes	
1 teaspoon pureed garlic (about 2 cloves)	*3* Meanwhile, make the tomato concassé by combining the tomatoes, garlic, chives, pine nuts, olives, and capers in a medium-sized glass mixing bowl. Set aside.
2 tablespoons thinly sliced chives	
2 tablespoons raw pine nuts	*4* Rinse the marinated root vegetable rounds in hot filtered water and towel dry. Lay half of them on a glass baking dish, close together but not overlapping. Using a pastry bag, pipe about 1 tablespoon of Basil Pesto in the center of each slice. Place another vegetable round on top and gently press together the edges of the two rounds with your hands to encapsulate the filling.
1 tablespoon chopped sun-dried olives	
1 tablespoon oil-packed capers	
1 recipe Basil Pesto	
	5 Serve the Raw-violi on a bed of tomato concassé.

Per serving: Calories 299 (From Fat 243); Fat 27g (Saturated 3g); Cholesterol 0mg; Sodium 414mg; Carbohydrate 14g (Dietary Fiber 4g); Protein 4g.

Tip: To serve warm, put the concassé and the vegetable rounds in separate glass dishes and place them in the dehydrator at 120 degrees for 30 minutes.

Note: You can find a recipe for Basil Pesto in Chapter 8.

Vary It! Try different fillings with this dish. Combine Sun-Dried Tomato Pesto (Chapter 14) and Almond Feta Cheese (Chapter 9) or use Not-Salmon Pâté for your filling and top with White Truffle Cream (both in this chapter).

Chapter 16

Snacks and Nutritious Nibbles

- -

In This Chapter

▶ Making snacks to enjoy at home

▶ Preparing take-along treats

- -

Some people avoid snacks in an attempt to control caloric intake. They believe that snacking adds extra calories, which in turn results in unwanted weight gain. And they're right — if the go-to snacks are fried chips and candy, foods full of empty, non-nutritive calories. Eating them doesn't fuel your body with the vital nutrients you need, and those calories are likely to induce unhealthy weight gain.

That said, snacking on nutritious foods is always a good idea. Raw snacks keep your body fueled and your brain fresh, ready to tackle a trail, a task, or even a difficult-to-please customer. Through the lens of a raw food lifestyle, watch for ways to make sure you're eating enough at fairly regular intervals.

When you follow a raw-food lifestyle and eat an abundance of raw plant foods, you don't need to count calories. Ever. That's one of the most popular benefits of this way of life. When you start fueling your body with nutritious, living, vital foods, you can eat a variety of raw plant foods (especially those that are high in water) and include good fats in reasonable amounts. When it comes to fresh, ripe, colorful, raw, and whole foods, it's all healthy, so enjoy!

In this chapter, we include recipes for terrific snacks that are pretty enough to share with a guest (Banana Boats on Fire, anyone?). And we give you ideas for make-ahead treats that travel well. Keep portable healthy snacks available to make maintaining your new raw lifestyle easier. When nutritious foods are close at hand, you are less likely to reach for an unhealthy option that's no doubt lurking nearby no matter where you are.

Making Fresh Nibbles and Nosh

If you feel a need for a snack in the afternoon, reach for one that is both healthy and delicious! Of course fresh fruit is always a great snack, and it travels well, but don't forget that leftovers make great snacks, too. Wrap leftovers up in a romaine lettuce leaf and dip it in your favorite dressing or sauce. Fruits and nut butters are also good snacks, especially for hungry kids coming home from school. What kid (or adult) can resist Red Ants on a Log? Healthy snack foods can be fun as well as delicious and nutritious!

Raw foodists are less rigid than conventional eaters about categorizing foods as snacks or entrees or sides. The recipes in this book are organized in a conventional way to help you get started with raw foods. But, truly, almost any recipe in this book can be considered a snack, especially if you're enjoying a small portion of it. If a snack-size portion of Caesar Salad (Chapter 13) or a Superfoods Green Smoothie (Chapter 10) is exactly the thing you need between lunch and dinner to keep you going, enjoy it! Don't feel like you can only eat certain foods at certain times.

Consider doubling some of the recipes in other chapters so you have leftovers for snacking. Here are some of our favorite recipe leftovers for snacking around the house:

- Better-Than-Eggs Salad Sandwich (Chapter 15)
- Buckwheat Granola and Almond Milk (Chapter 11)
- Fruit and vegetable juices (Chapter 10)
- Hemp-Seed Tabouli (Chapter 14)
- Mangoes in Lemon-Ginger Sauce (Chaper 11)
- Corn Tortillas (Chapter 15)
- Vitality Soup (Chapter 8)
- Wild Rice and Corn Salad (Chapter 14)

Cinnamon-Almond Apples

Prep time: 10 min • **Yield:** 2 servings

Ingredients	*Directions*
2 apples	**1** Core the apple, cut it in half, and halve the sections until you have 16 slices.
⅓ cup Sweet Almond Butter	
1 teaspoon ground cinnamon	**2** Spread 1 teaspoon of Sweet Almond Butter evenly on each apple slice and sprinkle with cinnamon.

Per serving (8 slices): Calories 220 (From Fat 81); Fat 9g (Saturated 1g); Cholesterol 0mg; Sodium 4mg; Carbohydrate 35g (Dietary Fiber 7g); Protein 4g.

Note: Turn to Chapter 9 for our recipe for Sweet Almond Butter.

Tip: Eat this treat immediately after preparing it so the apples stay crisp and bright. If you want to take this along on a hike or picnic, pack the apples, Almond Butter, and cinnamon separately. Pack a paring knife with a blade cover to slice your apples on the go.

Vary It! Try this recipe with peeled jicama or firm pears. You can also substitute different spices for the cinnamon; use cardamom for a taste of India or swap the cinnamon for ginger or nutmeg.

Picking apples

What's the best kind of apple to use in raw recipes? The kind you like to eat! Apples, especially their skins, are extremely high in a phytochemicals and nutrients that protect you from cancers and other diseases, help regulate blood sugar, protect against Alzheimer's, and may help slow or prevent bone loss. Here's a list of some of our favorites:

- **Braeburn** is a bi-color apple that's extremely juicy and crisp but not hard. It has a balanced sweetness that makes it a favorite for many.

- **Fuji,** a descendant of the Red Delicious apple, is dappled pink over a gold-green skin. It's delicious when chilled and has an exceptionally juicy, sweet flavor.

- **Honeycrisp** is a cold-hearty apple with a crisp, very pronounced sweet flavor. This apple is predominantly red with mottled green patches.

- **Jonagold** is a juicy apple with a mild sweetness.

- **Pink Lady** is a mildly sweet, juicy, crisp apple with pink and gold skin that has some brown speckling.

As with all produce, we recommend you purchase organic in-season apples whenever possible.

Banana Boats on Fire!

Prep time: 10 min • **Yield:** 2 servings

Ingredients	Directions
2 ripe bananas, peeled **2 tablespoons Sweet Almond Butter** **2 small sprigs of celery tops, including the leaves** **⅛ teaspoon ground paprika** **Pinch of ground cayenne pepper (or to taste)**	**1** Carefully slice off a sliver from the back (curved) part of the banana so it can sit upright without falling. Take a look at Figure 16-1 for help. Using a melon baller, scoop out a little bit of the banana to create a cavity (like the area of a canoe where a person sits). **2** Fill the banana cavity with Sweet Almond Butter. Stick a celery top in the middle to resemble the mast of a boat. Sprinkle generously with paprika, followed by a light dusting of cayenne pepper to set those boats on fire!

Per serving (1 boat): *Calories 152 (From Fat 36); Fat 4g (Saturated 0.5g); Cholesterol 0mg; Sodium 7mg; Carbohydrate 31g (Dietary Fiber 4g); Protein 3g.*

Note: The recipe for Sweet Almond Butter appears in Chapter 9.

Vary It! Instead of making boats, as shown in Figure 16-1, simply slice bananas and put them in a bowl (or on a plate, in a teacup, or whatever). Top the slices with Sweet Almond Butter and garnish with paprika and cayenne. If you serve this tasty snack to kids, skip the cayenne. They can enjoy the dusty red paprika garnish even if they might not appreciate the fiery heat of the pepper.

Figure 16-1:
Create a banana boat, fill it with Sweet Almond Butter, and add a celery mast.

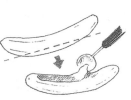

1. CAREFULLY SLICE OFF A SLIVER FROM THE BACK OF THE BANANA SO IT CAN SIT UPRIGHT WITHOUT FALLING, AND SCOOP OUT A LITTLE WITH A MELON BALLER.

2. FILL THE CAVITY WITH SWEET ALMOND BUTTER. STICK A CELERY MAST IN THE MIDDLE AND SPRINKLE GENEROUSLY WITH CAYENNE PEPPER.

Red Ants on a Log

Prep time: 10 min • **Yield:** 2 servings

Ingredients	Directions
4 celery ribs	*1* Slice off a sliver from the bottom of celery rib so it can sit flat without rolling over.
6 tablespoons Sweet Almond Butter	*2* Fill each celery rib with about 1½ tablespoons of Sweet Almond Butter.
24 sun-dried goji berries	*3* Place 6 goji berries in a row on top of the almond butter so they resemble red ants walking along a log.

Per serving (2 logs): Calories 204 (From Fat 90); Fat 10g (Saturated 1g); Cholesterol 0mg; Sodium 66mg; Carbohydrate 24g (Dietary Fiber 4g); Protein 7g.

Note: The recipe for Sweet Almond Butter appears in Chapter 9.

Vary It! If you don't happen to have goji berries handy, you can always use dried cranberries. They aren't quite as exotic (or as healthy), but they are red and delicious. And, of course, raisins are always a great choice.

Tip: To add these tasty treats to a buffet, make mini-logs by slicing each celery rib into 4 pieces.

Gotta get your goji berries

A Himalayan superfruit, goji (pronounced *go*-jee) berries have 500 times the amount of vitamin C in an orange. They've been used medicinally for thousands of years throughout Asia to boost immune function, protect vision, and slow aging, and they may even improve, ahem, sexual function for men *and* women.

Goji berries have shown ORAC (or *oxygen radical absorbance capacity,* which measures the ability of antioxidants to absorb oxygen "free radicals" in the body) values as high as 25,000. Compare this value to 2,800 for raisins and 1,200 for spinach. And one other must-have yet surprising component of these guys: They're a good source of protein and contain all the essential amino acids! Pretty sweet, right?

Speaking of sweet, goji berries have a deep flavor — not tart like some other berries and not super sweet like raisins. Soak dried goji berries and use the fruit and the soaking water in smoothies. You'll appreciate the subtle sweetness they bring to your foods.

You can find goji berries in most health food stores and online (see recommended retailers in Chapters 6).

Preparing Make-and-Take Snacks

Keeping a stash of healthy and portable snacks nearby and ready to eat is important to maintaining good health. Eating nutritious foods throughout the day ensures steady energy and also reduces temptation to hit a drive-thru or vending machine in a moment of weakness. Fresh fruit is an easy snack and doesn't require any time to make, but you do need to remember to pack it with you when you leave home. You can also prepare a few goodies on your day off and keep healthy raw snacks handy.

In this section, you find recipes for tasty treats that are easily portable. These foods are great in lunchboxes; they're also a great choice for camping because they keep well for several days without refrigeration. Use your dehydrator to make delicious trail mixes, spiced nuts, chips, and more. Then pack 'em up and head outside.

Dehydrated snack foods store well without refrigeration as long as they're fully dehydrated and no moisture is present. Confirm that your food is dry by breaking open a piece. If it's chewy or moist, it's not fully dehydrated. If it's crunchy and hard, it's dry. Be sure to store softer foods, with (any) moisture in them, in the refrigerator so they don't spoil. This, of course, reduces their portability.

Here are some favorite on-the-go treats:

- **Raw seeds and nuts:** Find out how and why to soak your raw seeds and nuts in Chapter 7.

- **Fruit:** Choose fruit that comes prepackaged from nature, such as oranges, clementines, grapes, apples, grape tomatoes, and bananas. For best results, keep them in their natural skin and peel when you're ready to eat.

  Save the delicate berries for home. They tend to get smashed during travel. Also skip fruits that require prep with a knife and cutting board (such as pineapple). Toting around a large kitchen knife can make other people a bit uncomfortable.

- **Crudité:** Carrot and celery sticks, whole snap peas, zucchini, cucumber and jicama slices, and broccoli and cauliflower florettes are delicious raw treats that provide crunch on the go. Full of phytonutrients and water, these snacks keep you energized and hydrated. Take a look at Chapter 18 for ideas on prepping veggies to make sure you have plenty of healthful grab-and-go options.

- **Dips:** Sweet Red Pepper and Zucchini Hummus (Chapter 12) packs a lot of protein and calcium in each serving, and it's easily portable in a resealable container.

- **Other finger foods:** Great Greek Olives (Chapter 13) and wraps (Chapter 8) are easy to take and eat anywhere.

Flip to Chapter 19 for other raw eating-on-the-go ideas.

PLAN AHEAD

Raw Power Trail Mix

Prep time: 15 min • **Waiting time:** 16–24 hr • **Yield:** 18 servings

Ingredients	*Directions*
½ **cup raw almonds**	**1** Soak the almonds and walnuts in separate bowls of unchlorinated water for 8 to 12 hours. During that time, soak the pumpkin seeds for 3 hours. Rinse and drain each. Dehydrate soaked nuts at 105 degrees for 8 to 12 hours or until completely dry.
½ **cup raw walnuts**	
½ **cup raw pumpkin seeds**	
1½ **cups chopped dried figs**	
½ **cup raw Brazil nuts**	**2** Combine all ingredients in a large bowl. Toss until well mixed.
½ **cup dried unsweetened coconut flakes**	
½ **cup raw cashews**	
½ **cup dulse flakes**	
½ **cup unsweetened dried blueberries**	
½ **cup dried goji berries**	
½ **cup unsulfured golden raisins**	
1 **tablespoon ground cinnamon**	

Per serving (½ cup): Calories 165 (From Fat 108); Fat 12g (Saturated 2.5g); Cholesterol 0mg; Sodium 12mg; Carbohydrate 14g (Dietary Fiber 2g); Protein 4g.

Note: Store your trail mix in an airtight container in the refrigerator for up to 1 week or in the freezer for 3 months.

Vary It! Change this recipe based on the ingredients you have handy. If you have sunflower seeds instead of pumpkin seeds, throw them in. If you're short on dried blueberries but have dried cranberries, it's all good. The nutritional information will vary, of course, but your trail mix will still be deliciously raw and healthy.

Savory Cashews

Prep time: 5 min • **Waiting time:** 8–12 hr • **Yield:** 16 servings

Ingredients	Directions
4 ounces unpasteurized tamari*	**1** Combine the tamari, onion powder, garlic powder, and cayenne in a small bowl. Pour the mixture over the cashews in a large bowl and stir until coated.
4 teaspoons onion powder	
½ teaspoon garlic powder	
½ teaspoon ground cayenne pepper	**2** Dehydrate the cashew mixture on a nonstick sheet at 105 degrees for 8 to 12 hours or until crisp.
8 cups raw cashews	

Per serving (½ cup): Calories 400 (From Fat 279); Fat 31g (Saturated 5g); Cholesterol 0mg; Sodium 512mg; Carbohydrate 22g (Dietary Fiber 3g); Protein 14g.

*Not raw

Trail mix: The universal grab-and-go snack

Trail mix, a combination of dried fruits, nuts, seeds, and grains, has been around for since the 17th century. Known by many names (including *scroggin* in New Zealand), trail mix can be a simple as raisins and peanuts. One of the most familiar terms for trail mix is GORP. Although generally believed to be an acronym for *good old raisins and peanuts* (or *granola, oats, raisins, and peanuts*), that's likely a *backronym*, or an acronym that was created after the fact. In Europe, the snack is commonly called student food, student feed, or student oats.

Tamari Almonds

Prep time: 5 min • **Waiting time:** 30–42 hr • **Yield:** 20 servings

Ingredients	*Directions*
5 cups raw almonds	**1** Soak the almonds for 12 to 18 hours. Rinse and drain.
½ cup unpasteurized tamari*	**2** In a medium bowl, combine the almonds and tamari.
	3 Spread the almonds on a dehydrator tray. Allow them to air dry. Then dehydrate at 105 degrees for 18 to 24 hours, until crisp.

Per serving (¼ cup): Calories 210 (From Fat 162); Fat 18g (Saturated 1g); Cholesterol 0mg; Sodium 403mg; Carbohydrate 8g (Dietary Fiber 4g); Protein 8g.

Note: Store in an airtight container in the refrigerator for up to 6 months.

*Not raw

Nacho-Cheese Kale Chips

Prep time: 10 min • **Waiting time:** 16–18 hr • **Yield:** 8 servings

Ingredients	Directions
½ **cup raw cashews**	*1* Soak the cashews in water for 4 to 6 hours. Rinse and drain.
½ **cup shredded carrot**	
¼ **cup filtered water**	*2* To make the cheese sauce, combine the cashews, carrot, water, nutritional yeast, chili powder, lemon juice, salt, garlic, onion powder, cumin, and cayenne in a high-performance blender and blend until smooth and creamy.
1 **tablespoon nutritional yeast***	
1 **teaspoon chili powder**	
¼ **tablespoon lemon juice**	
½ **teaspoon salt**	*3* Wash and towel-dry the kale and put it in a large bowl.
½ **teaspoon pureed garlic (about 1 clove)**	*4* Toss the kale with the sauce, making sure all the sauce is clinging to the leaves.
¼ **teaspoon onion powder**	
¼ **teaspoon ground cumin**	*5* Place the leaves on dehydrator trays covered with a nonstick sheet. Make sure that each leaf is separated from the others and none are on top of each other. This ensures that the leaves dry quickly and evenly. Dehydrate at 105 degrees until completely crisp, about 12 hours or longer.
pinch ground cayenne pepper	
1 **pound stemmed curly kale (about 3 large bunches)**	

Per serving: Calories 83 (From Fat 36); Fat 4g (Saturated 1g); Cholesterol 0mg; Sodium 69mg; Carbohydrate 10g (Dietary Fiber 2g); Protein 4g.

Note: These snacks keep for a month or more in the pantry if they're good and dry and stored in a sealed glass jar. If the chips are exposed to air, they become soft. If this happens, return them to the dehydrator for a few hours to crisp.

Tip: To stem a kale leaf, grasp the stem firmly with your primary hand. Using the thumb and forefinger of your other hand, slide the leaf down the stem, removing it easily. Or, place the leaf stem-side-up on a cutting board and use a sharp knife to trace the leaf along the stem to separate it.

Vary It! Try other raw sauces and dressings on these tasty chips; Tahini Dressing, Chili Colorado Sauce, Barbeque Sauce, and Creamy Dill Tartar Sauce are all terrific (see Chapters 13 and 15).

*Not raw

Chapter 17

Sweet Endings

In This Chapter

▶ Enjoying tarts, crumbles, and more

▶ Making raw ice cream at home

▶ Creating chocolate candies and truffles

You may be thinking, "Raw desserts, that's easy: fruit salad!" Indeed, fruit is always a great choice, but we know that sometimes you want a treat more decadent than a juicy orange or sliced grapes. Fortunately, you don't have to give up delicious endings like cheesecake, ice cream, and (gasp!) chocolate just because you want to embrace a raw food lifestyle. In fact, raw desserts are often tastier than cooked desserts because they're fresher and contain whole foods. For example, the nuts in many of these recipes take the place of wheat flour, which is tasteless. Nuts add a nice, rich flavor and great texture. Fruits are livelier when they are fresh, too.

In this chapter, we show you how to make raw versions of many of your favorite desserts, like baklava and brownies, and give you step-by-step instructions on making raw ice creams. You can also find out how to create memorable candies for any occasion.

Pitted dates are in many of the recipes in this chapter because they add a sweetness and texture that's perfect for crusts and fillings. Fresh dates are slightly dried but still soft and chewy. Even dried dates, such as deglets, are fairly soft but more wrinkled on the outside. For the recipes in this chapter, we use medjool dates, but deglets or any other soft date work fine. Just avoid dates plugs, which may not be raw.

Creating "Baked" Desserts

What's better than finishing a delicious meal with friends? We say it's satisfying the need for a little something sweet afterward. Many people, raw foodists included, love to enjoy a sweet with their savory, so in this section, we offer recipes for incredible sweet raw creations. Find out how to make a gooey, layered apple baklava with omega-3-rich walnuts and spices and how to create a delicious Peach Crumble, ideally served à la mode with homemade raw ice cream. Delish!

Most of these desserts require some chilling time to ensure they set properly. Don't skip this important step. Chilling makes the leap from a pile of fruit and nuts to a memorable dessert experience.

Why do you use extracts if they're not raw?

Some of the recipes in this chapter call for vanilla extract (and other kinds of extracts) to add a flavor boost. Strictly speaking, extracts aren't raw. Vanilla extract, for instance, is typically made from crushed vanilla bean pods that are soaked in a simmering mixture of alcohol and unchlorinated water. The solids are strained away, leaving the liquid extract, which isn't actually nutritionally beneficial. But many raw foodists use extracts to balance and flavor foods, especially desserts. This whimsical ingredient helps keep foods interesting; and, we believe, the flavor trade-off is worth the compromise. Only a very small amount of extract is ever used in raw recipes. In a serving of vanilla ice cream, for example, about ⅛ teaspoon of vanilla extract is included.

To avoid the extract and still get the vanilla flavor, you can use vanilla beans. Just purchase vanilla bean pods (typically labeled *vanilla beans*) in the spice section of the grocery store and follow these steps to use them:

1. **With a very sharp knife, cut the vanilla bean pod in half lengthwise.**

2. **Using the tip of the knife, carefully scrape the inside of the bean pod to remove the tiny black sticky beans.**

3. **With a rubber spatula, scrape the beans off the knife and into your recipe.**

4. **Reserve the empty pod to use for tea and to flavor smoothies, dressings, and other recipes.** Store the dried pod in a sealed glass jar in the pantry for up to 4 months.

If you're concerned about extracts and don't want to deal with using whole vanilla beans, consider purchasing a raw extract. These incredibly potent extracts are made with a cold-pressing technique without alcohol. Most list a conversion ratio to regular extracts on the label so you can easily substitute them in recipes. Somewhere between one and five drops could equal a teaspoon of traditional extract, so check the label.

Apple Baklava

Prep time: 20 min • **Waiting time:** 22 hr • **Yield:** 8 servings

Ingredients	*Directions*
2 cups raw walnuts	*1* Soak walnuts in unfiltered water for 8 hours; then rinse and drain. Dehydrate walnuts at 105 degrees for 12 hours or until thoroughly dry and crisp. Finely chop.
¾ cup coconut nectar* or light agave nectar*	
¾ cup minced unsulfured golden raisins	*2* Combine the coconut nectar, raisins, lemon juice, cinnamon, cloves, and cardamom in a high-performance blender and blend to form a smooth syrup. Set it aside.
1½ tablespoons lemon juice	
1 teaspoon ground cinnamon	
⅛ teaspoon ground cloves	*3* To assemble the dessert, evenly distribute ¼ of the apple slices in a 9-inch square springform pan and press gently. Drizzle ¼ of the syrup over the top of the apples and sprinkle ¼ of the walnuts and ⅓ of the currants evenly over the top, pressing each layer into place.
Pinch of ground cardamom	
4 apples, peeled and thinly sliced	
½ cup dried currants	
	4 Repeat Step 3 three more times until all the apples, syrup, and currants are used. Top with a final layer of apples arranged neatly (because they'll be visible). Add the remaining ¼ of walnuts to the top of the dessert. Press the final layer down gently.
	5 Lay a sheet of waxed paper on top of the baklava. Place a plate that fits into the springform pan on top of the waxed paper. Top with a glass jar filled with water to compress the layers of baklava.
	6 Cover and refrigerate the dessert for at least 2 hours (or overnight) prior to serving. Cut the baklava into small squares or triangles.

Per serving: Calories 74 (From Fat 0); Fat 0g (Saturated 0g); Cholesterol 0mg; Sodium 2mg; Carbohydrate 20g (Dietary Fiber 3g); Protein 1g.

Note: Store this dessert covered in the refrigerator for up to 5 days. We don't recommend storing the prepped ingredients separately, because the apples will turn brown.

*Not raw

Chocolate Mousse Tart with Strawberries and Bananas

Prep time: 30 min • **Waiting time:** 1 hr • **Yield:** 8 servings

Ingredients	Directions
1 cup dried unsweetened shredded coconut 1 cup raw macadamia nuts Pinch of salt ¼ cup pitted, chopped, and packed dates 2 ripe but firm avocados, peeled and pitted 5 tablespoons raw cocoa powder ½ cup coconut sugar* or evaporated cane sugar* 1 tablespoon vanilla extract* Pinch ground cinnamon 1 pint strawberries, thinly sliced 2 bananas, peeled and sliced	*1* To make the crust, place the coconut in a food processor outfitted with the S blade and process to a fine powder. Add the nuts and salt and blend to a coarse meal. *2* Loosely separate the dates and add them to the food processor. Process until the texture resembles a graham-cracker crust: The mixture should be loose and crumbly, yet hold together when pressed tightly. *3* Press the crust mixture into a 9-inch ungreased tart pan. Press firmly so the crust holds together. Place it in the freezer or refrigerator while you make the filling to chill the crust and reduce amount of time the pie needs to set. *4* Place the avocados, cocoa powder, coconut sugar, vanilla, another pinch of salt, and cinnamon in a food processor outfitted with the S blade and process until completely smooth. Set aside. *5* To assemble the tart, place the sliced bananas uniformly on top of the crust. Spread half of the filling evenly on top of the bananas and then place half of the sliced strawberries evenly on the filling. Spread the last of the filling on top of the strawberries, and then layer the remaining berries attractively on top. Chill for at least 1 hour prior to serving.

Per serving: Calories 324 (From Fat 198); Fat 22g (Saturated 6g); Cholesterol 0mg; Sodium 6mg; Carbohydrate 34g (Dietary Fiber 8g); Protein 4g.

Note: Store the tart in an airtight container in the refrigerator for up to 3 days or in the freezer for up to 2 months.

Note: For this recipe, use avocados that are ripe but slightly firm so the avocado flavor doesn't overpower the chocolate. Save the soft avocados for guacamole.

*Not raw

Peach Crumble

Prep time: 15 min • **Waiting time:** 17–21 hr • **Yield:** 6 servings

Ingredients	*Directions*
½ cup raw almonds	*1* Soak almonds, walnuts, and Brazil nuts in filtered water for 8 hours. Rinse and drain. Dehydrate the soaked nuts at 105 degrees for 8 to 12 hours or until completely dry.
½ cup raw walnuts	
½ cup raw Brazil nuts	
Pinch of salt	*2* To make the crumble topping, process the dehydrated nuts and salt in a food processor outfitted with the S blade until the mixture resembles a coarse meal.
¾ cup pitted, chopped, and packed dates, divided	
2 tablespoons filtered water	*3* Separate ½ cup of the dates and distribute them evenly over the nuts. Process again until the mixture just begins to stick together. Add the water and pulse for a few seconds. Set aside.
4 cups pitted and diced fresh peaches	
2 teaspoons lemon juice	*4* Blend 1 cup of the peaches with the remaining dates and lemon juice. Stir the mixture into the remaining peaches.
	5 To assemble the dish, pour the peach filling in a shallow glass baking dish that fits into your dehydrator. Press the crumble topping lightly on top. Put the baking dish in a dehydrator at 125 degrees for 1 hour before serving.

Per serving: Calories 314 (From Fat 180); Fat 20g (Saturated 3g); Cholesterol 0mg; Sodium 1mg; Carbohydrate 32g (Dietary Fiber 7g); Protein 6g.

Note: This Peach Crumble will keep in a sealed container in the refrigerator for up to 3 days.

Tip: Serve this dish with French Vanilla Ice Cream — the recipe follows.

Making Ice Creams and Frozen Desserts

Ice creams are typically made from a source of fat, such as nut cream, avocado, or young coconut. Sorbets are just fruit without a source of fat. And sherbets are a combination of the two — more fruit but less fat than ice cream, and less fruit but more fat than a sorbet. Juicers make great fruit sorbet, whereas blenders make great slushies. Food processors and ice-cream makers turn out the best ice cream and sherbet.

Making raw sorbet is child's play if you have a continuous feed, extruder juicer. (Check out Chapter 7 for the rundown on types of juicers.) Just use the *homogenizing plate,* also known as the blank plate, and then feed pieces of frozen fruit through the chute. Watch with awe as soft-serve sorbet comes out the other end!

Try these flavors for sorbet:

- ✔ Banana
- ✔ Strawberry
- ✔ Raspberry
- ✔ Mango
- ✔ Peach
- ✔ Apricot
- ✔ Kiwi
- ✔ Cherimoya
- ✔ Persimmon

We don't include a specific recipe for sherbet in this book, but if you want to take a crack at it, combine equal parts nut milk and very ripe fruit in a high-performance blender. Process until thoroughly combined, and then adjust the sweetness according to your preference. Place the mixture in your ice-cream maker and follow the manufacturer's directions for your appliance.

Experiment to find flavors you favor. For an added variation, try adding fresh herbs, like mint and basil. Mmmm!

French Vanilla Ice Cream

Prep time: 15 minutes • **Waiting time:** 3–5 hr • **Yield:** 10 servings

Ingredients	*Directions*
2 cups raw cashews	*1* Soak the cashews in cold filtered water in the refrigerator for 2 to 4 hours along with the young coconut meat. Rinse and drain the cashews.
2 cups young coconut meat	
1 cup cold filtered water	
1 cup light coconut nectar* or agave nectar*	*2* Put the chilled cashews, chilled coconut, cold water, coconut nectar, Irish moss gel, vanilla extract, vanilla seeds, and salt in a high-speed blender and blend until smooth and creamy. Add the lecithin powder and continue to blend until incorporated.
¼ cup Irish moss gel	
1½ teaspoons vanilla extract*	
1 vanilla bean pod, seeds only	*3* While the blender is running, slowly add the coconut oil to the mixture and blend for 15 seconds.
½ teaspoon salt	
2 tablespoons soy lecithin powder*	*4* Process the mixture in an ice-cream maker and chill according to the manufacturer's instructions.
¼ cup coconut oil, warmed to liquid	

Per serving (½ cup): Calories 324 (From Fat 189); Fat 21g (Saturated 7g); Cholesterol 0mg; Sodium 32mg; Carbohydrate 35g (Dietary Fiber 1g); Protein 5g.

Note: Extra ice cream lasts for up to 1 month in an airtight container in the freezer.

Tip: Raw ice creams freeze better when the ingredients are chilled first. When you combine the ingredients in a blender, the mixture generates a bit of heat that makes it tougher to freeze if the ingredients aren't pre-chilled. If you don't have time to chill the ingredients, allow extra time for freezing the finished ice cream at the end.

Note: Check out Chapter 7 for info on Irish Moss gel.

Note: If you don't own an ice-cream maker, freeze the mixture in ice-cube trays. After freezing, remove the cubes and allow them to soften slightly for about 15 minutes. Then, put the cubes in a food processor outfitted with an S blade and process to a soft ice cream.

*Not raw

PLAN AHEAD

Maple-Walnut Ice Cream

Prep time: 15 min • **Waiting time:** 9 hr • **Yield:** 10 servings

Ingredients	*Directions*
2½ cups raw walnuts 1 cup raw cashews 2 cups cold filtered water 1 cup chilled pure maple syrup* or amber agave nectar* ¼ teaspoon alcohol-free maple extract* Pinch of salt 1 tablespoon psyllium-husk powder	*1* Soak the walnuts and cashews separately in water in the refrigerator for 8 hours, and then rinse and drain them. Chop ½ cup of the walnuts and set aside. *2* Combine the 2 cups of unchopped walnuts, cashews, water, maple syrup, maple extract, and salt in a blender and blend until completely smooth and creamy. Add the psyllium powder and blend again for about 1 minute. The mixture should have the consistency of a thick milkshake. *3* Add the chopped walnuts and stir. Process the mixture in an ice-cream maker according to the manufacturer's instructions. *4* Serve immediately or freeze for up to 2 hours.

Per serving (½ cup): Calories 204 (From Fat 90); Fat 10g (Saturated 1.5g); Cholesterol 0mg; Sodium 5mg; Carbohydrate 27g (Dietary Fiber 2g); Protein 3g.

Note: Extra ice cream lasts for up to 1 month in an airtight container in the freezer.

Tip: Serve Maple-Walnut Ice Cream over Carob Brownies. Look for this delicious brownie recipe later in the chapter.

*Not raw

Creating Chocolaty Confections

If you're a fan of chocolate, rest assured that you can still satisfy your cravings with a raw food lifestyle. In fact, we highly recommend it. As with many raw ingredients, you need only look to your local health-food store or favorite online retailer to track down unsweetened raw cacao powder, which is less intense and a little more bitter than roasted cacao.

Technically speaking, the bean that chocolate comes from is the *cacao* bean; the powder made from it is often referred to as *cocoa*. However, many people, including some in the chocolate industry, use these terms interchangeably. Most raw cocoa powder is labeled *cacao,* and traditional chocolate makers use the word *cocoa.* After it's sweetened, the powder is referred to as chocolate.

Carob powder, on the other hand, is the dried, ground pulp of the carob plant, rather than a seed. It's naturally caffeine-free, sweeter than cocoa, and has three times more calcium than cocoa. Most people don't find carob to be as flavorful or as rich as chocolate, but why compare the two? Carob stands deliciously on its own! Carob doesn't contain the alkaloids and caffeine that chocolate has, so it's a far better choice for children and late-night snacking.

Many raw foodists enjoy the bitterness of cacao, but if you prefer sweet dark chocolate rather than the bitter variety, be sure to increase the amount of sweetener by 10 to 20 percent in these recipes.

The truth about raw chocolate

Chocolate has a wonderful seductive chemistry and can lead to feelings of euphoria, but it's also addictive due to a caffeine-related alkaloid called *theobromine.* Chocolate is touted by some to be a superfood due to its antioxidants qualities, but antioxidants can be found in other non-addictive foods, too, so we recommend thinking of chocolate as a celebration food.

In traditional chocolate-making, cacao beans are roasted in the first step of processing. When cacao is roasted, it loses many of its antioxidants and magnesium. Cooking cacao also destroys PEAs (*phenylethylamines,* the chemicals in chocolate that make you feel like you're falling in love) and its natural MAO inhibitors, which allow more serotonin to flow in your body.

Carob Brownies

Prep time: 10 min • **Waiting time:** 16–22 hr • **Yield:** 8 servings

Ingredients	*Directions*
4½ cups raw walnuts	**1** Soak the walnuts in filtered water for 6 to 8 hours. Rinse and drain. Dehydrate walnuts at 105 degrees for 8 to 12 hours or until crisp.
½ cup dried figs	
1 cup raw carob powder	
⅔ cup coconut sugar* or evaporated cane sugar*	**2** While the walnuts are being prepared, soak the figs for 15 minutes and then drain and mince them.
½ cup pitted and chopped dates	**3** Chop ½ cup of the dehydrated walnuts and set aside. Place the remaining walnuts in a food processor and pulse until they reach the consistency of meal.
2 tablespoons coconut oil, warmed to liquid	
2 teaspoons vanilla extract*	**4** Add the figs, carob powder, coconut sugar, dates, coconut oil, vanilla, and cinnamon and continue processing until well mixed and sticky. The mixture should hold together when pressed into a ball. If oil begins to separate from the mixture, it's overprocessed. (You can still use it, but it's not the desired effect.)
¼ teaspoon cinnamon	
	5 Transfer the mixture to a bowl. Add the ½ cup chopped walnuts and stir well. Press the mixture firmly into an 8-x-8-inch pan. Cover and chill for 2 hours before cutting into 8 equal pieces.

Per serving: Calories 203 (From Fat 72); Fat 8g (Saturated 3g); Cholesterol 0mg; Sodium 5mg; Carbohydrate 38g (Dietary Fiber 7g); Protein 1g.

Note: Store leftover brownies in a sealed container in the refrigerator for 1 week or in the freezer for 1 to 2 months.

*Not raw

Chocolate-Date-Nut Caramel Truffles

Prep time: 20 min • **Waiting time:** 1 hr • **Yield:** 15 servings

Ingredients	*Directions*
2 cups pitted and packed dates, divided **1 cup raw pine nuts or cashews** **1 teaspoon vanilla extract*** **½ cup unsulfured raisins** **¼ cup coconut oil, warmed to liquid** **⅝ cup unsweetened raw cacao powder** **Pinch of cinnamon** **30 raw pecan halves for garnish**	*1* For the caramel, loosely separate the dates and place 1 cup of the dates, the pine nuts, and the vanilla in a food processor outfitted with the S blade. Process until smooth. Place in the freezer for 10 minutes while making the fudge.
	2 For the fudge, place the remaining 1 cup of dates along with the raisins and coconut oil in a food processor outfitted with the S blade. Process until smooth. Add the cocoa powder and cinnamon, and process again for a few seconds until the cacao powder is fully integrated. Don't overprocess or the mixture will become oily.
	3 Roll the caramel into balls, using 1 teaspoon of the mixture for each. Do the same for the fudge, also using 1 teaspoon of mixture for each ball.
	4 Using your thumb, make a depression in the center of each ball of fudge that's large enough to hold a ball of caramel. Place a ball of caramel into each depression.
	5 Press a perfect pecan half on top. Repeat this process until all the candies are formed and chill for at least 1 hour. Serve each truffle in a paper candy cup.

Per serving (2 truffles): Calories 203 (From Fat 108); Fat 12g (Saturated 4g); Cholesterol 0mg; Sodium 4mg; Carbohydrate 25g (Dietary Fiber 4g); Protein 3g.

Note: Store the truffles in an airtight container in the refrigerator or freezer for up to 1 month.

*Not raw

Chocolate Almond Bark

Prep time: 20 min • **Waiting time:** 1 hr • **Yield:** 16 servings

Ingredients	*Directions*
1½ cups cacao butter, warmed to liquid	**1** Blend the warmed cacao butter, coconut sugar, scraped vanilla beans, and salt until all ingredients are completely emulsified and the mixture is warm.
¾ cup coconut sugar*	
2 vanilla beans, scraped to remove the center paste	**2** Pour the mixture into a food processor; add half the cacao powder and process until well combined.
¼ teaspoon salt	
2⅓ cups raw cacao powder, divided	**3** Add the coconut nectar to the food processor and continue to blend. Then add the remaining half cacao powder and continue to blend, scraping down the sides of processor, as needed, until the mixture is smooth and the cacao is well integrated, about 2 more minutes.
¼ cup coconut nectar* or agave nectar*	
½ cup slivered raw almonds	
	4 Divide the mixture in half and pour each half evenly onto a nonstick dehydrator sheet. Score each tray into 16 pieces (4 x 4). Sprinkle with almonds.
	5 Chill for 1 hour and then remove from the sheet and break into pieces along score marks.

Per serving (2 pieces): Calories 142 (From Fat 81); Fat 9g (Saturated 4.5g); Cholesterol 0mg; Sodium 10mg; Carbohydrate 16g (Dietary Fiber 1g); Protein 1g.

Note: Store bark in a sealed container in the pantry for up to 1 month.

Note: Find cacao butter in health food stores or online.

*Not raw

Chocolate Pecan Bars

Prep time: 20 min • **Waiting time:** 18–24 hr • **Yield:** 12 servings

Ingredients	*Directions*
¾ **cup pitted and packed dates (room temp)** ½ **cup plus ⅓ cup unrefined coconut oil (warmed to liquid)** ¾ **cup plus 2 tablespoons maple syrup* (room temp)** **1 tablespoon vanilla extract*** **1¼ cups raw pecan pieces** ¾ **cup raw cacao powder** **1 cup Candied-Pecan Crumble (see the following recipe)**	*1* Combine the dates, ½ cup coconut oil, 2 tablespoons maple syrup, and vanilla extract in the food processor and blend until smooth. Fold in the plain pecan pieces. Press the mixture evenly into a rectangular tart pan lined with parchment paper.
	2 Blend the remaining ⅓ cup coconut oil, ¾ cup maple syrup, and cacao powder in a high-performance blender to achieve a smooth consistency. Pour this chocolate mixture evenly over the bottom layer.
	3 Sprinkle the Candied-Pecan Crumble over the top of the wet chocolate and press gently to set the pecans firmly in place. Put the tart in the refrigerator to chill for 6 hours.
	4 Remove the tart from the pan and cut into 12 pieces. Place each piece on a piece of parchment paper to keep from sticking to the plate.

Candied-Pecan Crumble

¼ **cup maple syrup*** ½ **teaspoon cinnamon** **Pinch of nutmeg** **1 cup raw pecan pieces**	*1* Mix together the syrup, cinnamon, and nutmeg.
	2 Coat the pecan pieces with the mixture, spread on a nonstick sheet in a single layer, and dehydrate at 105 degrees for 12 to 18 hours, or until crisp.

Per serving: *Calories 343 (From Fat 216); Fat 24g (Saturated 14g); Cholesterol 0mg; Sodium 8mg; Carbohydrate 34g (Dietary Fiber 4g); Protein 3g.*

Note: Serve Chocolate Pecan Bars will last in an airtight container in the fridge for up to 1 week. You can store Candied-Pecan Crumble in a sealed glass jar in the pantry for 2 months.

*Not raw

Sweet Nut'ins 'n' Chocolate Kiss Cookies

Prep time: 30 min • **Waiting time:** 33–45 hr • **Yield:** 14 servings

Ingredients	Directions
2 cups raw almonds	**1** Soak the almonds and walnuts separately for 8 hours. Rinse and drain. Dehydrate at 105 degrees on a dehydrator tray lined with a nonstick sheet for 12 hours.
1 cup raw walnuts	
3 cups pitted and packed dates	
1 teaspoon vanilla extract*	**2** Pulse the almonds and walnuts in a food processor outfitted with the S blade until coarsely chopped. Add the dates and vanilla extract and process until well mixed. Put mixture in a bowl and knead in the cacao nibs by hand.
1 cup raw cacao nibs or vegan chocolate chips*	
	3 Using waxed paper or plastic wrap, roll the mixture into a log about 2 inches in diameter. Put the roll in the freezer for 1 hour. Cut into ½-inch slices, keeping a round shape. Cookies should be about 2 inches in diameter and ½ inch thick.
	4 Eat the cookies soft or dehydrate at 105 degrees on a dehydrator tray lined with a nonstick sheet for 12 to 24 hours, depending on how soft and moist or crunchy and dry you want them.

Per serving: Calories 366 (From Fat 207); Fat 23g (Saturated 5g); Cholesterol 0mg; Sodium 1mg; Carbohydrate 37g (Dietary Fiber 9); Protein 6g.

Note: Store the cookies in an airtight container in the refrigerator for up to 1 month or in the freezer for up to 4 months. If you dehydrate the cookies completely, with no moisture remaining, you can store them in the pantry for 2 weeks.

Note: Vegan chocolate chips are not raw. We include them here as an option if you're not a fan of raw cacao nibs. Many raw foodists enjoy the bitter taste of cacao nibs, but you need more time to acquire this taste.

Tip: Enjoy this raw version of a chocolate chip cookie with a glass of Almond Milk (see recipe in Chapter 11) or a cup of herbal tea in the afternoon.

*Not raw

Black Forest Cherry Brownies

Prep time: 30 min • **Waiting time:** 13–21 hr • **Yield:** 8 servings

Ingredients	*Directions*
2¼ **cups raw walnuts, divided**	*1* Soak the walnuts for 4 to 8 hours. Rinse and drain. Dehydrate at 105 degrees for 8 to 12 hours.
¼ **cup plus 2 tablespoons pitted and packed dates**	
¼ **cup plus 2 tablespoons raw cacao powder or carob powder**	*2* Put 2 cups of walnuts in a food processor outfitted with the S blade and grind them to the consistency of meal. Loosely separate the dates and add them to the food processor. Continue to process until the mixture is well combined.
1 teaspoon cherry extract*	
¼ **cup chopped unsweetened dried cherries**	*3* Add the cacao powder and the cherry extract and process to mix. Transfer the brownie mixture to a large mixing bowl.
3 tablespoons filtered water	
	4 Chop the remaining ¼ cup walnuts and add them and the cherries to the brownie mixture. Sprinkle with the water. Mix well with your hands.
	5 Pack the mixture firmly and evenly into a 7-x-7-inch pan. Chill for at least 1 hour before slicing and serving.

Per serving: *Calories 74 (From Fat 27); Fat 3g (Saturated 0.5g); Cholesterol 0mg; Sodium 3mg; Carbohydrate 11g (Dietary Fiber 2g); Protein 1g.*

Note: Store the brownies in an airtight container in the refrigerator for up to 1 week or in the freezer for 3 months.

Vary It! To change it up a bit, substitute almonds or cashews for the walnuts.

Coconut-Macadamia Rawcaroons

Prep time: 30 min • **Waiting time:** 12–36 hr • **Yield:** 24 servings

Ingredients	*Directions*
2 cups raw macadamia nuts	*1* Soak the macadamia nuts in water for 12 hours. Rinse and drain.
1 cup almond flour or finely ground raw almonds	
1 cup pitted and chopped dates	*2* Put the macadamia nuts and almond flour in a food processor outfitted with the S blade and process until coarsely chopped.
½ cup Coconut Butter	
½ teaspoon almond extract* or coconut extract*	*3* Loosely separate the dates and add them to the food processor along with the Coconut Butter and almond extract. Process until well combined.
1 cup dried shredded unsweetened coconut	
	4 Put the mixture in a large bowl and stir in the shredded coconut.
	5 Using a ⅛-cup measuring cup, form about 24 small mounds about 1-inch thick.
	6 Eat the cookies as they are or dehydrate at 105 degrees on a nonstick dehydrator tray for 12 to 24 hours, depending on how crunchy and dry you want them.

Per serving: Calories 147 (From Fat 108); Fat 12g (Saturated 3g); Cholesterol 0mg; Sodium 1mg; Carbohydrate 9g (Dietary Fiber 2g); Protein 2g.

Note: Store your Rawcaroons in an airtight container in the refrigerator for up to 1 month or in the freezer for up to 4 months.

Note: Our recipe for Coconut Butter is in Chapter 11.

Vary It! To make chocolate (or carob) Rawcaroons, add 2 tablespoons of cacao or carob powder to the ingredients in the food processor. Continue as directed.

*Not raw

Part IV

Taking Your Raw Lifestyle to the Next Level

In this part . . .

*F*ind out how to go beyond the basics with raw foods in these chapters. Discover how to eat raw in any situation — anytime and anywhere. We offer tips on introducing raw foods to non-raw friends and family members, planning menus (both simple and elegant), packing lunches, and even hosting a dinner party. And if you're feeling a bit lonely on your raw food journey, you'll be inspired by the ideas we offer for finding like-minded raw foodists to share your experience.

Chapter 18

Planning Menus in the Raw

*V*ery few people are satisfied eating the same food day after day or and experiencing the same textures. And fortunately, raw foodists don't need to endure such torment! With proper planning, you can create a wide array of delicious and satisfying meals for every occasion, to appeal to even the most discriminating palates. Raw cuisine can be simple, gourmet, or anywhere in between.

Providing the most nutrient-dense, well-balanced meals for yourself, your family, and even dinner guests takes a lot of planning whether you eat raw food only, vegetarian or vegan cuisine, or standard meat and potatoes. Most of us are happy if our families eat together at all! Sitting down to nutritionally sound meal is often a lower priority than accomplishing the feat of getting everyone around the table at the same time with food that they'll eat. Many families choose convenience over nutrition on a regular basis.

And then there's the budget to consider. This factor is more important in today's tough economy than ever. But just because money's tight doesn't mean that meals have to be less nourishing. In fact, meals need to be *more* nourishing when the grocery budget is limited. Most people can't afford to waste money on empty calories, so all calories need to count toward adequate nutrition. When times are tough, stocking up on in-season, garden-fresh foods is a good economic move that also benefits your health.

In this chapter, we show you how to plan weekday menus and prep ingredients ahead of time so you can create meals on the fly. And we point out how to make everyday meals feel like events with garnishes and gourmet touches. This doesn't mean, of course, that dinner parties and celebrations featuring raw food are overlooked; we help with those, too!

Coming Up with a Plan

A little organization and planning go a long way to reducing the time it takes to plan and prepare nutritious raw meals and to ensure that the money you invest in food and kitchen supplies is well spent. In other words, if you stock your kitchen with the equipment and staple ingredients we recommend in Chapter 5, then a plan to put it all to good use can go far.

Here are some different ways to plan your meals:

- ✔ **Plan a daily menu the night before:** This strategy is usually based on what's in the refrigerator or the garden, what's available at the market (if you have time to shop), and how much time you have to prepare the meal. Organizing a menu for the next day allows you a little advance preparation for steps like soaking nuts and seeds or dehydrating a component that requires more than a couple hours.

- ✔ **Create a weekly menu of meals:** This approach takes into consideration what's on sale or available at the farmers' market and in your garden as well as any leftovers from one day to the next. Planning a week's menu allows you time to shop and gather ingredients in advance, considers how much food-preparation time you need on particular days, and provides the opportunity to make a few items in advance. See Figure 18-1 for a ready-made week-long plan to get started.

- ✔ **Develop a rotating set of a dozen or more menus:** These menus vary little, except for seasonal ingredients that can be easily replaced by others that are available all year. Most families enjoy the same 10 or 12 meals and appreciate knowing what to expect. Having a set of rotating favorites takes some of the guesswork out of meal planning and ensures that you and your family stay happy with the food served. But this approach takes some time up front to organize, and if you want to try new dishes, you need to set aside a day specifically for that purpose.

As your family is developing a rotating menu, create a system for keeping track of what you eat when and choosing menus. Some families place favorite meals on index cards and shuffle the deck each week to decide what's for dinner each night. Or you can place the cards in a hat and randomly select dinners for the week. Other families let individual members choose one meal each week. Find a system that works for you and use it.

Making appealing choices

Deciding what to prepare for dinner is often quicker, easier, and more fun when you have pre-prepped food standing by and ready to serve. So when planning meals, consider using similar ingredients that are prepared in different ways to make meal decisions easier and shopping simpler. Also try making double or triple batches of foods that have good storage life, such as dressings, sauces, and fillings. Leftovers are always helpful, and being prepared with food to serve with little notice cuts down on kitchen tasks and ensures there's nutritious food to eat and serve — even when you aren't in the mood (or have no time) to be in the kitchen.

Here are a few rules of thumb to help you create healthy, satisfying, and nutritious menus:

- ✔ **Balance light and heavy foods to keep fat to less than 30 percent of the total menu.** You can include high-fat items, like dessert, as long as you balance them with fat-free foods like salad or juice. It isn't unusual for raw meals (and cooked meals, too) to be more than 50 percent fat, but this isn't a healthy balance. Keep an eye on how much fat you're including in your menu.

  Raw foodists don't usually need to count calories, but a high-fat diet contributes to obesity as well as other health issues. Some raw plant foods (including nuts and seeds, grains, legumes, avocados, and coconuts) are more calorie-dense and naturally lower in water content than most fruits and vegetables. So even raw meals that seem healthy can be far too high in fat.

- ✔ **Build flavors:** Serve mild dishes first and increase intensity of flavors with each new course to allow the subtle flavors of later courses to come through.

- ✔ **Be colorful:** The human appetite responds to color, and consuming a variety of natural colors ensures you're getting an abundance of phytonutrients. But make green your favorite color, because green leaves and vegetables provide the most variety of nutrients, including protein, calcium, and omega-3 fatty acids.

- ✔ **Consider needs:** Serve enough food to satisfy without encouraging people to overeat.

- ✔ **Plan for prep time:** Be realistic about how much time a menu takes to prepare. One gourmet item is enough to showcase the potential of raw food (and your culinary skill); the rest of a meal can be simple, easy-to-prepare, low-fat foods.

- ✔ **Set a budget:** Buy seasonal produce for the freshest, most nutritious, and least-costly menu. Choose common seeds like sunflower or pumpkin over more costly foods like macadamia or pine nuts.

- ✔ **Spin the flavor wheel:** Include all five flavor categories (sweet, salty, sour, bitter, and umami) plus some dramatic pungent flavors (such as onions, garlic, and ginger) in your menu. Find more on the flavor categories and how to balance and pair them to create appealing tastes in Chapter 7.

- ✔ **Support digestibility:** Follow food-combining principles (described in Chapter 3) and avoid overeating to avoid indigestion.

- ✔ **Emphasize nutrition:** Make sure your menu is nutritionally adequate. See Chapter 3 for help.

Narrowing your options

This checklist of options by category can help you get started with developing a daily or weekly menu:

✔ **Breakfast:** Choose one or two of the items from this list:

- ❑ Freshly prepped fruit or green juice
- ❑ Fresh fruit or a fruit salad
- ❑ Green smoothie
- ❑ Cereal with nut milk and bananas or berries

✔ **Lunch:** Choose one (or more) of the items on this list:

- ❑ One or two types of fruit with romaine lettuce and celery
- ❑ Large salad topped with seasoned seeds or olives
- ❑ Veggie wrap with favorite dipping sauce
- ❑ Nut/seed pâté, nut cheese, guacamole, or hummus with fresh vegetables and/or sesame chips
- ❑ Raw soup

✔ **Afternoon snack:** Choose one (or more) of the items on this list:

- ❑ One or two types of fruit with romaine lettuce and celery
- ❑ Freshly made fruit or green juice
- ❑ Trail mix
- ❑ Kale chips
- ❑ Cookies

✔ **Dinner:** Use the lunch options, one hearty option from this list, or choose two or three of the light items here:

- ❑ Vegetable juice
- ❑ Raw bread or a sandwich
- ❑ Wild rice salad
- ❑ Raw soup
- ❑ Large salad with pâté, nut cheese, guacamole, or hummus
- ❑ Wrap with favorite dipping sauce
- ❑ Hearty gourmet entree

Check out Figure 18-1 for specific meal ideas using recipes from Part III for an entire week. It's only an example, though, so make sure you're eating until you're satisfied. Also, include healthy snacks throughout the day to maintain consistent energy. Some days you may simply be hungrier, so don't be afraid to add more raw foods to your day as needed.

Week One	Breakfast	Lunch	Snacks	Dinner
Monday	Blueberry Hill Smoothie Date and Walnut Wheat-Berry Scones	Horiatiki (Greek Salad) Hummus and crudités	12 ounces To-Live-For Green Juice Sweet Nut'ins	Linguini with White Truffle Cream Large green salad with Italian Herb Dressing
Tuesday	Buckwheat Granola with Almond Milk and blueberries	Herbed Almond Cheese Spread and crudités Mixed green salad with Sweet and Spicy Dijon Dressing	Peach or other fresh fruit 12 ounces Green Juice	Creamy Red Bell Pepper–Chipotle Soup Mixed green salad with Pickled Red Onions
Wednesday	Cinnamon Oatmeal with Almond Milk, blueberries, and bananas	Rejuvelac Horiatiki (Greek Salad) Sweet Chili–Coconut Chips	12 ounces Rejuvelac Red Ants on a Log	Vegan Bay Crab Cakes with Creamy Dill Tarter Sauce Massaged Kale Salad Cinnamon-Almond Apples
Thursday	Buckwheat Granola with Almond Milk and bananas	Asian Fusion Salad Rolls Kelp Noodle Salad	12 ounces Wheat Grass Blast Herbed Almond Cheese and crudités	Zucchini Pasta Salad with Sun-Dried Tomato Pesto Greens with Cashew-Sesame Tofu and Sweet and Spicy Dijon Dressing
Friday	Fresh fruit Old-fashioned oatmeal with Almond Milk and bananas	Mixed green salad with Tahini Dressing Gazpacho Onion–Caraway Seed Bread	12 ounces Orange Jewels Bananas and Almond Butter	Guacamole and Salsa Vegetable Enchiladas
Saturday	Rise 'n' Shine Smoothie Date and Walnut Wheat-Berry Scones	Garden salad with Tahini Dressing Jalapeño-Onion Corn Bread	12 ounces Choconana Smoothie Apple Baklava	Root Vegetable Raw-violi Wild Rice Pilaf
Sunday	Leftover Apple Baklava and Almond Milk	Better-Than-Eggs Salad Sandwich Green salad	12 ounces Green Juice Maple-Walnut Ice Cream	Vegetable Antipasto Spinach Manicotti with Béchamel Sauce Mixed green salad with leftover dressing

Figure 18-1: Planning a week's worth of meals.

Getting Food Ready ahead of Time

Maintaining a health-promoting raw food diet requires convenient access to plenty of delicious, easy-to-prepare foods. Dedicating just a couple of days each week (on days off work) to prepare key ingredients and food items on your menu can dramatically reduce the time you spend working in the kitchen the rest of the week, and it ensures that you have food ready to eat when you need it.

This section offers do-ahead preparations that make mealtimes a snap. If you do nothing else to prepare food for the week, try to take care of the following tasks to give yourself some basic ingredients. These foods stay good for several days.

- ✔ Wash and cut all vegetables for morning juice (see Chapter 7 for juicing tips) and store in sealed containers in the fridge.
- ✔ Make a few batches of nut or seed milk (find out how in Chapter 11) and keep this staple in the fridge or freeze in jars.
- ✔ Peel and freeze ripe bananas for ice creams and shakes (check out Chapter 17 for details on raw frozen treats).
- ✔ Make a basic raw soup (find recipes in Chapters 8 and 13) and store a few servings in sealed glass jars in the fridge.
- ✔ Wash, dry, and prepare all greens and vegetables for salads. Seal and store them in the fridge.

Store veggies in Evert-Fresh Bags to extend their life in the fridge. You can find Evert-Fresh bags at health food stores, online retailers, and at www.evertfresh.com.

- ✔ Soak and rinse seeds and nuts. Store soaked nuts in the refrigerator until you're ready to use them. Sprout seeds on the counter (see Chapter 7 to find out how) and store the sprouts in the fridge until you need them.
- ✔ Make one or two salad dressings (see Chapter 13) and store them in glass jars in the fridge.
- ✔ Make a batch of nut cheese or pâté (flip to Chapter 7 to get started).
- ✔ Make a few raw entrees, dehydrated snacks, and/or desserts so they're handy and ready to eat. Anything in Part III is fair game!

Fully dehydrated foods can be stored in the pantry, but foods with high fat content (such as nuts, seeds, and olives) and oils (including flax oil and olive oil) should be stored in the fridge to prevent rancidity. Foods that contain moisture also should be stored in the fridge because bacteria and microorganisms thrive in moist conditions.

Prepping produce for salads

Salads are an easy and tasty way to get health-promoting, protein- and calcium-rich raw greens, vegetables, fruits, and whole-food fats into your diet. Plus, salads are simple; they don't require complicated techniques or hours in the kitchen. But when you eat salads daily, achieving enough variety to keep them interesting can be difficult.

To switch it up, people often try to include more and different veggies in their salads, but if you always include ten different vegetables in your salad, then you're probably eating the same packed salad every night! We recommend limiting the number of ingredients in a salad to greens plus a few different additions. That, plus a variety of salad dressings, keeps salads interesting and appealing; you create a very different salad every time.

Try adding acidic fruits to salads for a change of pace. These foods provide a wonderful flavor balance. A little touch of citrus helps brighten the flavor of foods and perks up your palate. And most of them keep really well, so you don't have to worry about them turning brown (like an apple or banana) when you cut them up.

Be sure to wash all fruits and vegetables thoroughly before using. If you're storing the item, be sure to dry it as well. (Find tips on how to wash produce in Chapter 7.)

Here are some specific ideas for prepping your produce ahead of time to make your salads quick and varied:

- **Beets and/or carrots:** Peel and thinly slice beets and carrots by hand or by using a V-slicer, or grate using a hand grater or the shredding attachment of a food processor.

- **Bell peppers:** Slice red, yellow, or orange bell peppers into rings, julienne strips, or dice. We don't recommend eating green bell peppers. They're unripe fruit and difficult for many people to digest. Ripe produce provides the most nutrition.

- **Berries:** Thinly slice berries or toss them in whole.

- **Broccoli:** Separate florets into small bites and thinly slice the stem.

- **Cabbage:** Quarter and core cabbage. Then shred with a knife, a V-slicer, or the 1- or 2-mm food-slicing blade of a food processor.

- **Celery:** Thinly slice celery using a chef's knife or the 1- to 2-mm attachment of a food processor.

- **Citrus fruit:** Peel fruit and section it using a serrated knife.

- **Cucumbers:** Thinly slice cucumbers into rounds or half-moons, or de-seed them and julienne or dice.

- **Herbs:** Remove stems from leaves and chop or mince the leaves with a knife or pulse chop using the S blade of a food processor. See Figure 18-2.

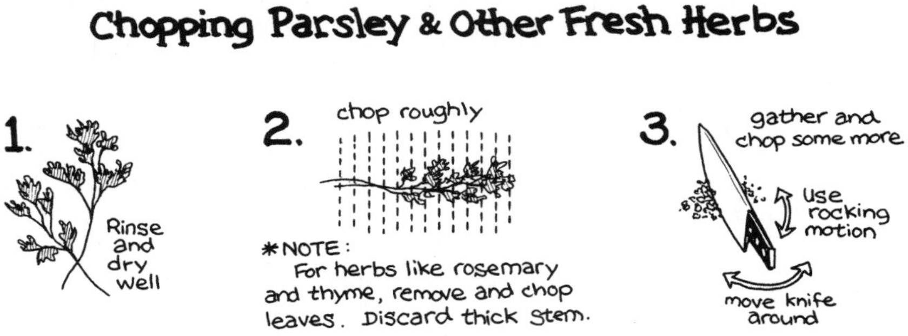

Chopping Parsley & Other Fresh Herbs

Figure 18-2:
The recom-
mended
way to chop
and mince
fresh herbs.

1. Rinse and dry well

2. chop roughly

✱ NOTE:
For herbs like rosemary
and thyme, remove and chop
leaves. Discard thick stem.

3. gather and chop some more

Use rocking motion

move knife around

Leafy, delicate herbs like basil have a tendency to turn black when they're cut. To minimize oxidation, hold off on preparing delicate herbs until just before serving.

✔ **Kale and tougher greens (like collard, mustard, or Swiss chard):** Remove stems, stack a few leaves, roll them up, and thinly slice into shreds. Another option is to tear leaves and pulse-chop them using the S blade of a food processor.

✔ **Lettuce and other tender greens (such as romaine, butter lettuce, green leaf lettuce, mesclun greens, spinach, arugula, frisse, and endive):** For head lettuces, discard the outer damaged leaves, and then separate the remaining leaves before washing. Spin-dry leaves or gently blot dry with paper towels. Tear into bite-sized pieces or cut into strips.

✔ **Onions:** Peel and thinly slice onions by hand or with a V-slicer. Rinse in warm water or soak in salt water for a few minutes to remove strong juices.

✔ **Pineapple:** Peel and core pineapple and thinly slice.

✔ **Zucchini and summer squash:** Thinly slice into rounds or half moons, grate using the hand grater or the shredding attachment of the food processor, or create long, thin noodles using a spiral slicer.

Keeping healthy fats ready for recipes

Fat is not a four-letter word. In fact, adding healthy, whole-food fats to your meals has health benefits and heightens *satiety,* a fancy word that means the state of being satisfied. So eating an appropriate amount of quality, healthy fat is a good thing. See Chapter 3 for details on the value of healthy fats.

Here are some prep tips for keeping nutritious sources of fat ready when you need them:

- ✔ **Avocado:** Keep a few avocados of varying ripeness at all times. Let them ripen on the kitchen counter. When ripe, store them whole in the refrigerator until you're ready to cut. Wrap cut avocado tightly in plastic and store in the fridge for a day or two. Mash avocado for dips and as a topping for salads; slice them and use in sandwiches, sushi, and wraps; and add them to blended soups. A little lemon juice helps to keep avocado from oxidizing and turning brown.

- ✔ **Coconut:** You can blend young coconut meat to make nut milk (see how in Chapter 11), cream, and yogurt — all great additions to sauces, soups, smoothies, and cereal. Plus, the tasty water from coconut can be enjoyed alone or added to smoothies. If you have extra coconut, freeze both the meat and the water for up to 3 months.

- ✔ **Nuts and seeds:** Soak nuts or seeds — choose walnuts, pecans, macadamias, almonds, pine nuts, pistachios, sunflower seeds, or pumpkin seeds — and toss ½ to 1 tablespoon of these protein powerhouses into salads and soups, or use them to garnish the dinner plate. They make great mid-day snacks, and you can blend with water to create delicious milk, yogurt, and cheeses.

- ✔ **Olives:** If you purchase salt-cured sun-dried olives, rinse and soak them in water to rehydrate them and remove some of the salt. Olives contain heart-healthy monounsaturated fat, so add them whole, sliced, or chopped to salads and other dishes.

Making Everyday Meals Special

Even the simplest meals can be more appealing with a few nice touches. Spending a few minutes to make a dish attractive shows that you've included the most important ingredient of all: love! Looking at a beautiful plate of food also starts the digestive juices flowing, so an attractive plate adds to good digestion and certainly enhances the enjoyment of eating the food on it. Plus, it's definitely rewarding to hear "oohs" and "ahhs" when you put a plate of food in front of people!

In this section, we help you conquer the sometimes formidable task of serving daily meals in a way that brings 'em running to the table. We show you how plating and garnishing even a simple meal can make it extraordinary.

The simplest foods can appear extraordinary if a dish is thoughtfully presented. Many factors influence desire for and satisfaction of food, including flavor, memories, expectations, textures, and, of course, appearance. Even various shapes of plates can add excitement and overall enjoyment of a meal.

In fact, we believe that the appearance of food can be as important as the flavor in maintaining a healthy raw plant-based diet in the long term because people respond to the way food looks.

If food isn't appealing to look at, it can be tough to get excited to eat it. For example, if you blend tomatoes in you green Vitality Soup, it turns an unappealing brown color, but if you add a dollop of chopped tomatoes to the soup instead, the color is much more appealing. The brown soup may taste good, but it can be a tough sell.

One of the best things about dining at a nice restaurant is seeing the food when it first arrives, artistically plated and garnished. *Plating* refers to placing food on a plate in an attractive way, and *garnishing* is dressing up the dish using decorations such as sprigs of herbs and artistically cut fruits and vegetables. Enjoying the beauty of a chef's creation tends to enhance excitement to taste it!

Why not take a cue from your favorite restaurants and dress up the dishes you prepare, too? Garnishing a plate with chopped nuts, colorful pepper confetti, minced or whole sprigs of herbs, and other ingredients in the food you prepare is an easy way to improve the visual appeal of any dish, especially if you have reluctant eaters. Just remember the number-one rule of garnishing: The garnish must be edible. Don't just throw something on a plate because it's within your reach. A garnish should add enjoyment of the flavors or textures of the dish — or be flavor neutral.

Here are easy garnish ideas to use with your raw creations:

- Sprinkle a dish with colorful vegetable powders, black sesame seeds, diced vegetable confetti, or flavored chopped nuts.

- Paint the plate holding a saucy dish with thicker sauces and create designs by dragging a brush or toothpick through it.

- Sprinkle capers over faux salmon and drizzle sweet chili sauce over coconut noodles to enhance the flavors and textures of these foods.

- Emphasize colors of ingredients in the dish. For example, a light dusting of chili powder is an excellent addition to a southwestern-inspired salad.

- Cut vegetables into different shapes to add interest. Try small dices, rounds, and sticks (see Figure 18-3 for ideas) or use small vegetable cutters and other kitchen gadgets to form little flowers, stars, or ribbons.

- Add texture where it's lacking, such as by pairing crispy with creamy. For example, top a pâté with a piece of flax cracker. And try using crunchy seasoned nuts or bits of fruits such as pomegranate seeds or raspberries to garnish a salad of bitter greens.

- Use fresh herbs to add color, fragrance, and flavor, but make sure they add to the overall flavor. A large sprig of oregano ruins the palate for other foods if it's accidentally eaten, but a sprinkle of mint, basil, or dill can be a nice surprise.

✔ Wrap lightly blanched leeks or chives around small bundles of vegetables.

✔ Add croutons, flavored oils, and drizzles, swirls, or dollops of cream to garnish soups. Pesto, salsa, coconut yogurt, and savory nut cream make a soup look lovely by adding contrast, color, and flavor.

Make a point of adding some form of a garnish to every dish, even if it's only for yourself. A garnish is a sign of the love you put into the food, and it takes very little extra effort.

Figure 18-3:
Formal knife cuts, shown in actual size.

Plating your way to culinary satisfaction

Plating refers to arranging food artistically on a plate, and proper plating adds to the overall enjoyment of a dish. So think of a dinner plate as a canvas and remember space, balance, color, design, and flow when you add food to it. Use these tips to make the foods you serve both appealing and health promoting.

- **Consider size:** Match food size with plates. A plate that's too small for the food it holds appears crowded and messy. And portions look skimpy on a plate that's too large.

- **Portion appropriately:** Strategically place high-calorie foods on top of greens or other low-calorie foods to make them appear more abundant. Serve enough food to satisfy without encouraging overeating. Drizzle sauce on the rim to visually expand the portion without increasing the calories.

- **Affect appetite with color:** People tend to eat less food if it's served on a dark-colored plate. White plates encourage increased food consumption.

- **Create a focal point:** Keep the center of attention on the entrée and consider everything else part of the supporting cast. Balance is essential, so place various colors and textures on the plate in a way that displays variety.

- **Spread color:** Make sure there are at least three colors on the plate and that they complement each other. Try not to place different foods of the same color side by side.

- **Use negative space positively:** Leave some empty space (also known as *negative space* in the world of design) on the plate to highlight individual foods and keep flavors separate. Lightly dot the empty space with flavored oils or drizzle with thin sauces.

- **Build layers:** Use sauces and marinated vegetables under the entrée and top the entree with spicy sprouts or candied nuts to allow the beauty of foods to show.

- **Play with shapes:** Use a variety of forms and shapes and sizes and heights to position food on a plate.

Feeding Friends and Family

Hosting friends and family for dinner and encouraging your children and spouse to eat more raw foods isn't as difficult as it may seem. The key is serving food that tastes great and looks beautiful. So find out what types of foods your loved ones normally enjoy, and take that direction with the raw foods you choose to offer them — even if the only risk you take at first is a decadent raw dessert. The goal is to satisfy your friends and family with delicious food that's raw and nourishing.

In this section we offer some guidelines for choosing a raw menu and ensuring that different dishes work together.

Deciding which dishes to serve

When deciding on a raw menu for others to enjoy, pick foods that most people appreciate, rather than items such as green soup or fermented dishes that require some getting used to. Luckily, everyone has raw food favorites. Guacamole, salsa, coleslaw, fruit salad, and green salad with great toppings and dressing are popular side dishes in conventional cuisine. And even kids love vegetable sticks. So include these favorites when introducing your friends and family to raw foods and add one or two more creative raw dishes with the meal. Consider including a healthy cooked choice as well if you think you need it to ensure that the meal is comfortable and enjoyable.

Consider a few of these guest-centric issues as you plan a menu.

- ✔ Elderly people tend to eat less than other groups and typically don't appreciate spicy foods or difficult-to-digest ingredients, such as beans.

- ✔ Children, like elderly people, eat far less than adults, usually don't care for very spicy foods, bitter foods, and food that are hard to chew. Many children are hesitant to try new foods, so stick to familiar foods when serving small children.

- ✔ Body builders and teenage boys tend to eat a lot of food, sometimes two to three times as much as older or sedentary adults, and they tend to favor heartier foods. At the salad bar, they may pile on the nuts and avocados and even have a second helping of dessert, so be preared with additional food if these big eaters are coming to the table.

- ✔ Body-conscious people tend to reject fatty food and load up on salads.

If one or more of your guests has a health challenge or special needs, consider making several items that he (and everyone else) can enjoy.

Avoid telling guests that the food you're serving is healthier than the foods they usually eat; no one wants to hear that they make poor food choices. Better to just offer a delicious meal and not make a fuss about it. Friends and family may ask what you're doing differently when they see positive change in you, but try not to preach about how others should eat. Adopting a raw food lifestyle is a personal choice that people need to make on their own.

Considering texture and mouthfeel

An important part of planning appetizing meals is ensuring pleasant mouth-feel and texture. *Mouthfeel* refers to food's physical and chemical interaction in the mouth, which, to most people, is as important to the experience of eating as visual appeal and flavor are.

Mouthfeel is not a topic that tends to stay top of mind or on the tip of tongues — people either experience pleasure from the texture of a food or they don't. When creamy food is contrasted with crispy (as in chips and dip) or hot food is mixed with cold (as in hot fudge sauce over ice cream), the experience is typically positive. But it's usually disappointing if food is gritty when you expect it to be smooth or if it's rubbery when you expect it to be crisp. In other words, satisfaction with mouthfeel definitely relates to expectations.

See Chapter 7 to find out how to prepare raw foods that meet certain kinds of mouthfeel expectations.

Celebrating raw with festive foods

Holidays and celebrations are a great time to enjoy friends and family. Many memories are made sitting around a table and enjoying each other and food. That doesn't stop because you've become a raw foodist. In fact, you may enjoy special times even more when you're not exhausted by trying to digest calorie-dense cooked food.

Here are a few ethnic-themed menus that use the recipes in this book. You may want to celebrate Valentine's Day with a romantic Italian-style dinner, or perhaps you can use items from the Mexican-themed menu for a Cinco de Mayo party. We also include a festive holiday menu that mimics some traditional dishes often served at Christmas or New Year's Eve.

Mexican theme:

- Piña Coladas
- Crudités and dehydrated corn chips with Guacamole and Pico de Gallo
- Corn Cakes with Chimichurri Sauce
- Jalapeño-Onion Corn Bread
- Green Burritos
- Vegetable Enchiladas with Chili Colorado Sauce
- Gazpacho

Asian theme:

- Creamy Coconut-Lemongrass Cocktail
- Soy-Ginger-Glazed Cashew-Sesame Tofu
- Asian Fusion Salad Rolls

✔ Mango-Avocado Wraps with Spicy Sweet-and-Sour Mango Sauce

✔ Thai Miang Kom (Thai-Style Spinach Tacos)

✔ Asian Slaw

✔ Mangoes in Lemon-Ginger Sauce

Italian theme:

✔ Hibiscus Rosé

✔ Root-Vegetable Raw-violi with Basil Pesto on Tomato Concassé

✔ Vegetable Antipasto

✔ Layered Herb Pesto and Almond Cheese Torte

✔ Spinach Manicotti with Béchamel Sauce

✔ Zucchini Pasta Salad with Sun-Dried Tomato Pesto, Black Olives, Capers, and Fresh Basil

✔ Caesar Salad with Garlic-Herb Croutons

Mediterranean theme:

✔ Seventh-Heaven Vegetable Cocktail

✔ Hemp-Seed Tabouli

✔ Great Greek Olives

✔ Dolmas (Stuffed Grape Leaves)

✔ Sweet Red Pepper and Zucchini Hummus

✔ Horiatiki (Greek Salad)

✔ Apple Baklava

American theme:

✔ Spicy Apple-Pineapple Cocktail

✔ Beefy Barbeque Sandwich

✔ Better-Than-Eggs Salad Sandwich

✔ Zucchini Pasta with Marinara and Pine Nut Parmesan

✔ Massaged Kale Salald

✔ Creamy Red Bell Pepper–Chipotle Soup

✔ Peach Crumble and Maple-Walnut Ice Cream

Holiday menu:

- ✔ Orange Jewels
- ✔ Lemony Zucchini Bisque with Shaved Fennel
- ✔ Holiday Wild Rice Pilaf
- ✔ Wild Rice and Corn Salad
- ✔ Vegan Bay Crab Cakes with Creamy Dill Tartar Sauce
- ✔ Onion–Caraway Seed Bread
- ✔ Waldorf Salad with Dried Cranberries and Walnuts

Chapter 19

Eating Raw on the Go

*A*fter exploring the raw food diet and experiencing the incredible improvements in how you look and feel, you may wonder how to maintain this lifestyle when you're away from home. Staying healthy and raw while traveling, dining in restaurants, eating at a friend's house, and even packing a lunch for work may seem like an insurmountable feat!

Sticking to your raw diet away from home does require some thinking ahead, but the benefits are worth it. In this chapter, we show you that maintaining your raw lifestyle is completely possible no matter where you are or how long you plan to be away. Find out how to choose restaurants that are likely to serve food that meets your needs and how to order raw restaurant meals.

We also point out how to take raw food and kitchen equipment along with you. For short trips away from your home turf, you may just need a cooler; for longer getaways, find out in this chapter how to create a simple, inexpensive portable kitchen.

Ordering Raw in Restaurants

People don't go to restaurants simply to eat. Of course, a restaurant's primary purpose is to feed hungry people, but the dining experience offers so much more. It's an opportunity to sample new foods, to relax while someone else prepares a meal and cleans the dishes, and to get together with friends and share a meal. Just because you're embarking on a journey to the world of raw doesn't mean you need to miss out on all the fun with your friends — or eat alone in your hotel room when away from home on business or vacation. This section can help you take your raw lifestyle into a restaurant.

Finding restaurants

Finding restaurants that accommodate a raw diet is getting easier all the time. Almost all restaurants have at least a few options for people looking to maximize nutrition; usually fresh fruit and vegetable options are available as well as a variety of green salads. The key is to think about the common ingredients in the type of cuisine that's offered on a restaurant's menu.

Restaurants that specialize in Mexican, Thai, Mediterranean, Japanese, and vegetarian cuisine are often terrific choices for raw foodists — say hello to guacamole, salad wraps, fresh tomato and cucumber salads, and seaweed appetizers. Even steakhouses often serve a variety of robust salads. Many restaurants are happy to put together a raw veggie plate for you if you ask.

 As you may expect, vegetarian restaurants offer the most possibilities for finding uncooked fruits, vegetables, and other plant-based foods. When you're choosing a restaurant, search for places categorized as vegetarian and/or raw with these online resources:

- ✔ www.happycow.net
- ✔ www.vegdining.com
- ✔ www.vegguide.org
- ✔ www.yelp.com
- ✔ www.urbanspoon.com

Here are some key words to use when exploring a restaurant's raw potential:

- ✔ Vegetarian
- ✔ Organic
- ✔ Gluten free
- ✔ Low fat
- ✔ Weight loss

Perusing the menu

When you sit down at a restaurant with hopes of finding a delicious, nutritious, and satisfying raw meal, be sure to take a look at the whole menu, not just the salad section. You may be surprised at what you find. Look for items that include fresh vegetables in season that you can enjoy raw. Also be on the lookout for sauces to grace your veggies or even your salad. Salsa, guacamole, and pesto are raw and make dynamite salad dressings. And if you don't mind adding a cooked sauce or dressing on your raw dish, try peanut sauce or marinara. Sautéed mushrooms are also a nice treat on occasion.

In the following sections, find tips on scoping out individual sections of the menu and adapting items to meet your raw desires. Don't be afraid to ask for what you want.

If you're worried about finding enough raw food to eat at a restaurant, eat a small snack before going out. Restaurants can be full of temptations that entice you to stray from your commitment to raw, and you're likely to make more healthful food choices when you aren't ravenous.

Appetizers

Restaurant starters, or appetizers, are often large enough to make a tasty and satisfying meal. Here are some best-bet raw options that may be among appetizers on a family-dining restaurant's menu.

- Gazpacho
- Fresh garden salad
- Fresh fruit or fruit salad
- Japanese seaweed salad
- Guacamole with vegetable sticks or lettuce leaves
- Pico de gallo (salsa) with vegetable sticks or lettuce leaves
- Olives or olive tapenade
- Sushi rolls with raw vegetables and no rice

If possible, keep some homemade raw chips in your travel bag and use them to enjoy the restaurant's raw sauces and spreads.

Salads

Ask your server for suggestions of salads and appetizers on the menu that can be modified to meet raw requirements. In addition to her suggestions, look for these keywords in the salad section to keep your meal as raw as possible.

- Tossed green salad
- Spinach or arugula salad
- Seaweed salad (available in Japanese restaurants)
- Papaya salad (available in Southeast-Asian restaurants)

- Mango salad (available in some Southeast-Asian restaurants)
- Cabbage salad (without mayonnaise)
- Greek salad (without feta)
- Chopped vegetable salads (common ones are cucumber-tomato-bell pepper or carrot-apple-celery)
- Chef's choice salad (made with fresh raw vegetables used in other dishes on the menu)

If all else fails, ask for a big, double salad with greens and a variety of raw vegetables (and maybe even avocado!) on it. Request extra-virgin olive oil and lemon wedges on the side to make a quick dressing or bring a small bottle of your favorite raw dressing.

Entrees

Finding raw options in the entree category of a typical restaurant menu can be challenging, but be sure to take a peek. You may get lucky! Look for vegetarian entrees that you can adapt:

- **Veggie sushi:** Order your rolls without the rice.
- **Spring rolls:** Ask for lettuce leaves instead of the processed rice wrapper.
- **Vegetable fajitas:** Order yours uncooked with lettuce leaves instead of tortillas.
- **Wraps:** Ask for the raw filling only; skip the tortilla and mayo. (Wrap chopped salads in lettuce leaves and use a dressing for dip.)

Desserts

Fresh fruit is likely your best bet for dessert. Fresh, in-season berries or oranges or a fruit salad may be the perfect sweet to end your restaurant meal.

A no-bake cheesecake may seem like a good idea, but it's likely made with refined sugar, tofu, and/or dairy. If it's essential for you to eat only raw foods, be sure to ask your server about any food preparation techniques for menu items that you're unsure about. Here are other desserts that may seem raw but aren't:

- Ice cream (even those made with tofu, coconut, or rice milk)
- Fruit sorbet
- Parfait

Making special requests

When you're living raw, don't be afraid to ask a restaurant to prepare your food in a way that meets your needs. Your dietary standards are just as valid as those of people who are gluten free, vegetarian, lactose intolerant, or observing food restrictions based on religion. Explain your dietary needs to your waiter and make certain he understands what you need. Quite often, chefs are happy to accommodate diners in this way. And if your requests are denied, then you know where not to go next time you dine out.

Here are other suggestions for ordering a raw meal in any restaurant:

- ✔ Order two house salads to be combined in one bowl or plate and topped with fresh avocado and raw seeds (if available). Bring your own seeds just in case.

- ✔ Ask the chef to puree two green salads and raw dressing. You just ordered green soup! Order a side of salsa, guacamole, pesto, diced vegetable concassé, or fresh fruit chutney; put a dollop on your soup.

- ✔ Order a plate of raw vegetables and natural sides, such as salsa and guacamole.

As with most considerations related to raw cuisine, advanced preparation is essential. If possible, call the restaurant in advance to see if kitchen staff can accommodate raw meal requests. Before calling, look for raw options on the restaurant's online menu, if available. You may need to politely explain what you mean by *raw* and offer meal suggestions. See the sidebar "Calling in food favors" for suggestions on asking a restaurant to prepare a raw meal for you.

Calling in food favors

If you decide to call a restaurant to ask for special accommodations to meet your raw food standards, try to place your call in the early afternoon or even a day in advance of your arrival, and ask to speak with the chef. Hosts and servers are limited in what they can promise from the kitchen.

Explain that you've heard wonderful things about the restaurant and that you want to request a special meal. Politely, clearly, and briefly tell the chef what your food needs are (100 percent raw or a combination of raw and cooked). Traditional chefs may think tofu,

bread, and yogurt are raw, because they don't cook them. So point out ingredients you need to avoid that the restaurant uses heavily (such as soy sauce, vinegar, or sugar). But don't make it too complicated!

Quite often, chefs are happy to accommodate special dietary requests, especially if your reservations are early in the evening (when the kitchen isn't so busy) and your meal doesn't require expensive ingredients or complicated preparation. Ask the chef for suggestions on what you may enjoy that's relatively painless to prepare.

Going prepared with a stash of goodies

Many raw foodists keep a little travel bag stocked with basic food items to supplement a restaurant's raw offerings or snack while away from home. We suggest including seasoned nuts and seeds (see Chapters 13 and 16), avocado, cayenne pepper or other favorite herbs and spices, flax crackers, raw bread (see Chapter 9), and/or even a small container of raw cheese or pâté (see Chapter 12). Nori sheets are also great for on-the-go bags because they have a fairly long shelf life and can be used to wrap up just about anything.

Here's a checklist of foods that you may want to have with you when you go to a restaurant:

❏ Seasoned seeds and nuts

❏ Dehydrated raw bread or croutons

❏ Kale chips

❏ Nut cheese or spread

❏ Favorite herbs and spices

❏ Sun-dried fruit

❏ Avocado

❏ Nori sheets

❏ Vegetarian-formula nutritional yeast

❏ Himalayan crystal salt

❏ Tea bags

❏ Agave nectar or coconut sugar

❏ Flavored organic extra-virgin olive oil or favorite dressing

Don't bring full meals from other restaurants or from home into a restaurant. Supplementing a meal that you purchase from a restaurant with some of your own ingredients is usually fine, but restaurants are businesses; packing in your own meals is a bit rude. Instead, encourage the restaurant to permanently offer raw options to earn your business.

Brown Bagging Raw Lunch

If you follow the recommendations in Chapter 7 regarding weekend food preparation, then assembling your weekday food should be a fairly light task. Dedicate some of your weekend preparation time to setting up away-from-home lunches.

When packing your lunch for work, consider toting your travel bag (as described in the earlier section "Going prepared with a stash of goodies") along with the following foods:

- ✔ Hardy greens, such as romaine lettuce, for salad
- ✔ Apples and other firm fruits with skin
- ✔ Dehydrated treats, such as bars, cookies, and trail mix

If you work in an office or other type of consistent area and have space for personal items, consider keeping some seasoned nuts and seeds, kale chips, well-dehydrated crackers, and other long-lasting items on hand (find ideas in Chapter 16) as well as your favorite seasonings, tea bags, and oil. You're less likely to make a stress-related run to the vending machine if you have your own healthy and delicious food nearby.

For kids' lunches, be sure to pack foods they can hold easily. If you can include foods that they helped to prepare, great! If you can't picture the Norman Rockwell version of working together each morning to assemble a nutritious lunch, ask your kids to help you put together batches of foods on the weekends. Store single portions in resealable bags for grab-and-go meals.

Here are some popular items for a child's lunch box:

- ✔ Raw Power Trail Mix
- ✔ Chocolate Pudding
- ✔ Kale Chips
- ✔ Red Ants on a Log
- ✔ Coconut Yogurt
- ✔ Sweet Nut'ins 'n' Chocolate Kisses
- ✔ Raw dips and veggie sticks
- ✔ Fruit salads
- ✔ Raw cookies
- ✔ Pinwheels (Any wrap sliced cross-wise into bite-sized pieces)
- ✔ Nut butter with apples or bananas
- ✔ Dehydrated apple chips
- ✔ Sugar snap peas
- ✔ Frozen grapes
- ✔ Clementines

Traveling Raw

Staying healthy on the road is always a challenge for people who want optimal health. Eating nutrient-dense foods when traveling takes a little bit of planning but is well worth the effort. Take a little time to think about how long you will be gone and how you can prepare yourself so you have what you need when you need it. Being prepared with some basic food-prep tools and other supplies can make all the difference in how you feel when you return home, too!

When making travel plans and preparing for your time away from home, do some homework online to find out where you may be able to find raw foods in the city or town you're visiting. Here are some suggestions:

- ✔ Search for raw food, vegetarian, vegan, or farm-to-table restaurants as well as health-food stores and farmers' markets in the area. Visit online raw food forums and ask for recommendations.

- ✔ Find supermarkets in the area with salad and juice bars. Smoothie and juice bars are popping up everywhere, and many even offer raw crackers and other goodies.

- ✔ Try to reserve a condo or hotel with a full kitchen (that has a blender) for your getaway so you can prepare raw meals. If this isn't an option, many standard hotel rooms have small refrigerators to keep your foods fresh.

- ✔ Check out www.localharvest.org to get a list of farms near your destination that sell to the public.

Program the addresses of restaurants and organic markets into your GPS so you're prepared with directions when you arrive at your destination. And if you don't discover places to eat and acquire raw, organic foods before you arrive, ask the locals for recommendations. Often, the hidden gems of an area never make it to the Internet.

Staying raw on road trips

Having access to a car during your travels gives you some flexibility. Pick up a salad at a nearby restaurant or drive to a whole-foods supermarket that has a salad bar with organic ingredients. If those options aren't available, go to a local grocery store and buy a few things in the produce section. You can make great wraps with romaine lettuce, a tomato, a bell pepper, an avocado, and goodies from your travel bag. If you need more excitement, buy hummus or another raw side item to enhance your meal. Or, if the season and geography permit, add to your eats by stopping at roadside fruit stands.

Create a list of your favorite travel foods to take with you. We recommend that you take along raw crackers, kale chips, fruit roll-ups, bars and cookies, trail mixes, raw nuts, dried fruit, and other favorite snacks when traveling. Check out Chapters 9 and 13 to find out how to make raw crackers, breads, seasoned seeds, and snacks.

You may also want to take a small cooler filled with some of these foods:

✔ Green smoothie for the day of your departure

✔ Frozen coconut water to drink when it defrosts

✔ Sprouts (rinse at morning and night to keep fresh for a couple days)

✔ Avocados (a ripe one for the day of departure and a slightly unripe one to eat later)

✔ Nut pâtés

✔ Romaine lettuce hearts in prewashed packages

✔ Green superfood powder

✔ Fresh and dried fruits

✔ Pre-cut vegetables

Finding raw food during air travel

On short domestic flights, airline meals are practically nonexistent. If one is offered on your flight, find out what options you have to pre-order a meal before you fly. Some airlines offer a raw, vegetarian, or vegan meal option. If yours doesn't offer a meal that matches your needs, bring your own food. Most airports have restaurants and kiosks that sell premade salads, which you can tailor to your personal needs with your homemade croutons, nutritional yeast, and seasoned nuts.

We suggest bringing a superfoods green powder packet with you and shaking it into juice or water that you buy pre-flight or on the plane. Flip to Chapter 6 to find out where to find these packets.

If you're planning to take food and beverages on a plane, be sure to check the current carry-on guidelines from the Transportation Security Administration (TSA) — available at www.tsa.gov — beforehand. Depending on the security threat level when you travel, you may be limited to a certain number and size of liquid containers allowed in your carry-on bag. You may have to purchase items after clearing security check points or choose to check some of your bags so they can undergo additional screening.

Considering coconut water

Young coconuts are filled with a clear, electrolyte-rich juice that contains zero fat and zero cholesterol. This juice is coconut water. With twice the electrolytes of a banana, coconut water is a great natural alternative to sports drinks. You can find coconut water in convenience stores, airports, and vending machines. Just be aware that some brands are pasteurized or have sugar added; look for raw coconut water with no sugar added.

Before your flight, hydrate yourself with coconut water, a natural electrolyte that keeps your body balanced. (See the nearby sidebar for more about coconut water.) Buy a large bottle of water after you go through security and, when onboard, ask an attendant for water, too. In fact, ask the attendant if you can have a full bottle of water. If you tell the attendant that you're on a special diet and need extra water, he'll likely accommodate you.

Eating raw at a hotel

If you're staying at a hotel while traveling, be sure you arrive with bottled water. Tap water contains bacteria-killing agents that take out beneficial bacteria as well as the bad guys, and very few hotels provide filtered water. Truly, even more important than making good food choices while traveling is staying hydrated. You need to maintain high levels of probiotics, your friendly flora, when you're away from home to aid in good digestion (see Chapter 3 for the details), so drink high-quality, chemical-free water.

Also, when selecting a hotel, be sure to book a room with a refrigerator to store your raw foods. And if the hotel has a complimentary breakfast bar, get your fill of fresh fruits each and every day!

If you happen to be traveling in luxe style and your hotel operates a full kitchen, ask if staff can make freshly squeezed orange juice, possibly for a fee. The kitchen may even have the ingredients to make a fruit smoothie or green soup for you, so have a recipe handy.

Packing a portable kitchen

If you're traveling for an extended period of time, it may be worthwhile to take a portable kitchen in addition to your normal travel bag. Here's a list of supplies to pack in an enhanced travel bag to offer you more food flexibility on your trip:

- ✔ A soft-sided cooler that's small enough to meet airline standards if you're traveling by plane
- ✔ Spoon, knife, fork, or chopsticks and cloth napkins for each person traveling (put in your checked luggage if traveling by plane)
- ✔ Small, flexible plastic chopping mat
- ✔ Wooden plate and/or bowl
- ✔ Beverage container with watertight lid
- ✔ One or more small containers for cereal or snacks
- ✔ One small leak-proof container for salad dressing
- ✔ One sealable container for salad
- ✔ Resealable plastic bags to hold dried fruit, nuts, fresh fruit, and veggies
- ✔ Favorite seasonings in small spice shakers
- ✔ Plastic bags for trash and compost
- ✔ Placemat or table cover

If you want to sprout while traveling, bring a mesh sprout bag and some seeds. Clover seeds are easy to sprout and take about five days. Legumes such as lentils are ready in only three days and are a great addition to salads.

If you're traveling internationally, you likely won't be able to pack produce or sprouting seeds. Check the website for customs and border patrol (in the U.S., www.cbp.gov) for current rules and regulations before you travel.

If you're planning an extended trip or simply want to take more complicated food preparation tools on your trip, consider adding these items to your traveling kitchen:

- ✔ Small blender made of lightweight plastic
- ✔ Extension cord
- ✔ Rubber spatula
- ✔ Kitchen towel and sponge
- ✔ Knives: 6–8-inch chef's knife, small paring knife, and/or serrated knife (must pack in check-in luggage if traveling by airplane)
- ✔ Cloth bag with drawstring for sprouting seeds and straining nut milk
- ✔ Plastic produce spinning bag for washing salad greens

Chapter 20

Gathering with a Raw Community

....

In This Chapter

▶ Looking for friends to support your new raw foods lifestyle

▶ Finding support online

▶ Hosting raw foods events

....

*E*njoying excellent health and vitality is the best motivator for continuing a raw food journey, but the road is much more pleasant when you have friends who share your lifestyle. You may know that raw foods nourish your body and spirit, but how do you find others who are as passionate about eating this way as you are? In this chapter, we help you find (or create!) a raw foods support structure and meet other people who are making the choice to eat raw. We promise, you aren't alone! Many more people eat this way than you may think, and still more want to but don't know where to start. Perhaps you'll inspire this positive change in someone you meet.

Joining a Local Group

You may feel alone or misunderstood when you begin to eat a diet of raw foods. So finding other like-minded people can really help keep you motivated to maintain the raw lifestyle.

A raw food support group can take various forms. Some have monthly meetings; some offer an online forum through social media; and others are just friends or family who gather casually to talk about the raw food lifestyle and its benefits (or challenges). The important thing is for the group to supply information and encouragement to folks who are curious about the lifestyle along with insight about how to make it easier and most satisfying.

Joining a raw food support group has many benefits, including making friends; sharing recipes, foods, and ideas; and trying new restaurants and travel destinations together. Members of a raw food group can likely relate to your experiences and answer questions about various aspects of this way of living.

Some groups are specialized, focusing on a specific aspect of living raw, such as weight loss, cancer support, pregnancy, child rearing, or environmental steward-ship. A group may motivate you to improve other aspects of your life — beyond your food choices — to become even healthier. And groups often form buying clubs to purchase items in bulk to save money on organic foods (see Chapter 6).

The benefits of joining a local raw-food community may include some of the following perks:

✔ Monthly or weekly meetings and potlucks

✔ Recipe and book sharing

✔ Food swaps

✔ Social events

✔ Support for various health and life goals

✔ Online discussion boards and blogs

Find a group near you by serching online. Enter "Raw Food Group" and the name of your city. Or check your local newspaper, organic markets, and health-food store calendars for raw food group meetings and other raw-centered events. And don't be shy about starting up a conversation with people you meet at farmers' markets and yoga classes. Often, these people know people who are raw foodists, or perhaps they themselves live raw!

Logging In to Online Support

Cyberspace offers nearly limitless opportunities to learn more about raw foods; and the more you know, the more likely you are to be successful at maintaining this nutritious lifestyle. So get online and take advantage of social networking. Check out raw food blogs, network on Facebook, post questions and follow raw foodists on Twitter, and watch YouTube videos to find inspiration and learn new ways to prepare raw meals.

If you discover websites or blogs you find interesting, don't be afraid to write to the authors and ask questions. If people are developing content and pub-lishing it online, they're likely willing to share information with you — for free. But if you're looking for personal service such as one-on-one coaching, consider hiring a professional raw food coach. You can find some options at http://therawfoodcoach.com, http://rawfoodeducation.com, and www.rawfoodchef.com.

Search for raw food classes or a raw culinary school — sounds fancy, right? — to find opportunities to pick up new tricks for raw food prep. Many raw culinary schools offer classes for individuals with no aspirations to become a chef as well as advanced instruction for people who hope to create a career with raw foods.

Here are a few trusted raw food communities online:

- ✔ **123 Raw** (http://123raw.ning.com) welcomes people who are curious about, new to, or fully committed to raw foods and features forums, events, and videos.

- ✔ **30 Bananas a Day** (www.30bananasaday.com) is geared toward 100 percent low-fat raw vegans.

- ✔ **G Living** (www.glivingmembers.com) is a stylish raw food community that features information on the lifestyle along with posts about nature, technology, food, and music.

- ✔ **Gone Raw** (www.goneraw.com) is an online community where members post raw vegan recipes.

- ✔ **The Living Foods Community** (www.living-foods.com) speaks to new raw foodists and features recipes, forums, a marketplace, and personal ads.

- ✔ **My Crazy Sexy Life** (http://my.crazysexylife.com) is the community forums of Kris Carr, a *New York Times* best-selling author and wellness warrior.

- ✔ **Raw Food Rehab** (http://rawfoodrehab.ning.com) is an online raw community that focuses on healthly weight management.

- ✔ **Raw Food Network** (www.rawfoodnetwork.com/supportgroups. html) facilitates the development of raw food support groups and meet-ups in cities throughout the world.

- ✔ **Raw Food Boot Camp** (www.rawfoodbootcamp.com) is a support group for obese women who are interested in transitioning to diet containing more raw food to manage food addiction and obsession while losing weight.

Look for a feature on the websites you find to search for affiliated groups near you. Often you can search by zip code.

Creating a New Community

If you can't find a raw food group in your area, begin your own group and draw like-minded people to you. It can be a lot of fun to organize a new raw food meet-up group. Truly, it's less challenging than you may think. Start by thinking about the type of group and people you want to gather as well as what you want to do with the group.

Consider the possible ways for your group to interact, and write down your goals. Think about what you want to gain from meeting with the new group and what members can expect when joining. Also decide how often you want to meet and what you want to do at meetings.

Some groups have a membership fee of $25 to $35 for the year, which can be used to pay for certain offerings such as supplies for dinner gatherings, educational events, newsletters, and even group recipe e-books.

To attract members, consider using an online service like Meetup (www. meetup.com). As the organizer on this site, you choose from 15 different topics to serve as a group identity. If you're starting a raw food Meetup group, you can list your group under a variety of tags, including Raw Food, Raw Vegan, Organic, Vegetarian, or any other key words that flag what your group is about.

For a first meeting, choose a well-lit public place. A local coffee shop or juice bar is an excellent first meeting place — comfortable, nonthreatening, and inviting to new members. At this initial meeting, encourage people to talk, get to know each other, and tell the group why they're interested in raw foods. You can also share food and dietary goals and get a sense of everyone's interests, abilities, and experiences.

Don't worry about making a firm agenda. Allow the first interaction to flow naturally. Ask the group what kind of gatherings they want to organize and attend. Some people may prefer small weekly meetings in addition to a monthly rawluck. Some may be interested in visiting a local organic farm or local resturants, and others may be focused on preparing foods together. Figure out what is and isn't doable and formulate a plan to begin working with the group to meet its needs.

Ask for volunteers. Find out who might be interested in handling various tasks for the group. For instance, are a few people available to arrive early for the next gathering to set up the space or bring water and other supplies? Anyone want to take the lead on arranging a farm visit? Some of the most robust meet-up groups have a volunteer web manager and social media person, a newsletter designer and editor, and even someone who plans events such as culinary demos and health talks. Announce opportunities for tasks that the group may require.

Before parting ways, suggest an event, such as a raw potluck, for the next gathering to center on, and choose a date with the group.

Hosting a Dinner Event

Hosting a raw potluck, or *rawluck,* featuring raw vegan dishes is an ideal way to gather a raw foods group, meet other raw foodists, and try out new raw recipes. Rawlucks are also a fun way to support the raw food community and provide information to people who are interested in adding more raw foods to their diet.

Before your dinner event, be sure to establish specific dietary guidelines for the event. Will the group enjoy organic foods only, strictly vegan cuisine, all raw, or other standard? If some of your guests are new to the raw foods lifestyle and they're contributing to the dinner, make sure they understand what's considered raw and what isn't.

Deciding on a menu

Ideally, rawlucks contain a variety of courses, including appetizers, entrees, and desserts, as well as a beverage. The event can center on a haphazard assortment of dishes or a well-orchestrated spread. To avoid a meal consisting of only desserts (unless that's your theme), ask guests to contribute a specific course.

Because we feel it's so important, we include an entire chapter (Chapter 18 to be exact) on menu planning. Take a look at it for tips on choosing foods for your rawluck.

Here are some raw foods that are especially appropraite for a rawluck:

- ✔ Raw salads of all kinds are always a hit! Top organic greens with a nice raw dressing.

- ✔ Fresh fruit salad or fresh, ripe, in-season organic fruit is sure to please.

- ✔ Spreads, such as Not-Salmon Pâté or Almond Cheese Spread, with raw chips or bread are great as an appetizer or with salad.

- ✔ Salsa and Guacamole are ultimate party favorites. Dig into them with Sweet Pepper Sesame Chips or freshly cut veggies.

- ✔ A fresh veggie platter with sliced cucumbers, zucchini, cherry tomatoes, carrots, and radishes offers tasty treats for everyone.

- ✔ Raw lasagna and other casserole-like dishes make satisfying fare.

- ✔ Apple Baklava is a great choice for dessert.

Some groups divide the menu and use a rotating list to determine who brings what kind of dish. For instance, guests with last names starting with A–E bring an appetizer, F–L bring dessert, and M–Z bring an entree. If you have a Meetup site, Facebook page, or blog, you can post the menu so guests can see what other people are bringing.

Other groups choose a theme, such as Mexican Fiesta or Mediterranean Flavors, or a course, as in Just Desserts. You can also hone in on a specific ingredient, such as Zucchini Extravaganza, or a holiday: Raw Holiday Traditions or Sweet Valentines go over well.

If this level of planning is a bit much for you, just have everyone bring a dish and allow the menu to be divinely guided, so to speak. After all, that system puts the *luck* in *rawluck*.

Keep in mind that not everyone understands the ins and outs of raw, so if a guest shows up with a non-raw dish, be a gracious host and use the opportunity to talk about foods that are commonly mistaken for being raw and why they don't measure up. Also make sure people know they can just bring a bag of juicy organic grapes to share if they don't want to prepare a dish.

To keep trash to a minimum, ask guests to bring their own plates, utensils, and cup. Have extra handy in case someone forgets. Also ask guests to bring a copy of their recipe so you can assemble and share them in the group newsletter or e-recipe book. At the very least, ask guests to list the ingredients in their dish on a note card that you can place near the food to alert those with food sensitivities.

Preparing the venue

Potlucks are usually hosted in someone's home, but parks and meeting rooms at supermarkets, public libraries, and community centers also make good locations.

If you're hosting an event and inviting people you don't know well, consider choosing a public location rather than your home. Think carefully before you post your home address online.

Arrive at the location early so you have plenty of time to clean and set up for the event. Here's a list of set-up items to get your rawluck off to a great start:

- Extra plates, utensils, and napkins
- A pen and paper for writing recipes or ingredient lists
- Name tags
- Sign-in sheet asking for contact information
- Pitchers of filtered water
- Small collection of raw food books and other reference materials
- Trash, recycling, and compost bins

Enjoying the event

Potlucks are always more successful if the host is organized. Be sure to have the room set up with the buffet table ready, serving utensils at the ready, and a greeter at the door with name tags.

Create an agenda so everyone is clear on what time to start eating. If a speaker, social circle, video, or food demo is going to be featured, make sure everyone knows whether it will be before or after the meal. Most of the time it's best to have special events after eating unless the event is a peace or thanksgiving meditation.

After your guests arrive and begin to mingle, encourage people to introduce themselves. When it's time to eat, gather around the food and ask each guest to announce his or her dish and mention if it contains any common allergens. Near the end of the meal, ask if there are any "first-timers." If so, ask them to stand and introduce themselves.

Following the meal, ask for suggestions about how to communicate with the group about the next gathering and, if you want to grow the numbers, how to extend the invitation to others. These events tend to work best with groups of 20 to 30 people.

Here are a few ideas for communicating with the group:

✔ **Use a phone tree.** Ask volunteers to divide a list of phone numbers to call and remind people about the next gathering. Encourage people to bring a friend if you want to expand the group.

✔ **Create an e-mail list.** Gather e-mail addresses at the event and send periodic messages with information about upcoming gatherings.

Before your guests leave, ask for volunteers to help clean up, pack up, and remove trash. Establish early that the group is a cooperative experience in which all members need to contribute in some way.

Creating an Educational Event

Consider organizing an informational event for your raw support group. Lectures provided by raw food experts, classes on the raw vegan lifestyle and food-preparation techniques, and guided tours of facilities that center on organic foods can offer valuable information to people who are interested in the raw foods lifestyle as well as those who've been living raw for years.

After you choose an event type, pick a date and time and publicize the event through social media like a relevant Meetup group, Facebook, and Twitter. (Check out the section "Logging In to Online Support" earlier in this chapter for other online resources for communicating your event to the raw food community.)

Get in touch with local vegetarian and vegan groups, too. They may be able to provide a potential audience for your event. Posting flyers on community bulletin boards in local health-food stores, CSAs (community-supported agriculture networks), cooking schools, yoga studios, colleges, organic gardening groups, animal-rights groups, co-ops, farmers' markets, hospitals, libraries, and health clubs can't hurt.

And if you're feeling ambitious, also consider writing a brief press release about the event and sending it to health or food calendar contacts at your local newspaper. Include a brief description of the event with a date and time, venue address, and your contact information.

Part V
The Part of Tens

The 5th Wave   By Rich Tennant

RAW FOOD HUNTERS

"Easy—there it is. The wild rutabaga, and I think you've got a clear shot."

In this part . . .

If you turn to the end of any *For Dummies* book, no matter what the topic, you can find the Part of Tens. Here, this part gives you small (but mighty!) and easily digestible tips for beginning and following a raw food lifestyle. The first chapter emphasizes the immediate and long-term benefits of eating raw foods. The second points out foods that are best eaten raw, whether your diet consists of a little or all raw food.

Chapter 21

Ten Reasons to Go Raw

In This Chapter
▶ Enjoying better health
▶ Being kind to the environment and animals

*T*here are as many compelling reasons to go raw as there are raw foodists. All raw foodists have personal stories about how raw foods helped them lose weight, heal, gain more energy or mental clarity, look better, feel better, or achieve some other benefit or goal. But most people go raw and stick with this lifestyle for the following reasons. (Check out Chapter 2 for other benefits of living raw.)

Looking and Feeling Better

Most people report improved health and general well-being within weeks of switching to a raw food lifestyle. The nutrient-rich raw diet is high in antioxidants, phytochemicals, vitamins, minerals, fiber, and healthy fats (such as omega-3 fatty acids), so it maximizes health and vitality.

It's not uncommon to hear about health-conscious people — including movie stars and other celebrities — who are embracing a raw food lifestyle to maximize their health, increase energy, and build a strong immunity system.

Raw foods are available in abundant variety and present delicious food choices, especially compared to diets that focus on calorie restriction and deprivation. Temporary diets are often very unhealthy and doomed to failure because people cannot maintain the regimen as a lifestyle. However, the raw diet is abundant with fresh produce as well as nuts, seeds, grains, and legumes.

Reducing Health Risks and Healing from Disease

The facts are indisputable; a raw plant-based diet leads to lower risk of heart disease, cancer, diabetes, high blood pressure, rheumatoid arthritis, and obesity. Even beyond people who eat other types of vegetarian diets, including lacto, lacto-ovo, and even cooked vegan, people who eat a raw vegan diet are less prone to obesity, coronary disease, high blood pressure, cancer, and type 2 diabetes because it's rich in nutritious plant foods, contains omega-3 fatty acids (from flax, chia, and nuts), and has low levels of saturated fats but no hydrogenated fats or cholesterol.

Cancer, which is responsible for killing more than 568,000 Americans each year, can be reduced and even reversed when the following foods are eliminated from the diet:

✔ Beef

✔ Duck

✔ Chicken

✔ Fish

✔ Pork

✔ Turkey

✔ Wild game

✔ Processed meat and fish products (even if not heated)

✔ Dairy cheese

✔ French fries

✔ Potato chips

✔ Beer

Avoiding Premature Aging and Promoting Longevity

Many raw foodists look 20 years younger than people of the same age who eat cooked foods. This youthfulness is due in part to the nutrient density of raw foods, which are rich in antioxidants, phytonutrients, and vitamins that protect the body from free radicals, which attack healthy cells. (See Chapter 3 for details.) People who are well nourished tend to feel good and maintain a healthy body weight well into their golden years.

Achieving an Ideal Body Weight

With a diet that's high in fiber and essential nutrients, you feel satiated sooner than when eating foods that contain empty calories. Many people believe that the body continues to feel hungry until nutrient needs are satisfied. Therefore, even if you eat enough calories to fuel your body, you're still hungry — for nutrients! In this situation, your metabolism slows down, you stop burning fat, and you crave more food. If you have an addiction to sugar and fat, you'll most likely reach for these foods to achieve a feeling of satiation.

The fast-food industry is in business to provide people with lots of opportunities to eat sugary and fatty foods, and many people are addicted to these foods. But with a raw plant-based diet, you can eat all you want of fresh, ripe, and raw foods without worrying about counting calories. After eating a mostly raw diet for a few weeks, your body begins to naturally regulate how much food you need by turning off its hunger-response mechanism when you have had enough.

Increasing Energy, Vitality, and Stamina

When the human body is well nourished, it's healthy and active and has an abundance of vitality. Fats, especially heat-processed oils, slow you down because they require long periods of digestion, which steals energy from your body. Light foods, such as fruits and vegetables, digest easily and leave you with energy for activity.

Also, less sleep is required when you eat foods that are fresh and light; when you consume heavy, cooked foods, especially in the evenings, several hours of sleep time is spent digesting food rather than moving you to the deep sleep zone that's required to reach beta levels and the dream state. Raw foodists often report that they sleep one to three hours less and still have more energy and stamina than when they ate mostly cooked foods.

Enhancing Memory and Mental Clarity

Your brain needs nourishment, and whole, ripe, raw organic plant foods provide the power you need for strong mental acuity. The essential fats that the brain needs, such as omega-3 fatty acids, are in leafy greens, flaxseed, chia, hemp, and walnuts as well as many other raw plant foods. The human brain also needs plenty of water, magnesium, and organic sodium; whole raw foods offer an abundance of these nutrients. When nutrient- and water-deficient foods (including pasta, pizza, and other fare that's laden with hydrogenated, saturated, and cooked fats and salt) are replaced with nutrient-dense whole plant foods and healthy fats, brain function improves.

Reducing Colds, Flus, and Allergies

Most raw foodists find that replacing toxic foods with wholesome nourishing plant foods reduces or even eliminates their respiratory problems, colds, flus, and allergies. A raw diet is especially great for people who are intolerant of dairy, wheat, and soy because raw foods have virtually no hidden ingredients. Apples and carrots, for instance, are dairy- and lactose-free, wheat- and gluten-free, soy-free, egg-free, grain-free, and even corn-free.

Check out the recipes in Part III to find out how to make luscious desserts without dairy, eggs, or wheat; prepare raw lasagna and enchiladas with delicious nut cheese; and, if you're allergic to gluten, delight in eating sandwiches again with raw breads made with heart-healthy flaxseed and vegetables.

Peanuts and tree nuts are also common allergens and cause life-threatening reactions. Peanuts are typically roasted, so you won't find any of those in this book, but raw foodists do use other kinds of nuts and consider them health-promoting when used in reasonable amounts. But even the tiniest speck of nuts can be problematic for people who have serious nut allergies. If you have allergies to nuts, we recommend that you replace nuts with young coconut in many of our recipes.

Forgetting about Cleaning Dirty Pots and Pans

A raw diet frees you from cooking! And raw food preparation is (for the most part) quick and easy with meals that are a breeze to clean up. No greasy stoves and no hot ovens or fryers.

Of course, any gourmet food takes time to prepare — raw foods included. But you can make satisfying raw meals without a lot of fuss. A knife and a blender are all that's required to whip up smoothies, soups, sauces, and even desserts in a flash (see Chapter 8). And if you spend just one day a week making foods for the pantry and fridge, you can ensure that food prep is quick and easy for the rest of the week — even for a working person. (Find a 31-day menu with food-prep prompts in Chapter 4.)

Demonstrating Kindness to Animals

Although some raw foodists do consume small amounts of meat and fish, we recommend following a raw vegan diet, which includes only plant foods. All the recipes in this book are vegan; no animal suffering is involved in these foods. The animal husbandry industries can be quite cruel to animals, and chickens, cows, lamb, sheep, pigs, rabbits, and other sentient beings that are used for food feel pain and fear, just as we do. These creatures become ill without proper living conditions, and the fact is, we're healthier when we don't eat meat, so why do it?

Protecting the Environment

A raw lifestyle supports sustainable farming, creation of healthy topsoil, protection of watersheds, and reduction of your carbon footprint. A vegan diet also protects natural resources by not contributing to the deforestation that's inherent in the meat industry. Greenhouse gases, loss of natural habitat, depletion of topsoil, and contamination of the precious water supply are directly linked to the meat and dairy industries, which uses nearly 20 percent of all energy use in the U.S. and more water and fossil fuels than any other industry.

Moreover, raw food, when purchased in its natural state, contains little to no packaging; it's packaged by nature. Cooked and processed foods in cans, plastic containers, and plastic-coated boxes add to the volume of hazardous waste. Most raw foodists support organic agriculture, eschewing the use of pesticides, fungicides, and other chemicals. They know the importance of composting and recycling and many make purchase decisions based on the packaging, human rights, fair-trade standards, and other criteria that support the earth and its inhabitants.

Chapter 22

Ten Foods Best Eaten Raw

In This Chapter

▶ Picking out foods to only eat raw

▶ Seeing the connection between heating food and damaging its nutrients

Cooking kills bacteria that may be present in food. In fact, people probably started cooking food as a means to kill harmful bacteria. But unfortunately, cooking also destroys vital nutrients, including antioxidants and phytochemicals, which are essential for repairing your body and keeping you strong. (Check out Chapter 3 for the whole lowdown on nutrition.)

Cooking and processing food definitely results in nutrient loss, but how long it is stored after picking also plays a role in the benefits received from food. The longer fresh, ripe food is stored after harvest, the more vulnerable it is to nutrient loss, even if it's prepared with raw food techniques, such as juicing and blending. Foods that continue to ripen off the tree, like avocados, bananas, and tomatoes, can be held without refrigeration until they are ripe; then they must be refrigerated to maintain freshness and nutrient value. This chapter points out foods that are best enjoyed raw and as quickly after harvest as possible.

Nuts and Seeds

Nuts and seeds are a powerhouse of nutrition. Macadamia nuts, cashews, pine nuts, pistachios, Brazil nuts, flaxseeds, and chia seeds all contain vitamin B1 (thiamine), which helps cells convert carbohydrates into energy. This nutrient is essential for healthy function of the heart, muscles, and nervous system. Most fruits and vegetables do not provide a significant amount of thiamine, so eating a few raw nuts and seeds every day helps you get this important nutrient.

Almonds contain vitamin B2, or riboflavin, an important nutrient for repro-duction, red-cell production, and body growth; walnuts, chia, flax, and hemp seeds have a significant amount of omega 3, an essential fatty acid and anti-inflammatory that the body needs for good cardiovascular health and beauti-ful skin and to guard against aging.

Many nuts and seeds also contain omega-3 fatty acids, a good fat that can be harmed by heat and light. All their oils, but particularly flax oil and hempseed oil, are susceptible to rancidity, which is accelerated by heat. Raw nut butters, nut milk, nut pâtés, and fermented nut cheeses contain important nutrients and definitely have a place in a healthy diet, but enjoy them in moderate amounts because they contain a significant amount of fat.

Store raw nuts in the pantry for up to one month. If you need to keep them longer, store them in an airtight container in the freezer for up to six months.

Avocados

Avocados are delicious raw but not so great when cooked. When exposed to the air, this fruit begins to turn brown, or *oxidize,* losing much of its flavor and appeal. Time can also be a killer — of nutrients. A browned avocado won't kill you, but a perfectly ripe avocado is much more attractive and tasty.

If you have leftover avocado, do your best to keep it from coming into contact with air. Press plastic wrap directly on the surface of guacamole. Keep an unused half of an avocado intact and wrapped tightly; cut it when you're ready to eat it.

Dark Leafy Greens

Greens, such as spinach and kale, contain phytonutrients and folate. Both of these important nutrients leech into cooking water if boiled. And as boil time increases, nutrition diminishes. Greens lose 51 percent of their folate in 5 minutes of boiling, 58 percent in 10 minutes, and 68 percent in 15 minutes.

If you must cook your greens, lightly steam them. Studies show that steaming greens for 5 to 15 minutes results in no significant decrease in folate, so enjoy your greens raw or lightly steamed.

If you're looking for a non-salad way to enjoy raw leafy greens, look to Chapter 7 for details on how to juice them. Find recipes for smoothies that call for greens in Chapter 10, and Chapter 16 includes a recipe for kale chips.

Broccoli

Broccoli is a great source of protein, phytonutrients, vitamin C, beta caro-tene, and calcium. It's rich in fiber and, like all cruciferous vegetables, con-tains powerful cancer-fighting chemicals. Not many vegetables can compare to the nutritional punch of broccoli.

Cooking quickly destroys vitamin C. And as cook time grows, vitamin C levels plummet. Broccoli loses 48 percent of its vitamin C after 5 minutes of boiling, 56 percent after 10 minutes, and 65 percent in 15 minutes. Steaming broccoli for 5 to 15 minutes doesn't significantly decrease its vitamin C content, so if you can't consume raw broccoli, enjoy it lightly steamed rather than not eating it at all.

Use a mandoline or sharp knife to julienne raw broccoli to make it more palat-able in its raw form.

Citrus Fruits

Lemons, limes, grapefruit, and oranges are refreshing and contribute impor-tant nutrients, especially vitamin C, which is necessary to building a strong immune system as well as collagen, muscle, bones, teeth, and connective tissue. Without enough vitamin C, you're vulnerable to premature aging, cancer, and other degenerative diseases.

Cooking vitamin C even at low temperatures destroys it, so orange juice lovers should make their own fresh-squeezed orange juice. Commercially available juices are *pasteurized,* meaning they've been cooked. Not only does pasteurizing destroy vitamin C, it also transforms alkaline-producing citrus fruit into an acid. This change can interfere with your ability to digest the juice and use its nutrients. Find juice and smoothie recipes using citrus fruits in Chapters 8 and 10.

Berries

Berries contain heat-sensitive vitamin C and various B-complex vitamins and are particularly high in phytonutrients, which are only in plant foods. These essential nutrients provide protection from cancer, degenerative diseases, and premature aging. Both vitamins C and B-complex help maintain normal nerve and brain function, support the formation of red blood cells, and facili-tate creation of antibodies, red blood cells, and DNA.

Buy berries in season when possible to enjoy them at their peak of ripeness and sweetness; then refrigerate them immediately! Buy extras to freeze and enjoy year-round in smoothies, salads, dressings, and sorbets. Wash berries before freezing and lay them on a flat sheet pan in the freezer. After the individual berries are frozen, put them in a sealed container. They last in the freezer for several months.

Sauerkraut

Sauerkraut, fermented cabbage, has a tangy, bold flavor that most people come to love. Consuming raw, naturally fermented foods such as sauerkraut provides you with beneficial probiotics.

A single ¼-cup serving of sauerkraut contains 10 percent of the RDA (recommended daily allowance) for vitamin A and 25 percent of the RDA for vitamin C. Both of these nutrients as well as the probiotics, enzymes, and phytonutrients in sauerkraut are damaged by heat. Raw sauerkraut aids digestion, boosts immune function, and contains disease-fighting isothiocyanates. The Center for Cancer Research reports that sauerkraut even has a profound effect in preventing and healing breast cancer.

Sea Vegetables

Raw sea vegetables, including algae, chlorella, and spirulina, provide an abundance of vitamins, minerals, essential amino acids, carbohydrates, enzymes, and chlorophyll. In their raw state, sea vegetables are highly digestible superfoods that contain about 60 percent vegetable protein, which is higher than any other food.

The outstanding nutritional profile of sea vegetables also includes essential fatty acids, GLA fatty acid, lipids, the nucleic acids (RNA and DNA), heat-sensitive B-complex and vitamin C, vitamin E, and phytochemicals — such as carotenoids (an immune booster), chlorophyll (a blood purifier), and phycocyanin (a protein that's known to inhibit cancer). Chlorella and blue-green algae may also contain high levels of vitamin B12. Blue-green algae is an especially powerful brain stimulant, providing enhanced mental clarity.

Some spirulina and chlorella powders are heat processed for commercial distribution, making them difficult for digestive enzymes to penetrate during digestion. As a result, the body can't assimilate the amazing proteins and other nutritional components in the vegetable. And isn't that why you're eating it in the first place? Be sure to purchase fresh, non-heat-processed algaes, such as frozen E-3 live blue-green algae, which contains active B vitamins, carotene, and chlorophyll.

Green Juices

Green juices contribute to good health in a variety of ways, and they should always be consumed fresh and raw. Most green juices are made from vitamin, antioxidant, and phytonutrient-rich grasses and dark leafy greens, including kale, spinach, and parsley, which are all harmed by heat. Heat-sensitive antioxidants protect your cells from damage by *free radicals,* cells that attack healthy cells and can lead to cancer and heart disease (see Chapter 3).

Free-radical damage accumulates with age. So the older you get, the more important it becomes for you to eat antioxidant-rich foods like green juices.

Green juice is rich in chlorophyll, which gives greens their color. Chlorophyll helps your body detoxify and circulate oxygen. It also helps balance your body's pH by reducing acidity. Low-grade acidosis can zap your energy and contribute to many health challenges, including kidney stones.

Nonsweet Fruits

Bell peppers, cucumbers, tomatoes, and zucchini are examples of fruits that are low in sugar and high in phytonutrients and vitamins B and C. We often treat these fruits like vegetables, but they're more fragile than most vegetables and contain heat-sensitive nutrients that are vital to good health and longevity. If cooked, they lose important nutrients.

Bell peppers are especially high in vitamin C — even higher than oranges! Add them to juices, soups, sauces, dressings, salads, pasta dishes, raw crackers, breads, and even desserts.

Green bell peppers are unripe fruits and therefore difficult to digest, so choose red, orange, or yellow bell peppers.

Appendix

Metric Conversion Guide

• •

Note: The recipes in this book weren't developed or tested using metric measurements. There may be some variation in quality when converting to metric units.

Common Abbreviations

Abbreviation(s)	What It Stands For
cm	Centimeter
C., c.	Cup
G, g	Gram
kg	Kilogram
L, l	Liter
lb.	Pound
mL, ml	Milliliter
oz.	Ounce
pt.	Pint
t., tsp.	Teaspoon
T., Tb., Tbsp.	Tablespoon

Volume

U.S. Units	Canadian Metric	Australian Metric
¼ teaspoon	1 milliliter	1 milliliter
½ teaspoon	2 milliliters	2 milliliters
1 teaspoon	5 milliliters	5 milliliters
1 tablespoon	15 milliliters	20 milliliters
¼ cup	50 milliliters	60 milliliters

(continued)

Volume *(continued)*

U.S. Units	Canadian Metric	Australian Metric
⅓ cup	75 milliliters	80 milliliters
½ cup	125 milliliters	125 milliliters
⅔ cup	150 milliliters	170 milliliters
¾ cup	175 milliliters	190 milliliters
1 cup	250 milliliters	250 milliliters
1 quart	1 liter	1 liter
1½ quarts	1.5 liters	1.5 liters
2 quarts	2 liters	2 liters
2½ quarts	2.5 liters	2.5 liters
3 quarts	3 liters	3 liters
4 quarts (1 gallon)	4 liters	4 liters

Weight

U.S. Units	Canadian Metric	Australian Metric
1 ounce	30 grams	30 grams
2 ounces	55 grams	60 grams
3 ounces	85 grams	90 grams
4 ounces (¼ pound)	115 grams	125 grams
8 ounces (½ pound)	225 grams	225 grams
16 ounces (1 pound)	455 grams	500 grams (½ kilogram)

Length

Inches	Centimeters
0.5	1.5
1	2.5
2	5.0
3	7.5
4	10.0
5	12.5

Inches	Centimeters
6	15.0
7	17.5
8	20.5
9	23.0
10	25.5
11	28.0
12	30.5

Temperature (Degrees)

Fahrenheit	Celsius
32	0
212	100
250	120
275	140
300	150
325	160
350	180
375	190
400	200
425	220
450	230
475	240
500	260

Index

● *T* ●

& Mac

 For Dummies,
...ition
...118-17679-5

...e 4S For Dummies,
...ition
...118-03671-6

...ouch For Dummies,
...ition
...118-12960-9

...S X Lion
...ummies
...118-02205-4

...ing & Social Media

...le For Dummies
...118-08337-6

...ook For Dummies,
...ition
...118-09562-1

...Blogging
...ummies
...118-03843-7

...r For Dummies,
...dition
...470-76879-2

...Press For Dummies,
...ition
...118-07342-1

...ess

...Flow For Dummies
...118-01850-7

...ing For Dummies,
...ition
...470-90545-6

Job Searching with Social
Media For Dummies
978-0-470-93072-4

QuickBooks 2012
For Dummies
978-1-118-09120-3

Resumes For Dummies,
6th Edition
978-0-470-87361-8

Starting an Etsy Business
For Dummies
978-0-470-93067-0

Cooking & Entertaining

Cooking Basics
For Dummies, 4th Edition
978-0-470-91388-8

Wine For Dummies,
4th Edition
978-0-470-04579-4

Diet & Nutrition

Kettlebells For Dummies
978-0-470-59929-7

Nutrition For Dummies,
5th Edition
978-0-470-93231-5

Restaurant Calorie Counter
For Dummies,
2nd Edition
978-0-470-64405-8

Digital Photography

Digital SLR Cameras &
Photography For Dummies,
4th Edition
978-1-118-14489-3

Digital SLR Settings
& Shortcuts
For Dummies
978-0-470-91763-3

Photoshop Elements 10
For Dummies
978-1-118-10742-3

Gardening

Gardening Basics
For Dummies
978-0-470-03749-2

Vegetable Gardening
For Dummies,
2nd Edition
978-0-470-49870-5

Green/Sustainable

Raising Chickens
For Dummies
978-0-470-46544-8

Green Cleaning
For Dummies
978-0-470-39106-8

Health

Diabetes For Dummies,
3rd Edition
978-0-470-27086-8

Food Allergies
For Dummies
978-0-470-09584-3

Living Gluten-Free
For Dummies,
2nd Edition
978-0-470-58589-4

Hobbies

Beekeeping
For Dummies,
2nd Edition
978-0-470-43065-1

Chess For Dummies,
3rd Edition
978-1-118-01695-4

Drawing For Dummies,
2nd Edition
978-0-470-61842-4

eBay For Dummies,
7th Edition
978-1-118-09806-6

Knitting For Dummies,
2nd Edition
978-0-470-28747-7

**Language &
Foreign Language**

English Grammar
For Dummies,
2nd Edition
978-0-470-54664-2

French For Dummies,
2nd Edition
978-1-118-00464-7

German For Dummies,
2nd Edition
978-0-470-90101-4

Spanish Essentials
For Dummies
978-0-470-63751-7

Spanish For Dummies,
2nd Edition
978-0-470-87855-2

...ble wherever books are sold. For more information or to order direct: U.S. customers visit www.dummies.com or call 1-877-762-2974.
...K. customers visit www.wileyeurope.com or call (0) 1243 843291. Canadian customers visit www.wiley.ca or call 1-800-567-4797.
Connect with us online at www.facebook.com/fordummies or @fordummies

Math & Science

Algebra I For Dummies,
2nd Edition
978-0-470-55964-2

Biology For Dummies,
2nd Edition
978-0-470-59875-7

Chemistry For Dummies,
2nd Edition
978-1-1180-0730-3

Geometry For Dummies,
2nd Edition
978-0-470-08946-0

Pre-Algebra Essentials
For Dummies
978-0-470-61838-7

Microsoft Office

Excel 2010 For Dummies
978-0-470-48953-6

Office 2010 All-in-One
For Dummies
978-0-470-49748-7

Office 2011 for Mac
For Dummies
978-0-470-87869-9

Word 2010
For Dummies
978-0-470-48772-3

Music

Guitar For Dummies,
2nd Edition
978-0-7645-9904-0

Clarinet For Dummies
978-0-470-58477-4

iPod & iTunes
For Dummies,
9th Edition
978-1-118-13060-5

Pets

Cats For Dummies,
2nd Edition
978-0-7645-5275-5

Dogs All-in One
For Dummies
978-0470-52978-2

Saltwater Aquariums
For Dummies
978-0-470-06805-2

Religion & Inspiration

The Bible For Dummies
978-0-7645-5296-0

Catholicism For Dummies,
2nd Edition
978-1-118-07778-8

Spirituality For Dummies,
2nd Edition
978-0-470-19142-2

Self-Help & Relationships

Happiness For Dummies
978-0-470-28171-0

Overcoming Anxiety
For Dummies,
2nd Edition
978-0-470-57441-6

Seniors

Crosswords For Seniors
For Dummies
978-0-470-49157-7

iPad 2 For Seniors
For Dummies, 3rd Edition
978-1-118-17678-8

Laptops & Tablets
For Seniors For Dummies,
2nd Edition
978-1-118-09596-6

Smartphones & Tablets

BlackBerry For Dummies,
5th Edition
978-1-118-10035-6

Droid X2 For Dummies
978-1-118-14864-8

HTC ThunderBolt
For Dummies
978-1-118-07601-9

MOTOROLA XOOM
For Dummies
978-1-118-08835-7

Sports

Basketball For Dummies,
3rd Edition
978-1-118-07374-2

Football For Dummies,
2nd Edition
978-1-118-01261-1

Golf For Dummies,
4th Edition
978-0-470-88279-5

Test Prep

ACT For Dummies,
5th Edition
978-1-118-01259-8

ASVAB For Dummies,
3rd Edition
978-0-470-63760-9

The GRE Test For
Dummies, 7th Edition
978-0-470-00919-2

Police Officer Exam
For Dummies
978-0-470-88724-0

Series 7 Exam
For Dummies
978-0-470-09932-2

Web Development

HTML, CSS, & XHTML
For Dummies, 7th Edit
978-0-470-91659-9

Drupal For Dummies,
2nd Edition
978-1-118-08348-2

Windows 7

Windows 7
For Dummies
978-0-470-49743-2

Windows 7
For Dummies,
Book + DVD Bundle
978-0-470-52398-8

Windows 7 All-in-One
For Dummies
978-0-470-48763-1

Available wherever books are sold. For more information or to order direct: U.S. customers visit www.dummies.com or call 1-877-762
U.K. customers visit www.wileyeurope.com or call (0) 1243 843291. Canadian customers visit www.wiley.ca or call 1-800-567-4797
Connect with us online at www.facebook.com/fordummies or @fordummies

Wherever you are in life, Dummies makes it easier.

From fashion to Facebook ®, wine to Windows®, and everything in between, Dummies makes it easier.

Visit us at Dummies.com and connect with us online at www.facebook.com/fordummies or @fordummies